Houses and Cottage

Origins and Development of Traditional Domestic Buildings

Professor R. W. Brunskill, OBE, of De Montfort University, Leicester, was formerly Reader in Architecture at the University of Manchester. He trained as an architect and has been deeply involved in the study of vernacular architecture for many years. He was formerly a Commissioner of English Heritage and Vice-Chairman of the Royal Commission on the Architectural and Historical Monuments of Wales. Married and with two married daughters and three grandchildren, Professor Brunskill lives in Wilmslow, Cheshire and Harlech, Gwynedd.

Houses and Cottages
of Britain

R. W. Brunskill

Victor Gollancz *in association with* Peter Crawley

Also by R. W. Brunskill

Traditional Buildings of Britain
An Introduction to Vernacular Architecture
Timber Building in Britain
Brick Building in Britain
Traditional Farm Buildings of Britain and their Conservation
Illustrated Handbook of Vernacular Architecture
Vernacular Architecture of the Lake Counties

To Cameron James Campbell – my grandson

First published in Great Britain 1997
This paperback edition published 2000
in association with Peter Crawley
by Victor Gollancz
an imprint of The Orion Publishing Group
Orion House, 5 Upper St Martin's Lane
London WC2H 9EA

A catalogue record for this book
is available from the British Library

ISBN 0 575 07122 2

Typeset in Great Britain by
Rowland Phototypesetting Ltd,
Bury St Edmunds, Suffolk
Printed in Great Britain by
Butler & Tanner Ltd, Frome and London

Title page photograph, Dedham, Essex

Contents

List of Plates

Chapter 2

Large Houses
1 Priory Place, Little Dunmow, Essex (RCHME)
2 Manor House, Boothby Pagnell, Lincolnshire (RCHME)
3 Woodhouses Bastle, Northumberland (RCHME)
4 Manor Farm, Feckenham, Worcestershire (PSC)
5 Cochwillan, Llanllechid, Caernarvonshire (RCAHMW)
6 Hall i' th' Wood, Bolton, Lancashire (RCHME)
7 Trewern Hall, Trewern, Montgomeryshire (RCAHMW)
8 Ty-Faenor, Abbey Cwmhir, Radnorshire (RCAHMW)
9 Talgarth, Trefeglwys, Montgomeryshire (RCAHMW)
10 Bodwrdda, Aberdaron, Caernarvonshire (RCAHMW)
11 Manor House, Hammoon, Dorset (PSC)
12 Gunby Hall, Lincolnshire (PSC)
13 The Latin House, Risley, Derbyshire (PSC)

Small Houses
14 Synyards, Otham, Kent (PSC)
15 Old Cloth Hall, Smarden, Kent (PSC)
16 Preston Cottage, Alderley Edge, Cheshire (RWB)
17 House at Old Glasson, Lancashire (RCHME)
18 Houses at Porlock Weir, Somerset (PSC)
19 Home Farm House, near Devizes, Wiltshire (PSC)
20 House in Stoke-by-Nayland, Suffolk (PSC)
21 House at Fittleworth, Sussex (PSC)
22 Bryn-yr-Odin, Maentwrog, Merionethshire (RCAHMW)
23 House in Beaminster, Dorset (PSC)
24 House at Over Kellett, Lancashire (PSC)
25 House near Earl Soham, Suffolk (PSC)
26 House at Walton, Cumberland (PSC)
27 House near Banks, Cumberland (PSC)

Cottages
28 Cottage at Corfe Castle, Dorset (PSC)
29 Plas Bach, Rhoscolyn, Anglesey (RCAHMW)
30 Cottage at Muchelney, Somerset (PSC)
31 Cottages at Hatfield Broad Oak, Essex (JMcC)
32 Cottages at Ware, Hertfordshire (PSC)
33 Cottages at Crayke, Yorkshire, NR (PSC)
34 Cottage at Bampton, Oxfordshire (PSC)

Chapter 7

Key to credits

GDB	G. D. Bold
GW	Geoffrey Wheeler
JMcC	J. McCann
PSC	Peter Crawley
RCAHMW	Royal Commission on the Ancient and Historical Monuments of Wales
RCHME	Royal Commission on the Historical Monuments of England
RWB	R. W. Brunskill

Unless otherwise stated, buildings illustrated are in private occupation and readers are asked to respect that privacy.

Note on the Diagrams

The various diagrams constitute a major part of the book and a note on the intentions behind their preparation may be helpful. There are six sets:

1. Development of simple house-plans. This is a theoretical diagram showing the variations in position of door, staircase, and principal hearth or fireplace likely to be found in a small house of rectangular plan-shape. It is followed by an example of variations coming from use of different door and fireplace positions given a constant doorway location.

2. Summary diagrams of Rural and Urban plan-types. These attempt to show on one sheet each the main plan-types that are elaborated in other diagrams. Rural house-plans are divided between Large Houses, Small Houses and Cottages. While the plans within each size-type are arranged roughly in chronological order there are many overlaps and some parallel developments. Urban house-plans have been divided between earlier houses (generally with open halls), later houses (generally multi-storey) and urban cottages. In all the diagrams, the position of doorway, fireplace or hearth and (where appropriate) staircase are indicated, but purely diagrammatically. These are summary diagrams only and are not intended to deal with variations within each plan-type.

3. Diagrams of individual plan-types. These are in more detail but are still intended to show plan-types and not plans of actual buildings. Generally a ground-floor plan, a cross-section and an isometric sketch are included together with examples of common variations. The plans etc. are drawn approximately to scale but not to a uniform scale. Conventional indication of building materials is given but usually the same plan-type could be used with any walling or roofing material. In some of the earlier plan-types both for town and country there was no certain position for the staircase which may be omitted or conventionally indicated in the diagram. The time-scales are intended to show the range of dates during which the plan-type was commonly in use; no attempt has been made to distinguish between advanced and backward regions or between inferior and superior versions of the same plan-type. The diagrammatic distribution maps, where included, are intended to give only the broadest indication of where a plan-type may be found, as known from current information; they do not necessarily indicate a former distribution. Where no map is given, then generally the plan-type may be found in any part of the country.

4. Diagrams of methods of construction. These show only a selection of the constructional systems and materials used in domestic buildings.

5. Diagrams of development of various plans over a long period. These are idealised, and not based on specific examples but on combinations of examples.

6. Diagrams of Scottish house-types and methods of construction. Again only a selection is shown, and not all the types noted in the text are illustrated.

All diagrams have been prepared and drawn by the author.

Preface

This book is about houses and cottages as subjects for study and appreciation and as seen mainly through their plans. It is about the houses of ordinary people in countryside and town. It is based on study in the field. The houses of important and wealthy people may be studied primarily by historical methods and secondarily on the site, but the humble dwellings of ordinary folk are best understood initially by field study supported later by library and archive work. This book concentrates on plans rather than materials and construction; for however vital may be the peg-holes and straight joints in elucidating the complex history of quite unpretentious structures, ultimately the most detailed investigation is intended to discern the relatively simple arrangement of spaces on plan and in section which the designers intended at each phase.

Although my background is architectural rather than archaeological, I have ignored matters of proportion and decorative detail. This is not because the buildings lack architectural merit – indeed it is the beauty which stems from simple but consistent proportions and sparse but well-controlled ornament which makes their study so agreeable – but rather because we must assume that these houses were intended to be utilitarian first and decorative only secondarily.

The main purpose of this book is to draw together the basic information on standard house- and cottage-plans that were used or intended by unknown designers at various times in the past. The rapidly growing body of literature on minor domestic architecture is producing many published house-plans, and the archives, especially of the National Monuments Records of England, Wales and Scotland are swelling with large numbers of such plans; but most of the archaeological, architectural or historical reports are based on single buildings, covering in greater or lesser degree the sequences of development on a single building site, and it is not always easy to see to what extent the example studied is typical or unique. Many village or district surveys which study all the houses and cottages in a locality have been published over the past ten or twenty years, but here again the focus tends to be on the detail rather than on the overall picture. The growing number of published regional or national surveys take the broader view, but even here there is sometimes a tendency to detail the early and the exceptional, along with the variations that have been discovered, rather than concentrate on standard plans covering all periods.

Although I have concentrated on house-plans I have included a basic introduction to building materials and methods of construction. Most type-plans may be found clothed in timber, stone, clay or brick according to period or location, and so constructional matters have been omitted as far as possible from the main text and illustrations.

For maximum clarity, the classifications of plan and section have been prepared and illustrated as if all houses and cottages were built from scratch and never altered. This, of course, is rarely the case even in the most modern domestic property; and if it were, much of the archaeological detective work which generates so much enthusiasm for the subject would be eliminated. Examples have been included, therefore, of some of the more common sequences of development, recognising always that the story is taken back only as far as the earliest substantial surviving structure in the sequence, and that excavation might well reveal even earlier stages. Few essays in total archaeological investigation of small houses and their sites have yet been made.

Both the plan-types and the typical sequences of development are of types and the typical. They are not meant to illustrate specific buildings.

The book deals with the geographical entity of Great Britain but is mainly about England and Wales, which it has been found convenient to take together. Although study of the subject is rapidly developing in Scotland, it is still not as advanced as in the two other parts of the Kingdom. At the same time, the separate topography, economics, history and culture of Scotland demand recognition; and so a separate chapter gives a brief account of minor domestic buildings and their construction in the town and countryside of Scotland.

The period covered in the book extends mainly from the early 14th century to the late 19th century. Some of the plans were used rather earlier, however, and a note about more recent domestic planning has been included.

Since all the buildings were designed with traditional measures in mind, Imperial dimensions have been used throughout, but with metric versions added.

This book is based on an earlier book which I wrote and which was published in 1982 in the series of Collins Archaeologies. That book has been out of print for more than a decade and an updated version seemed worth the preparation. Comparison of the select bibliographies of 1982 and 1995 shows how the subject has advanced in the interval. Although the original selection of type-plans has been justified, there has been some correction and some addition while some diagrams have been made clearer. The Notes and References have also been expanded.

A summary work such as this is bound to depend very considerably on the published works listed in the bibliography and especially on those by N. W. Alcock, the late M. W. Barley, P. Eden, B. Harrison, B. Hutton, R. Machin, E. Mercer, S. Pearson, P. Smith, J. T. Smith, W. J. Smith, and the late R. B. Wood-Jones. Grateful acknowledgement is made to all listed in the bibliography and notes. Considerable benefit has also been gained from discussions with members of the Vernacular Architecture Group and the Scottish Vernacular Buildings Working Group, too numerous to list.

I would like to thank my daughter, Robin, for all her help with typing the ms. and Anthony Turner for his meticulous work and helpful suggestions as sub-editor.

Once again I am indebted to Peter Crawley for the majority of the photographs, for his faith in the book, and his tolerance of delays in its preparation.

R. W. Brunskill
Wilmslow, 1995

Chapter 1

The Study of Houses and Cottages

The process of design and construction of houses nowadays is straightforward and well understood. The architect or other designer takes instructions from his client, be he private individual, local authority, housing association or speculative developer, agrees a brief and then presents proposals which take into account the client's requirements, the opportunities and limitations presented by the site, the suitability and feasibility of materials and methods of construction, the requirements of a hundred and one regulatory bodies, the factor of cost, and matters of aesthetics. All the necessary compromises having been made and the proposals agreed, the house is erected. It is then occupied by an individual or family practising a particular life-style within a particular social and economic setting.

Since we are all familiar with the life-styles and socio-economic circumstances of our own time, we see in each newly erected house confirmation of what we know. Thus the vulgarly opulent mansion of the tycoon confirms what we know or suspect about him just as the plain anonymity of the council house inhabited by his chauffeur confirms what we know about his life-style and position on the social scale. The enthusiasm with which members of the public buy magazines full of illustrations of houses which they could not afford and in which they would not be comfortable, or visit show houses on estates to which they have no intention of moving, shows that the comparison of artefacts (in the form of houses) and needs or aspirations (which may be formalised in clients' briefs to architects) is a constant delight.

Many people are equally fascinated by old houses. They flock in their hundreds of thousands to visit the stately homes of this country and overseas, they attend in surprisingly substantial numbers the excursions of archaeological and historical societies which include visits to houses not normally accessible, and their tours of the Cotswolds and Cumbria are planned as much to see the villages and farmhouses as to see the hills and mountains. Their interest may be purely architectural; but one suspects that more often than not the visitor is concerned to observe a life-style, still perhaps perpetuated as a shadow of itself in certain stately homes or remote farmsteads or to be sensed from the bricks and mortar, the timber-frame and thatch of houses erected by past generations.

Any examination of an old house begins to put into reverse the process of construction and design: given the artefact one may, in theory at least, deduce the circumstances in which it was created. Anyone making a systematic observation of a building such as a house or cottage would record the plan and section of the building on its site, note the materials used and the way in which they had been put together, establish what appear to be the levels of extravagance or economy, and, comparing the house with others, ascertain which features appear to be conservative or even archaic and which are innovatory. From such a study the factors that had been considered by the original designer may begin to come to light, the brief or set of requirements given to the designer may, in the right circumstances, be deduced, and, one hopes, the way of life which determined that brief may be ascertained and understood. To this study of the building would be added what could be discovered by way of documentary evidence: information about the building and the people who had been its inhabitants.

The systematic study of old houses and cottages has been developing over the past hundred years or so and with increasing intensity over the past forty or fifty. It has attracted the attention of many scholars and each one has brought the techniques of study developed in his own field to the overall task. Social and economic historians have balanced evidence of phases of house construction with other data to gain a better understanding of the accumulation and dispersal of capital. Geographers have examined the distribution of houses at various periods in the past as essential data in their studies of areas and groupings. Sociologists have begun to relate developments in house planning to the changing pattern of family life. Students of folk life can see in certain aspects of house construction and detailing further evidence of the web of mystery and superstition that quite recently enveloped life in the countryside. Archaeologists see in surviving houses pieces of evidence that are essential to the understanding of the pattern of house design and construction, of the sequence which culminates in above-ground elements but which must be pursued in excavation.

While each approach to the study of houses brings with it a particular method of study, there are really two main groups of methods: those which involve study of the buildings themselves and those which involve searching for information *about* the buildings. Legal documents, diaries and travellers' descriptions, long-beards' memories, folk tales and superstitions are usually pieces of evidence about houses in general; plans, sections, elevations and photographs are pieces of evidence stemming from specific houses. It is with the latter study that we are concerned.

The possibilities of archaeological study of houses and cottages were demonstrated by Sir Cyril Fox and Lord Raglan in the influential *Monmouthshire Houses*, the first volume of which was published in 1951. The possibilities of documentary [1] study of houses and cottages, especially by way of probate inventories, were demonstrated by M. W. Barley, in *The English Farmhouse and Cottage* published ten [2] years later. Both had their predecessors and both have set examples magnificently followed by their successors, but these two books were most influential.

It is not my intention to explain the processes to be followed in making surveys of houses: there are handbooks available which do this, but it is important to note that there are various stages or levels of recording which are selected according [3] to the objectives in any study of houses and according to the resources available. If a quick and acceptably superficial impression of the general characteristics of houses in an area is required, then a survey based on photographs and a set of notes on each house, based on external observation and with the aid perhaps of a check-list, may be all that is needed and all that can be afforded. If a rather more comprehensive record of a smaller number of selected examples is required, then sketch plans or small-scale measured drawings supplemented by notes and sets of photographs would be prepared. Where a full record is to be made of a house or cottage about to be destroyed, re-erected or substantially altered, then a painstaking survey will be necessary, every stone and peghole being recorded on large-scale drawings and every nail and window-catch being measured, photographed and catalogued. Many houses have, of course, been recorded at the first level; village surveys are being published which have been made at the second level; understandably, few archaeological surveys have been made at the third level, though folk museums such as the Welsh Folk Museum and the

Development of simple house-plans

A. *Position of main door*

    1. In end wall
    2. In front wall near one corner
    3. Near centre of front wall

B. *Position of staircase*

    1. At one end against fireplace
    2. In rear wall
    3. In middle of plan:
        (a) transversely
        (b) longitudinally
        (c) dog-leg stair
    4. At one end away from fireplace

C. *Position of source of heat*

    1. Open hearth near middle of plan
    2. Fireplace at one end wall
    3. Fireplace in middle of plan
    4. Fireplace in rear wall
    5. Fireplace in front wall

D to G show plan variations given a constant position for the main door but with variations in the positions of the staircase and fireplace. H = hall or kitchen/living room, P = parlour.

D. *Door near corner, fireplace in end wall*

    1. Staircase associated with fireplace
    2. Staircase in rear wall
    3. Staircase near middle of plan
    4. Staircase in end wall, far from fireplace

E. *Door in corner, fireplace near middle of plan*

    1. Staircase associated with fireplace
    2. Staircase in rear wall
    3. Staircase near middle of plan
    4. Staircase in end wall

F. *Door in corner, fireplace in rear wall*

    1. Staircase associated with fireplace
    2. Staircase in rear wall
    3. Staircase near middle of plan
    4. Staircase in end wall

G. *Door in corner, fireplace in front wall*

    1. Staircase associated with fireplace
    2. Staircase in rear wall
    3. Staircase near middle of plan
    4. Staircase in end wall

H. *Cross-section*

    1. One-storey
    2. One-and-a-half-storey
    3. Two-storey

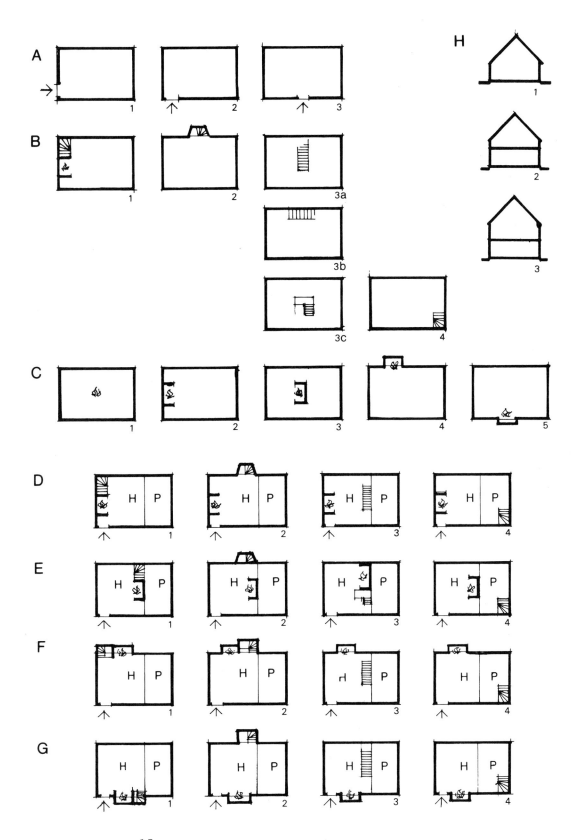

15

Weald and Downland Museum are doing such work as part of the dismantling and re-erection of the buildings which are their exhibits. 4

It is the custom of archaeologists and others to classify their findings. By grouping the artefacts which have been discovered and recorded into a set of types and then arranging the types into a series, the haphazard collection of objects with which the study begins may be converted into a logical sequence – either as an end in itself or as preparation for a further set of studies. As more and more has been discovered about more and more, precise classifications of design, constructional methods and architectural details have been made.

The major part of this book consists of a classification of smaller houses and cottages according to plan-types. 5

The first stage in the classification was the division into houses and cottages of the countryside on the one hand and those of the towns on the other, on the grounds that, until quite recently (and to some extent even now) economic and legal differences led to different lines of development. The next stage was to eliminate, both in town and country, the houses of the very rich. These, the Great Houses, were taken to be those of royalty and nobility, great magnates of church and state, major landowners, rich and powerful merchants and industrialists and so on. People of such standing would expect in all periods to be able to command houses of unique design from professional designers, and these buildings would be erected in circumstances that produced the documentary evidence which would allow each building to be studied primarily by historical methods. The most recent houses have also been omitted. The remaining houses are mostly of the type which is now generally called vernacular. When found in the countryside, they have been divided into the Large Houses of people of some local importance, the Small Houses of ordinary farmers and people of like quality who had some stake in the land, and the Cottages of those on the lowest rungs of the social and economic ladders. When found in the towns, they have been divided into the earlier and later groups of plans adopted by the minor merchants, shopkeepers and members of the urban middle class generally, and the cottage plans adopted by those who worked for others. Finally the classification has been directed towards 6 distinguishing plans or room arrangements which appear to have sufficient characteristics to be called types.

Each plan-type has been described and illustrated with separate mention of such variations as seem to occur within the type. Where possible some indication has been given of the dates at which the plans were in common use and those parts of the country where examples can be found. The term 'plan' is also taken to imply 'section' since all houses have a vertical dimension as well as a horizontal one, and changes in the number of storeys, development of roof space, provision of staircases to give access to upper storeys and cellars are as significant as other matters in the development of plans. The plan-type is taken to be the basic arrangement of customary dimensions, it always being accepted that members of a particular social class differed at any given time in the resources that they could devote to buildings and the degree of individuality which they felt disposed to give to a plan which they shared with neighbours; the plan might be the same, the size generally similar, but individuality could still be expressed in some little extravagance of decoration. The date-range has to take into account that even in a pretty rigid society some houses were forward-looking while others were backward, and that some districts tended to accept the example of nearby sources of influence while others heard about plan developments reluctantly and late. The distribution

16

maps are very generalised and are based on published maps which must in some cases reflect the haphazard progress of regional studies. The diagrams are of types and not of specific buildings, though the photographs are, of course, of buildings illustrating as far as possible the various plan-types. While the various parts are drawn in proportion to each other, the houses and cottages are not drawn to a common scale.

The classification of plan-types is supported by notes on the building materials and methods of construction. This is consciously offered as supporting material: it is considered axiomatic that the plan reflects the demands and hopes of the client's brief, that the building materials were chosen according to circumstances of economy, custom or fashion, suitability of purpose, etc., but that they were chosen to clad and support a set of spaces which themselves reflected the intended uses. Many good studies of traditional structures and building have been made, whereas the balance of the present book depends on plan-types. Similarly, no attempt has been made to explore the fascinating avenue of architectural decoration, important even at this level.

As some token of the fact that very many houses have come down to us in the form of the latest in a series of modifications and that many sites are very ancient – much older in human occupation than the houses which stand upon them – a chapter has been included which explains very briefly some of the common transformations whereby one plan-type has become another on the same site.

The majority of the book is based on England and Wales taken together, but a chapter has been included giving a very brief account of plan-types and constructional methods and materials in Scotland.

Although generally the house has been treated as a building type separate from all others, it must be acknowledged that nearly all rural dwellings were related to agriculture, both as an industry and as a way of life, and most houses were farmhouses. Some of the plan-types listed here incorporated farm buildings, while others would have been adjacent to farm buildings – either attached, as part of a farmstead group, or carefully detached from the farmyard on which they depended.

No one could pretend that this classification and its supporting material constitute a history of house design in Great Britain. For this the archaeological study itself is quite inadequate. The results of fieldwork must naturally be balanced against other sorts of evidence. With the rapidly increasing momentum of the study of house design and vernacular architecture, generally, evidence is being contributed by specialists in all the participating fields and our understanding of trends and particular aspects is that much more comprehensive. The concept of the 'Great Rebuilding', set forth more than forty years ago as a result of fieldwork combined with documentary investigation, has recently been modified by further work in both library and village street. The process of design and construction of these humble buildings about which we make such assumptions is beginning to be clarified through better understanding of the documents and ever closer attention to detail in the buildings. I hope that the present classification will provide a starting point for still further study of the houses themselves and for still more diligent search for material about them.

Chapter 2

Rural Houses and Cottages

The evolution of rural house-plans generally

It may be a truism that house-plans should reflect the way of life of the people for whom they are intended, but the plans of houses and cottages for members of the rural population of England and Wales do much more than reflect a single set of functions. Not only do the functions vary according to the wealth and social status of the inhabitants, but they also vary with time and are modified by the changes of a generally improving standard of living at each social level. The functions vary according to the occupation of each family: virtually all rural inhabitants were tied to the land in some way, most being full-time farmers but many, from priests to blacksmiths, combining farming with some other occupation. The functions also vary according to fashion, or rather the changing conventions of domestic behaviour; what was considered essential to a high standard of living at one time might be considered less important at another. The functions to be housed, then, varied in many ways, but since they were essentially quite simple functions it is to be expected that certain standard solutions to the problems were devised and widely adopted.

Even if function were the principal determinant of house-plans (and not everyone would accept this), it was certainly not the sole determinant: siting, security, structure and available materials were also important, and the humbler the dwelling the more significant would be such factors when weighed against the otherwise ideal method of housing certain domestic activities.

Siting might seem less important in the countryside than in the towns; whether rural houses were built as isolated dwellings, in hamlet groups or in villages, one would expect the sites to allow ample freedom to the designers. In the less crowded days of the past the countryside was indeed relatively empty and building land in total must have seemed more than adequate; but study of villages and hamlets would suggest that available building land was not much more plentiful than now. Building sites were precise in extent and their use was limited by law and custom; the late 18th-century and early 19th-century Small Houses and Cottages of the villages were often contorted in shape because adequate sites were not in fact available in locally crowded communities.

The squatters' cottages of that period were confined to the restricted sites that custom or boldness allowed on open waste land, or were squeezed into odd pockets and corners between plots whose legal owners could forbid encroachment. Even where some freedom in siting was enjoyed by the house-builder, there were fashions in siting and especially in orientation to be observed. At one time the fashion might be for houses to face the street or village green, at another time a position at right angles seems to have been popular; at one time houses were built to face the sun, later it was more customary to face the view, prospect taking preference over aspect. At certain times, places and social levels, houses were mixed with farm buildings, at others they were deliberately, almost self-consciously, set apart.

Security was an important factor in house planning at various times and at various social levels. For the small farmer or cottager with little to lose, the security of the individual dwelling might not seem a major factor in planning, whereas for his contemporary lord – subject to feuds in disorderly times – security might seem all-important. For the master and tenant the communal security of living in villages rather than scattered in isolated settlements might dictate the house site and so, indirectly, the house-plan. During the period from which most smaller houses in the countryside survive, rural society was at peace, the stable conditions being interrupted only occasionally by disturbances and the Civil War. For the ordinary householder no more precautions than shutters or bars at ground-floor windows would be necessary: the defensible high-walled farmyards of some European countries are rarely to be found in England or Wales. There were, however, periods of general unrest, especially during the Middle Ages when any landowner or occupier of an isolated house would need a refuge in which he could protect his family, stock and goods. There were also localised areas of insecurity, especially on the Scottish border until the mid-17th century and sometimes in the south-west of England, in which quite modest proprietors required defensible dwellings, and at times in such areas the tenant had even less occasion than elsewhere to build anything other than a house which could be swiftly re-erected if it had been destroyed.

Structural limitations and available building materials affected architectural form, but do not seem to have affected house planning to any great extent. Obviously a householder could have a particular arrangement of rooms only to the extent that technology and materials would allow, but it is hard to believe from the plans of surviving houses that the choice of materials seriously inhibited design: the same plans may be seen in timber-frame, stone and brick and under thatched, slated or tiled roofs. For the very largest houses, the limitations on span may have encouraged the use of, say, the aisled hall, while for the very smallest houses the stage of primitive building may have been extended until cheap manufactured materials became available to supplement poor-quality local materials of natural origin.

Fashion, however, is definitely an important determinant of house-plans. For those at the highest levels of society the choice of plan seems increasingly to have been guided by fashion rather than function; for those at the lower levels the desire to imitate their social superiors was evidently very strong and may be seen as getting stronger all the time. Over and over again one can see a plan arrangement as well as architectural detail working its way through all social levels. The influence of fashion is easy enough to understand once pattern books and eventually journals and magazines were freely circulating; it is less easy to accept during those periods in which the dissemination of ideas committed to paper was difficult and expensive. Yet in the absence of elaborate drawings, the model for each house-builder would most conveniently be an existing building modified as necessary; the traditional plans would be improved or altered following experiments made by those at higher social levels who had both the incentive and the means to make innovations.

What applies to the ground plan of a building applies also to its cross-section in relation to the method of access from floor to floor, the number of storeys, the roof construction and materials. Limited sites encouraged building upwards, security

Rural house-plans: summary of the main plan-types

A. *Large Houses*

   1. Ground-floor halls, aisled halls
   2. First-floor halls and bastle houses
   3. Tower houses
   4. Single-ended halls
   5. Double-ended halls
   6. Multi-storey houses
   7. Compact houses with projecting wings
   8. Double-pile houses

B. *Small Houses*

   9. Wealden and other open-hall houses
   10. Small houses with lateral chimneys
   11. Longhouses
   12. Cross-passage Small Houses
   13. Lobby-entrance houses and houses with back-to-back fireplaces
   14. Houses with central service rooms
   15. Internal cross-passage houses
   16. Two-unit houses
   17. T-shaped and L-shaped houses
   18. Two-unit houses with an extra bay
   19. Continuous-outshut houses
   20. Double-pile houses

C. *Cottages*

   21. One-unit cottages
   22. One-and-a-half-unit cottages
   23. Single-storey and croglofft cottages
   24. Double-pile single-fronted cottages
   25. Other multi-storey cottages

D. *Special-purpose houses*

   26. Laithe houses
   27. Almshouses

---

suggested height as protection, fashion determined that an imposing elevation should be several storeys high. The open hall of the medieval Large House appeared as the principal living room of the Wealden house and could be seen again as the basis of the croglofft cottage in Wales; the tall rooms of the 18th-century mansion required a staircase of two flights as did the mid-19th century farmhouse and the remarkably tall rooms of the late 19th-century cottage. Plan and section go together. Both ultimately depend on the way of life to be housed, site conditions and cultural factors such as the acknowledgement of fashion.

A. LARGE HOUSES

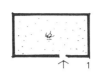

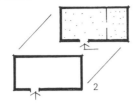

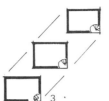

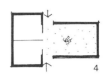

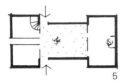

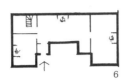

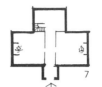

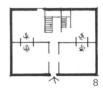

B. SMALL HOUSES

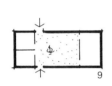

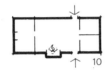

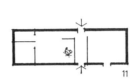

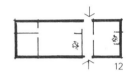

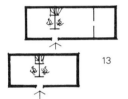

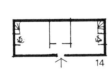

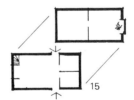

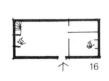

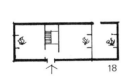

C. COTTAGES

D. SPECIAL-PURPOSE HOUSES

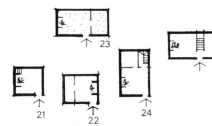

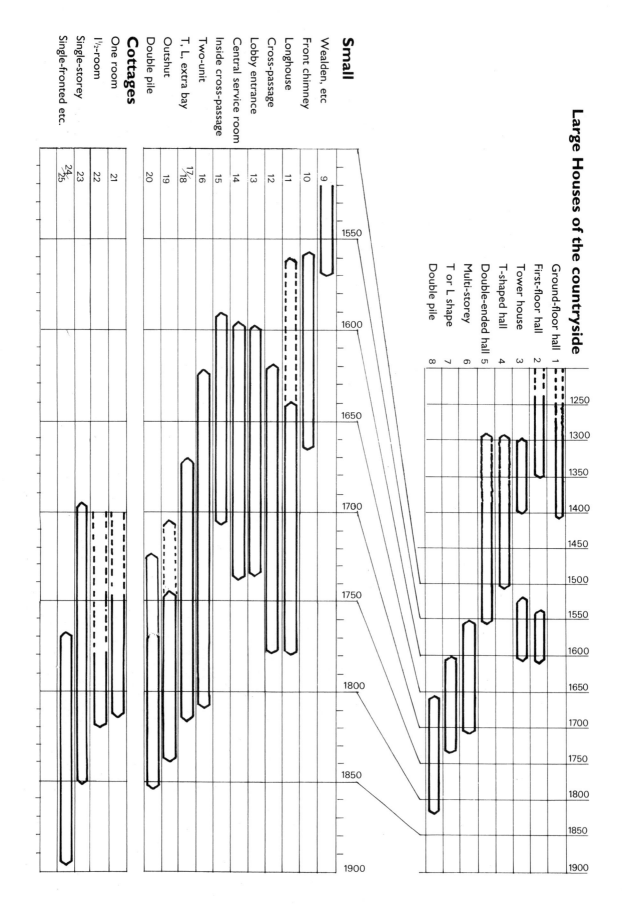

Large Houses of the countryside

Ground-floor hall 1
First-floor hall 2
Tower house 3
T-shaped hall 4
Double-ended hall 5
Multi-storey 6
T or L shape 7
Double pile 8

1250
1300
1350
1400
1450
1500
1550
1600
1650
1700
1750
1800
1850
1900

Small

Wealden, etc 9
Front chimney 10
Longhouse 11
Cross-passage 12
Lobby entrance 13
Central service room 14
Inside cross-passage 15
Two-unit 16
T, L, extra bay 17/18
Outshut 19
Double pile 20

Cottages

One room 21
1½-room 22
Single-storey 23
Single-fronted etc. 24/25

1550
1600
1650
1700
1750
1800
1850
1900

Large Houses of the countryside

1 Ground-floor halls

The ground-floor hall was the nucleus of most pioneering house-plans at every social level from medieval Great Houses to 18th-century Cottages. At every level except the lowest, a proportion of ground-floor halls had one side or both sides aisled.

The essential characteristics of a ground-floor hall were its rectangular shape and its undivided section, the room rising open and unobstructed to the ridge or apex of the roof. In the basic hall, the roof was carried by the walls or by piers or posts set in the walls so that the whole floor area was unobstructed, but in the aisled hall the roof-loads were carried by way of trusses on to a series of stone piers or timber posts that ran along the length of the hall, dividing the floor space into a central nave and flanking narrower aisles.

In the basic hall the rafters were carried by the walls, perhaps with the aid of trusses and purlins; in the aisled hall the great arcade plates or braced beams ran from post to post while carrying rafters on their journey down to the low side walls. The forest of timber members, all exposed to view in the dim light of the fire or half-shuttered windows, dominated the interior of the ground-floor hall just as the great roof dominated the exterior, sweeping down from ridge to eaves of an aisled hall almost to the exclusion of visible walls.

In the earlier examples no clear distinction between superior and inferior ends to the hall may be distinguished, nor does there appear to have been any substantial division to indicate zones of different use, though entrance was normally into one of the long sides and a temporary division into two spaces could be contrived without difficulty. Heat was provided by an open fire burning on an open hearth located somewhere near the middle of the floor.

In later examples it seems that one end was partitioned from the rest, and eventually one can see in some instances that the single hall has become two

1. Priory Place, Little Dunmow, Essex
An example of a double-ended hall house incorporating an aisled hall. The steeply inclined pitched roof falls to a low eaves and is extended to include a further addition to the side aisle.
(RCHME © Crown Copyright)

1 Ground-floor halls, aisled halls

a. Plan of an aisled hall of four bays on the ground floor, showing two rows of aisle posts (1), with an open hearth heating the main part of the plan (2), a space at one end (3) sometimes partitioned off the main room, and the entrance (4) near the middle of one wall.

b. Cross-section showing the trusses based on aisle posts (1) and the roof sweeping down to cover the aisles and carried on the low outer walls (5).

c. Isometric sketch of a timber-framed aisled hall; in this instance the roof has a half-hip and gablet (6) at each end but sweeps over the aisles on the side walls (7).

d. Plan of an aisled hall with stone piers serving in place of aisle posts.

e. Sketch of a stone-walled and gabled aisled hall.

f. Plan of a small single-aisled house of four bays with a cross-passage (8), hearth near the cross-passage (9) and inner room (10).

g. Plan showing such a house hidden within a later set of stone or brick walls.

h. Sketch showing the incorporation of a single-aisled hall in later walls.

---

spaces: a larger space presumably intended for more public functions and a smaller space giving greater comfort and privacy. It has been suggested that the larger was the courtroom reflecting the lord's public duties as governor, administrator and arbitrator while the smaller was his private house accommodating his family life. There seems to have been no practice, even in the largest halls, of dividing nave from aisles as was done through the development of screened chapels in parish churches. Although many, perhaps most, aisled halls served as the nucleus of a farmhouse, the north German practice of making the hall the physical nucleus of a complete farmstead maintained entirely under one roof did not develop in this country.

At one time it was thought that the aisled hall was a building type confined to the higher social levels and only found in the south-east of England, but more recent research has shown that the type was more widespread socially as well as geographically: fairly humble farmhouses in the Pennines and Vale of York were built to this design. Nevertheless it is still agreed that earlier examples belong to higher social levels and are most likely to be found in such counties as Suffolk, Essex, Kent and Sussex.

2

2 First-floor halls

As the name implies, the characteristic feature of this group of houses was a room open to the roof and raised substantially above ground level. Normally the hall occupied most of the first floor of an elongated building, a smaller room (which might be ceiled) occupying the rest. Entrance was by an external staircase up to the hall, the smaller room being entered through the hall, and there was usually no intercommunication between the hall and the space beneath. The ground floor, which was sometimes undivided and sometimes had two rooms corresponding with those above, often had a stone vault to carry the upper floor. The hall usually had a side-wall fireplace but the ground floor was often without a fixed heating source, though the larger room sometimes had a side-wall fireplace smaller than

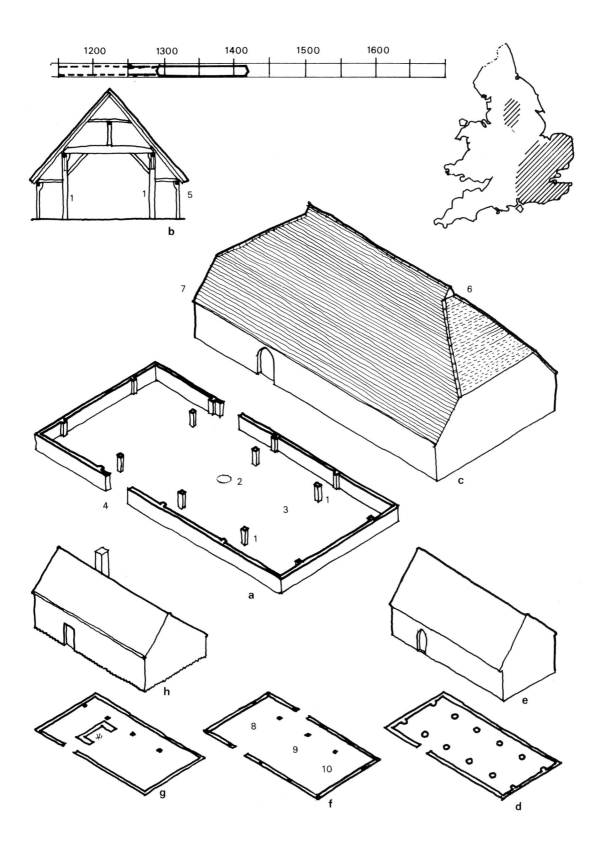

1200 1300 1400 1500 1600

b
1 1 5

c
7 6

a
4 2 3 1 1 1

h

e

g

f
8 9 10

d

2 First-floor halls and bastle houses

a. Ground-floor plan showing larger room (1) and smaller room (2), which in this case are entered through separate doors (3 and 4). The larger room has a fireplace (5).

b. First-floor plan showing larger room (6) which is the first-floor hall and, opening off it, the smaller room (7) or solar. The larger room has a fireplace (8) in the side wall and is approached by a door (9) from an external staircase. In this example there is no intercommunication between ground and first floors.

c. Cross-section showing ground-floor room (10) and first-floor hall (11) carried here on a set of vaults (12).

d. Sketch showing first-floor hall approached by its external staircase.

e. Plan showing barrel-vaulted undercroft beneath a first-floor hall; here there are three interconnecting rooms with entry into one (13) and a mural staircase (14) rising to the first-floor hall.

f. Ground floor of a bastle house with direct entry into the cowhouse (15) which occupies the whole of this floor.

g. First floor of a bastle house with the door (16) reached by an external staircase or ladder leading into the first-floor hall (17) off which opens the ceiled inner room (18).

h. Plan of small bastle house, almost square in shape.

i. Cross-section showing gable fireplace and a timber intermediate floor.

2. Manor House, Boothby Pagnell, Lincolnshire
A well-preserved example of what appears to be a first-floor hall but which may have been the solar wing of a former ground-floor hall now demolished.
(RCHME © Crown Copyright)

that serving the hall above. It is likely that the larger first-floor room served as a public room or court space and the smaller as a private or domestic space; the ground floor may have been devoted to storage (though of what is not clear), but alternatively the floor may have provided domestic accommodation for a separate and inferior household.

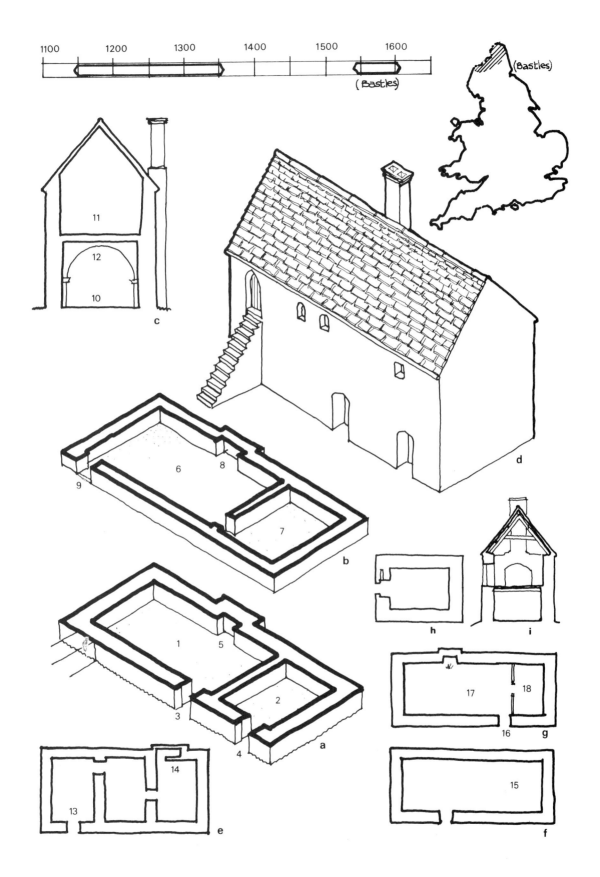

The first-floor hall was generally a mark of high status: most castles from the early 13th century to the middle of the 14th had at least one; much domestic accommodation in monasteries may be seen as a series of first-floor halls, with the church as an aisled ground-floor hall and the chapter house as a ground-floor private room. Comparatively few secular examples of first-floor halls survive and these are nearly all of stone; one can only speculate as to how many timber first-floor halls may once have existed and have since been destroyed.

First-floor halls are sometimes called 'King John's houses', and a proportion of those surviving date from the second half of the 12th century; but such halls were built throughout the 13th century and well into the 14th, especially in Wales and the Marcher counties.

Recently doubt has been cast on the number of first-floor halls that were independent dwellings. Many seem more likely to have been the private blocks originally attached to ground-floor halls that were subsequently demolished or replaced. ³

2a Bastle houses

There is another sort of first-floor hall, much later in date and rather smaller in size than the others but of which many hundreds of examples survive complete or in part. This is the bastle house, the defensive dwelling of the most substantial farmers of the Scottish Borders, erected mainly during the period of border raiding during the 16th century and the beginning of the 17th century. The bastle house consisted of a first-floor hall with a smaller room at one end which was usually

3. Woodhouses Bastle, Northumberland
A bastle house with entry for animals through the gable, and for humans at first-floor level in the hidden side wall.
(RCHME © Crown Copyright)

ceiled and sometimes had a garret room over. Both hall and smaller room were raised over a ground floor which was equipped for the accommodation of cattle and, probably, horses. Access to the first floor was by a retractable ladder which has been replaced in surviving examples by an external stone staircase; access to the ground floor was through a stout door protected by a drawbar; there was often no apparent means of intercommunication between the two floors. The intermediate floor was sometimes vaulted in stone, but more commonly a timber floor made of boards, joists and beams in the conventional manner was provided. Walls were of stone, usually about 4 ft (1.2 m) thick, doors were stout, windows small and protected with iron bars, but there was usually a conventional pitched roof without battlements or, indeed, any provision for active defence.

Clearly the bastle house form represented a direct response to the specific needs of certain people in a certain district at a certain time. The first-floor position for domestic accommodation raised the household above direct attack by assault or battering ram while the thick defensive walls meant that both family and stock were secure against sudden raids by small bands who might smoke out less well-protected families. The circumstances on the Scottish border were exceptional but perhaps not unique: family feuds and inter-communal rivalry were not unknown in other parts of the country, especially during the Middle Ages, and so buildings resembling bastle houses may yet be discovered in other remote and sparsely populated districts. 4

3 Tower houses

The tower house was another special version of the first-floor hall, but one whose development and importance justifies a separate category. Such buildings were found in many parts of England, and occasionally in Wales, both at the upper social levels in the late 12th and early 13th centuries and, in the 14th and 16th centuries, lower down the social scale.

A tower house consists of a first-floor hall which is raised over an undercroft, has one or two chambers above, and usually terminates in battlements around a flat or pitched roof. In the larger and earlier examples the first-floor hall was extended to run through two storeys; in the smaller and later examples the hall was not substantially different in either interior arrangement or external expression from the other upper rooms. Entrance was normally to the hall at first-floor level, from which mural staircases, or a winding staircase in one corner, led up to the chambers and down to the ground-floor cellar. It is customary to regard the stone vaulted cellar space as a prison or storage chamber, though it is not clear what could be stored in a damp, ill-ventilated space reached only by way of a narrow winding staircase, or what would be securely stored in a prison cell apart from a prisoner.

It may be that the principal function of the cellar space was simply to raise the hall to a comfortable and relatively secure position: comfort could have been obtained if the upper rooms had been raised on posts or piers but security required as solid and fireproof a base as possible. In the larger examples the ground-floor level could have been occupied by a separate household, as beneath first-floor halls, but surviving examples suggest that this was uncommon. Apart from a few brick buildings, all the surviving tower houses were built of stone, wall thicknesses varying from about 4 ft (1.2 m) to as much as 10 ft (3.1 m) and many had a stone vault beneath the hall, protecting the main part of the house from attack by fire.

3 Tower houses

a. Ground floor or undercroft, shown here as reached only by a winding staircase from above, unheated and lit by narrow slits.

b. First floor containing hall (1) heated by an end-wall fireplace (2) with an external door (3) reached by a ladder or external staircase. A winding staircase partly built into a corner (4) connects the various floors. There is a garderobe (5) in the opposite corner.

c. Second floor containing, in this instance, a single heated chamber with its own garderobe. (6)

d. Cross-section showing a stone-vaulted undercroft (7) with hall (8), chamber floor (9) and garret (10) which have timber floors between.

e. Alternative cross-section showing timber floors throughout and a hall (11) which rises through two floors.

f. Sketch showing a gabled roof hidden behind battlements.

g. Plan to show a longitudinal wall dividing each floor into two flanking apartments and with a fairly spacious winding staircase housed in a projecting wing.

In some of the largest examples there is a transverse wall dividing each floor into two long and rather narrow spaces. These walls may have been military in purpose, ensuring that a breach in one part of the wall did not automatically give access to the whole tower, but equally they may have had a domestic basis, dividing the hall floor into a larger and smaller room for more public and more private use and dividing the chamber floors into similar accommodation for other households. Again, many of the larger tower houses had rooms hollowed out of the thick walls of the upper levels, preserving the stout appearance of the whole tower but leaving only the bottom storey with a truly defensive wall thickness.

In some of the smaller examples, the so-called 'pele towers', the entrance was at ground level, a stout door and a wrought-iron 'yett' protecting the entrance against sudden attack by battering ram or fire. A narrow winding staircase rose up through the various floors linking entrance with hall, chambers and a roof walk. In English examples the staircase was usually tucked into a corner of the building; the projecting staircase turret of Scottish examples, which eventually led to the L- and Z-shaped tower-house plans, was rarely found south of the border.

Although in their abandoned and often ruined state the tower houses now stand isolated, they were, in fact, usually built as part of a complex of walls, courtyards and subsidiary buildings and served as the fireproof defensive refuge, amid more flimsy and expendable buildings, within the curtain walls of a castle or the barmkin walls of a border strength.

4 Single-ended halls

Sometimes known as the T-shaped hall or the end-hall house, the single-ended hall-plan consists of a one-storey open hall with a two-storey private or domestic block attached at one end. The hall may be aisled or without aisles and was usually designed to have an open hearth, but may have a fireplace along the rear side wall. The domestic block consists usually of a small first-floor hall or solar, open to the roof and raised over one or more subsidiary rooms. The upper room

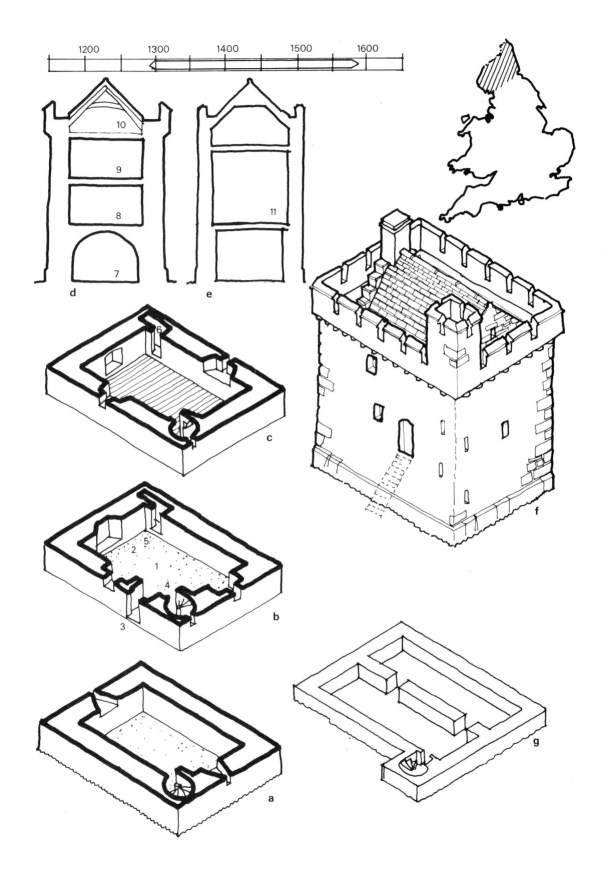

1200   1300   1400   1500   1600

10
9
8
7
d

11
e

6
c

2 5
1
4
3
b

a

g

f

4. Manor Farm, Feckenham, Worcestershire
A T-shaped hall (now two-storey throughout) with entrance near the junction between hall range and cross-wing.
(Peter Crawley)

may have had a fireplace but often had no fixed form of heating; the lower rooms did not usually have any heating provision at all. Access to the domestic block was often by an external staircase; at least in the earlier examples, there might be no intercommunication between upper and lower rooms or between upper rooms and the hall.

The single-ended hall may be seen as representing the combination of the public duties and private activities of a minor lord; the large assemblies of local courts, major social activities, etc., taking place in the ground-floor hall while ordinary domestic life was enjoyed in a first-floor hall. We have the two traditions of first-floor hall and ground-floor hall coming together in one house. In so far as the entrance position became established at the junction of the two parts of the house, we have an instance of the convenient location also expressing the double nature of such a house-plan.

Usually the multi-storey wing was roofed at right angles to the single-storey main block, just as the wing usually projected from the walls of the hall; but this was not essential, as one could have a T-shaped roof over a rectangular plan and even, in the smaller examples, a rectangular roof over a T-shaped plan.

Most T-shaped halls were built either of timber-frame or stone and, at least on the evidence of surviving examples, it could not be said that use of the one material preceded use of the other. However, a stone wing and a timber hall must have been a fairly common arrangement. This would have been reasonable both struc-

32

turally and functionally: stone being used for the multi-storey structure where height and stability were important and span of roof- or floor-beams less significant, and timber for the hall where desire for width and uninterrupted height dominated the planning. It would also have been a reasonable arrangement where occasional need for defence might occur, the stone wing serving as a defensible tower while the timber main block made use of more readily available building materials.

Transitionally, a few late T-shaped halls had a hall not open to the roof but chambered over. In this case a half-bay accommodated a staircase at the junction of the two wings.

As a plan-type the T-shaped hall originated in the late 12th century, developed in the 13th and 14th centuries and was used at slightly lower social levels in the 15th and early 16th centuries. Examples may be found practically anywhere in England and Wales. Most have an inserted intermediate floor in the hall while many gained a multi-storey porch to mark the entrance.

5. Cochwillan, Llanllechid, Caernarvonshire
A hall open to the roof, seen from the dais end. The two doors serving the cross-passage may be seen at right angles to the wooden muntin-and-plank partition with its door leading to service rooms.
(British Crown Copyright: Royal Commission on the Ancient and Historical Monuments of Wales)

4 Single-ended halls

a. Plan showing hall (1) with open hearth (2), screens passage (3) stretching between opposite doors, buttery (4), pantry (5) and kitchen passage (6); a winding staircase (7) leads to the first floor of the cross-wing.

b. Upper-floor plan showing the upper part of the hall (8) and first-floor hall or solar in the cross-wing (9).

c. Cross-section looking towards the cross-wing and showing the spere truss (10).

d. Sketch which shows the different eaves-lines of the hall and the two-storey cross-wing. A saddle louvre is shown over the hall (11).

e. Plan showing a common method of improving a single-ended hall in the 16th century by the insertion of fireplaces and an intermediate floor. The cross-passage is blocked by an inserted fireplace and staircase (13) while the lower part of the cross-wing (12) has become a habitable room with its own fireplace.

f. Sketch showing the chimney-stacks serving the new fireplaces and dormer windows lighting the chambers formed in the upper part of the hall.

g. Sketch showing how the roof formation reveals that a rectangular plan is really that of a single-ended hall.

h. Plan showing timber-framed hall and stone solar wing.

i. Multi-storey porch at entrance to cross-passage.

j. Multi-storey throughout and with half-bay for staircase.

---

5 Double-ended halls

The H-shaped or double-ended hall was developed at the same time as the single-ended hall-plan but had a longer period of popularity as a house-plan and became the basis for many further developments in domestic planning. The plan allowed the hall to serve more than one set of domestic rooms, and it gave the larger houses a unity and potential symmetry that became more and more to be desired as the medieval period gave way to the Renaissance.

The early medieval manorial headquarters had comprised a collection of buildings each serving a separate use, only loosely related to one another, with differing degrees of permanence and loosely or tightly enclosed by a wall, fence or moat according to circumstances that varied with place and time. The connection of two buildings to make the single-ended hall marked one step in the assembly of all domestic functions within one building. Use of the vacant end of the hall to serve another set of domestic accommodation marked a further step: it emphasised the communal function of the hall and was a reminder of its non-domestic uses since, at least in the earlier examples, the wing at each end of the hall was capable of functioning independently as a basic domestic unit.

There developed, however, a standardisation, almost a formalisation, in the planning of the hall which may be detected in the single-ended hall and which led to the further development of the hall as a domestic room, but which remains to a large extent the basis of planning of other halls for certain public uses. One aspect of the standardisation was the increasingly complete distinction between

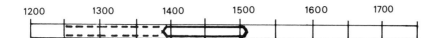

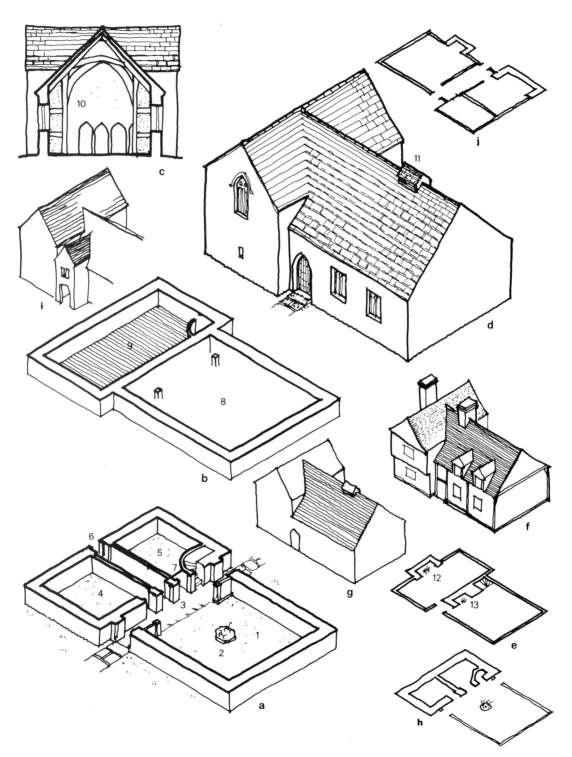

6. Hall i' th' Wood, Bolton, Lancashire
This is a late 16th-century house with hall and cross-wing, except that the hall range has been two-storey from the beginning and is served by fireplaces in a chimney-breast in the side wall. There is a half-bay at the junction between the hall and cross-wing. The upper floor is jettied on three sides.
(RCHME © Crown Copyright)

the 'upper' or socially superior end of the hall and the 'lower' or socially inferior end, between parts above and below the salt.

At the lower end there was a concentration of circulation space. Entrance to the whole building was at the junction between the lower end of the hall and one of the cross-wings; opposed doors led into a cross-passage which was taken from the lower end of the hall and defined by the short partitions of the spere truss and by the free-standing screen in between. Across the passage, doors led into the lower portion of the cross-wing and here accommodation became standardised as buttery and pantry (for liquid and dry goods respectively) with a corridor in between leading to an outside kitchen. There was also in many examples a winding staircase which led from the passage to the room on the upper floor of the wing.

Thus the circulation space at the lower end of the hall contained front and back doors, the doors to buttery, pantry, kitchen and staircase, and the two openings which led into the main part of the hall; it served as an inner porch, protecting the hall from the worst of the draughts, as an ante-room when the hall was used as a courtroom and as a servery space when the hall was used for those banquets that many can picture and some try to recapture.

At the upper end of the hall developments took rather longer to get under way. The socially superior status was marked by the provision of a dais, a platform raised slightly above the general floor level, and those sitting on the dais were protected by a covered canopy of timber or plaster from the worst of the smutty down-draughts that resulted from the use of a central open hearth. In later examples status was further marked by a bay window, sometimes of complex plan and elaborate decoration, which gave light and distinction to the upper end of the hall. Doors were provided at each end of the dais to give access to the cross-wing at the upper end of the house, and sometimes there were short screens giving further protection to the occupants of the dais from any draughts that might come through the doors. With a public entrance and assembly space at one end, an unobstructed main area capable of being furnished in various ways and a raised platform at the other end, panelled, protected and with its own doors to private retiring rooms, one can well see how the medieval hall became the courtroom, council chamber and even parliament hall of subsequent centuries. Indeed, this part of the tradition is so strong that it helps to prevent the British Parliament from adopting the horse-shoe pattern of Continental assemblies.

The earlier halls had a central open hearth with smoke rising to the rafters and emerging through uneven tiles or slates, being absorbed in thatch or passing fitfully through a draughty louvre. Some such halls still survive. The central position meant that heat was evenly distributed throughout the room. Later halls and improved earlier halls had a fireplace, usually located on the rear side wall where its heat was still quite well radiated; only in a few small and northern halls

7. Trewern Hall, Trewern, Montgomeryshire
A multi-storey Large House, this highly decorative timber-framed building has a multi-storey porch bearing the date 1610 and appearing to open on to a lobby against the fireplace jamb. The upper floor and gables are jettied, except in the presumed service wing on the right.

5 Double-ended halls

a. Ground-floor plan showing hall (1) with side-wall fireplace (2), entrance by way of cross-passage or screens passage (3) off which leads the kitchen passage (6) running between the buttery (4) and pantry (5) and a staircase (7) leading to the upper floor of this wing. At the opposite end of the hall is the dais (8) with flanking doors leading to a heated parlour (9) which has its own staircase to a solar above.

b. Cross-section looking towards the dais and its canopy (10).

c. Sketch to show the single-storey hall and cross-wings.

d. Ground-floor plan of a semi-fortified hall: the open hall (11) has a fireplace (12) which backs on to the cross-passage (13) off which opens a kitchen (14) now brought into the house. There will be a chamber above, but in this example the two-storey portion does not project as a wing. At the opposite end of the hall is a service room (15) with solar and chamber above; all this projecting wing is strengthened so as to act as a place of refuge or defence.

e. Sketch showing the defensible wing, the hall chimney and the massive kitchen chimney-breast.

f. A late example of a double-ended hall showing on the ground floor the hall (16) which might have a gallery joining the upper floors of the two wings or might already have an inserted floor. The hall is heated by a fireplace (17) which backs on to a cross-passage (18) off which opens a kitchen (19) and service room (20). At the 'upper' end of the hall there are parlours, staircases, and chambers above (21). The porch at the front end of the cross-passage is built into the adjacent wing.

g. Sketch showing the appearance of such a house.

h. The dais end of a hall was often marked externally by use of a bay window.

was the fireplace made to back on to the cross-passage.

Later developments affected the main entrance and the dais, for it became the practice to give architectural acknowledgement to the importance of these two ends of the hall. The dais had its bay window becoming ever more pretentious, the most magnificent example being probably that at Hampton Court Palace, but then changing to become a link with the cross-wing rather than a separate projection. The entrance door was given more emphasis and was made more effective as a projection from the hall by the provision of a porch, usually of two or three storeys. Previously the front and back doors to the cross-passage were given equal attention and it might be difficult to decide which side of the hall was considered the front. Now all doubt was removed. The porch that was related to one cross-wing and the bay that was related to the other clearly distinguished one side of the whole house as the front and another as the back. Furthermore, within that front elevation preparation had now been made for the receding planes and balanced disposition which was to mark the transition to design under Renaissance influence.

The wings contained small separate rooms, buttery and pantry, with a solar or great chamber at one end, withdrawing rooms and another chamber at the other end. Apart from the service rooms, all had fireplaces and were distinctly more comfortable than the hall could ever be. Separate staircases at each end gave direct access to most of the rooms, a hint of that other tendency – towards privacy and comfort – which was to mark the house designed under Renaissance influence.

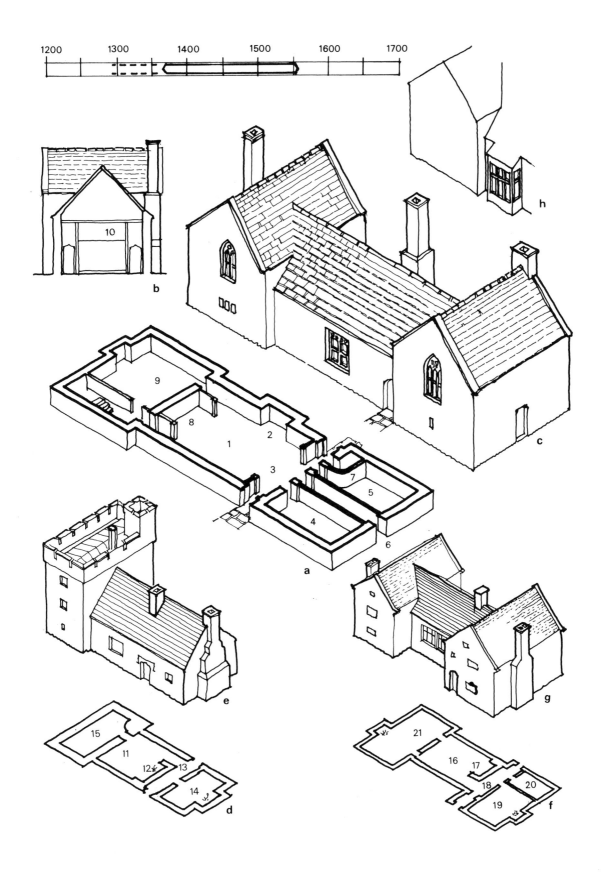

The H-shaped house of open hall and storeyed cross-wings was found throughout the country. The plan developed during the 14th century and, although generally transformed in the late 16th century, continued in use in the central Pennines to expire with a flourish a whole century later.

6 Multi-storey houses

The revolution in Large House design that took place in the second half of the 16th and early part of the 17th century meant the elimination of the open hall, the shift of architectural emphasis from ground floor to first floor, and a tendency towards a symmetrical front elevation. The result of the revolution was storeyed designs for houses which were two-storeyed throughout and often with a third storey in the wings; which located an important room on the first floor and had staircases of appropriate size, convenience and ostentation to reach it; which had many separate rooms each served by a fireplace, so that tall, highly decorated chimney-stacks enlivened a roof already marked by gables and finials; and which had a distinct front, back and sides so organised that the front at least was symmetrical, or as nearly symmetrical as function would allow.

The hall complete with screens passage survived, but as a room with a comparatively low ceiling and usually without a distinct dais. In the largest houses the porch, doorway and screens passage were moved to the centre of the elevation; but in rather smaller houses the hall occupied its conventional position between the wings, porch being balanced by bay window and the centre of the more or less symmetrical elevation being marked by an extra gable or dormer window. The room above the hall was comparable in importance to the solar of the medieval house, but it took over some of the semi-public functions of the hall and was not open to the roof but ceiled and heated by a side-wall fireplace, both modifications giving extra comfort. The cross-wings generally remained, bringing some more of the service activities into the lower end of the house (the kitchen, for instance, was no longer detached) and multiplying the number of parlours and chambers elsewhere. All these developments increased the opportunity for privacy; more and

8. Ty-Faenor, Abbey Cwmhir, Radnorshire
A multi-storey Large House of three floors and a full-height basement accommodated in the fall of the ground. On each floor there are two rooms, one each side of a dog-leg staircase. The building is unusual, possibly unique, in the distinct entasis (slightly curved taper) on the end walls and the chimney-breast.
(British Crown Copyright: Royal Commission on the Ancient and Historical Monuments of Wales)

9. Talgarth, Trefeglwys, Montgomeryshire
This also is a multi-storey Large House, but the timber-frame is jettied only on the end wall. The chimney-pots suggest that as many as eight fireplaces are served by the one stack.
(British Crown Copyright: Royal Commission on the Ancient and Historical Monuments of Wales)

more rooms opened off landings or corridors rather than off each other, and the greater comfort that this allowed added to the improved condition of rooms ceiled with plaster, lined with panelling and heated by fireplaces.

Stone and timber continued to be the main building materials: stone used less in mass and more in moulded mullions and transoms for the newly popular large square windows; timber used with an extravagance which hardly suggested its increasing scarcity, and especially to produce the jettied floors that helped to emphasise the upper storeys.

10. Bodwrdda, Aberdaron, Caernarvonshire
This multi-storey Large House with boldly projecting wings was built in 1621. It is practically symmetrical, only the front door being slightly off-centre. The use of brick at that time in such a remote location in north Wales is very unusual.
(British Crown Copyright: Royal Commission on the Ancient and Historical Monuments of Wales)

6 Multi-storey houses

a. Ground-floor plan showing a diminished hall (1), unheated or with a rear-wall fireplace, remnants of a screens passage (2) with a prominent multi-storey porch (3), and kitchen (4) and pantry (5) in a cross-wing. At the opposite end of the hall is a multi-storey bay window (6). A parlour (7) occupies part of the ground floor of a wing which balances the service wing.

b. Cross-section showing hall (8) with tall great chamber (9) and garret rooms above (10).

c. Sketch to show the broadly symmetrical arrangement of facets receding to the wall of the hall and great chamber.

d. Alternative with hall (11), kitchen (12), heated parlour (13).

e. Sketch to show the two storeys and a garret storey.

f. Elevation of a timber-framed house with continuous jetty at the front.

g. Cross-section of such a house with jetty.

---

7 Compact houses with projecting wings

A house-plan which is represented by comparatively few examples, but is important in the stages of development to the standard Renaissance plan, is that in which a compact central block, several storeys high, had a number of projections from each face making a more or less balanced collection of elements and a set of more or less symmetrical elevations. This sort of house was forward-looking in being symmetrical (often about both axes) and having the lines of symmetry architecturally emphasised, but it was backward-looking in that the symmetry was usually marred by such elements as windows introduced for functional or traditional reasons (even though their position might be architecturally inconvenient) and in that the roof-line was punctuated by gables, dormers, turrets and chimneys in a lively and not always well-ordered profusion. Internally such a house was forward-looking in the importance of staircase and upper rooms but backward-looking in that elements of hall and parlour sometimes remained.

One version of the plan had hall and parlour or withdrawing room in the central block with a kitchen wing at the rear, a projecting multi-storey porch at the front, and possibly staircase turrets at each side. Another, larger version had two principal and two service rooms on the ground floor, chambers above, and either a front porch and rear staircase turret or front and rear porches and staircase projections on each side. There were several experiments, but the most significant examples had a centralised entrance/lobby/staircase system that allowed all the rooms on each floor to be separately entered. It has been observed that the combination of a multi-storey porch at the front, staircase and kitchen at the rear and hall or other circulation space in the centre, together with bold projection of fireplaces and chimney-breasts from the end walls, 'produced the characteristic cruciform plan of the mid-17th-century gentry house' in Wales, but this is also true in England. 6

There is one further point about this plan that deserves note: the medieval house often had no front, both sides being of comparable importance; the multi-storey house had a front on which all attention was lavished, giving a back and sides

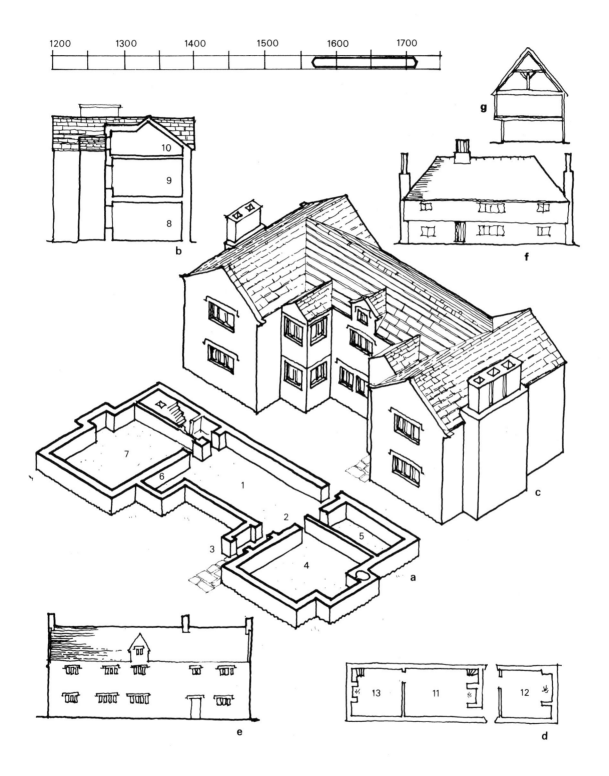

7 Compact houses with projecting wings

a. Ground-floor plan showing hall (1), parlour (2) and kitchen (3). A staircase (4) gives easy access to the chambers and garret floor. The multi-storey porch (5) marks the approximate centre of the front elevation. The fireplaces (6) are back to back and their flues combine in a single tall chimney-stack.

b. Sketch to show the main block and projecting wings which produce a cross-shaped plan.

c. Alternative ground-floor plan which also has hall (7), parlour (8), kitchen (9), staircase (10) and porch (11). In this case the main fireplaces (12) are on the gable walls and so the compact block of flues is missing.

d. Sketch to show the distribution of chimney-stacks as well as the cross-shaped plan.

e. Ground-floor plan of a house with internal chimneys and projecting staircase wings. Entrance through the porch is directly into the hall (13) off which a staircase rises to the chambers on one side of the house (14). In this example the house is two rooms deep as well as two rooms wide.

f. Sketch to show that a stubby cross-shape emerges from use of porch and staircase wing.

11. Manor House, Hammoon, Dorset
A compact house with a porch projecting to the front and a wing projecting to the rear combines the T-shape with the L-shape. The continued use of thatch in a house of such quality is notable.
(Peter Crawley)

44

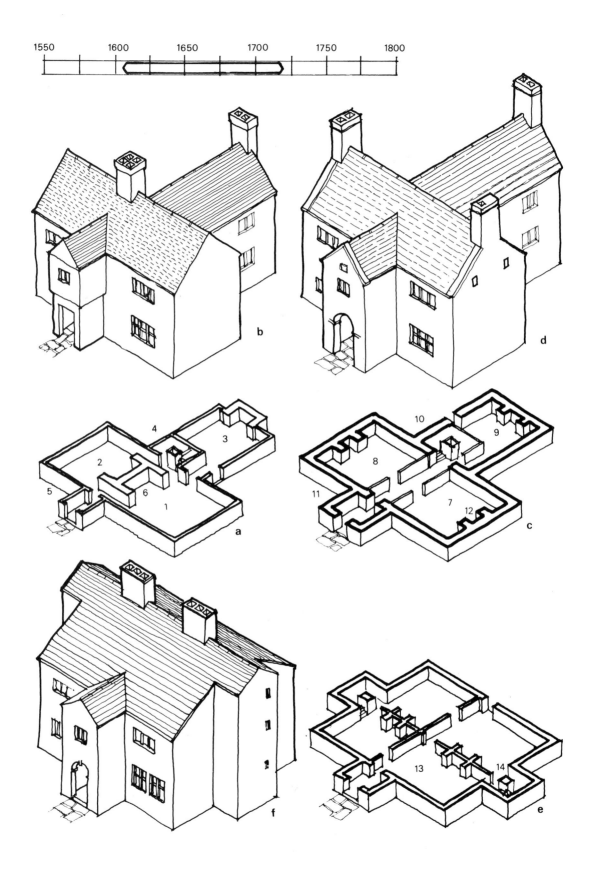

1550 1600 1650 1700 1750 1800

12. Gunby Hall, Lincolnshire
This brick double-pile Large House of 1700 has a carefully composed symmetrical elevation, but is unusual in its flat roof.
(Peter Crawley)

13. The Latin House, Risley, Derbyshire
Small in size but definitely a Large House in pretension, this brick house of 1706 is of double-pile plan, with its roof hipped all round a small lead flat. The cruciform chimney-stacks serve fireplaces back to back in a spine wall.
(Peter Crawley)

which were ignored architecturally; but the compact house with projecting wings often had four fronts, each elevation receiving attention from the designer and establishing its own symmetry.

In cross-section these houses advanced the development of the garret floor, the accommodation in the roof space that gave greater privacy to more members of the household. They also began the development of the semi-basement which gave an impressive approach to the front door, encouraged the use of a dry boarded floor to the principal rooms, and extended the service accommodation.

8 Double-pile houses

Medieval houses had tended to symmetry about the long axis. Inside the hall there was symmetry about an imaginary line leading from the centre of the screens passage to the centre of the dais; viewed from the entrance or garden fronts, the disposition of rooms and windows was generally asymmetrical. The short axis was paramount in the Renaissance house, even though there might be subsidiary symmetries about the long axis on the end elevations. Medieval houses were conceived as one room in depth: the hall spanned from front wall to back, the wings, though placed at right angles, were composed of rooms of full depth. The Renaissance house, however, was conceived as a compact, centralised, cubiform block two rooms in depth, and for this the contemporary term 'double pile' is appropriate.

The normal arrangement of the double-pile Large House gave a central entrance lobby leading to a double-flight fully exposed staircase at the rear. The two principal living rooms were at the front, one on each side of the entrance lobby; the two

46

47

8 Double-pile houses

a. Ground-floor plan which shows a central entrance door leading to a lobby (1) off which open the living room (2) and parlour (3), kitchen (4) and dairy or pantry (5), with main staircase (6) and service stairs (7).

b. First-floor plan showing the bedrooms (8), many with fireplaces.

c. Cross-section showing ground- and first-floor rooms and the garret storey; in this example the double-pile plan is roofed by means of two parallel roofs and a valley gutter between (9). Sometimes there is a cellar beneath the front rooms (10).

d. Sketch to show the arrangement of roofs and gable chimneys.

e. An alternative ground-floor plan with fireplaces back to back rather than in the gable walls.

f. Another version of the plan with all fireplaces grouped together in the centre of the building and the staircase in one corner.

g. Sketch showing how a simple roof of shallow pitch covers the whole depth of the plan.

h. An alternative roofing system giving a clean eaves at the front and two gables at the rear. This method of roofing is suitable for steeply pitched roofs and also for a plan with internal chimneys as in plan (e).

i. Another roofing system used with low-pitch roofing material and for plan (f).

j. Sketch showing the rear of a house that approximates to the double-pile plan but has two wings a few feet apart rather than a continuous run of rooms.

k. Flat roof behind parapets.

---

principal service rooms were at the rear, one on each side of the staircase; the principal bedrooms were on the first floor, subsidiary bedrooms were above, partly in the roof space, and subsidiary service rooms were below the entrance level and partly underground. There were variations in the position of the main staircase, which was sometimes at the side between living and service rooms. The fireplaces were usually on the side walls, but might be placed back to back on spine walls and were sometimes clustered together in a massive stack in the middle. In houses of such a deep plan there were roofing problems; these were solved either by having two parallel roofs with a vulnerable gutter in between, by having a hipped or gabled roof at the front and two short stretches of roof at the rear, by having a hipped roof at the front leading to a central flat roof with a cupola, balustrade and 'widow's walk', or by having a deep overall roof of shallow pitch making use of good quality slate. The aim in fact was to diminish the importance of the roof in a composition which was as compact as possible on every plane; gables, finials and ornate chimney-stacks were quite alien to such a composition.

The double-pile house-plan came into use in the late 17th century, was universally used in the 18th century and lasted through much of the 19th, albeit in Greek, Gothic or Italianate dress. Stone remained in use for such houses, timber passed out of use, but brick became quite the most favoured material.

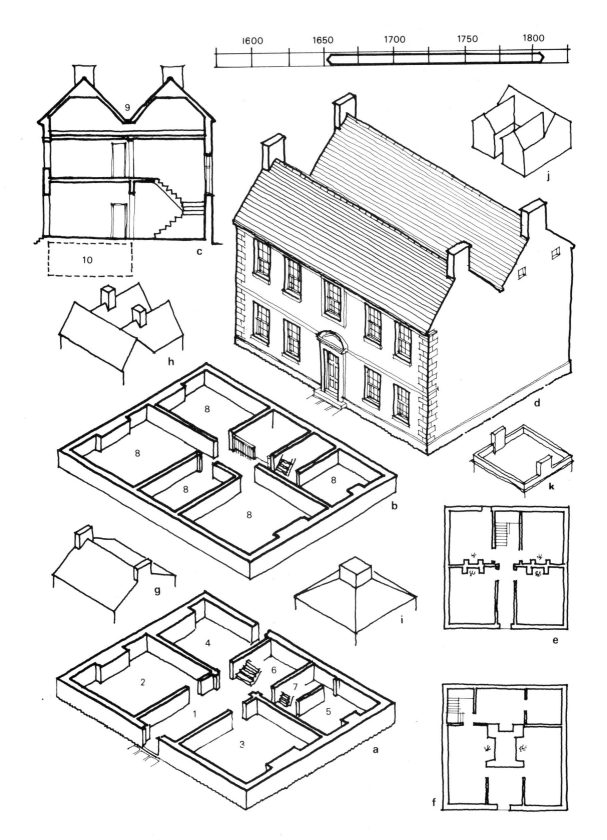

1600   1650   1700   1750   1800

9

10

c

h

8

8

8

8

8

b

d

k

e

g

i

4

6

2

7

1

5

3

a

f

Small Houses of the countryside

The design of Small Houses generally

Although most Small Houses were farmhouses, the dwellings of working yeoman or tenant farmers, nearly all existing examples of this size-type have domestic buildings separated from the farm buildings – either physically separated as a free-standing building, structurally separated by way of a solid party wall, or functionally separated by means of a cross-passage. Small Houses were therefore essentially domestic buildings and, as the ordinary farmer was spared the public duties of his social superior, the lord of the manor, they may indeed be considered as purely domestic buildings. As such they show the two-part division between more public and more private areas which is fundamental to domestic planning even today: one part accommodated the more public activities of eating, cooking, and entertaining guests; the other accommodated the more private activities of sleeping and storing valuable goods. The developments in Small House planning may be seen as responding to the tendency towards increased specialisation in the accommodation of these activities: as more and more rooms were provided, ever greater specialisation in the use of the separate rooms was achieved, with ever greater privacy for the users.

However, development was neither steady nor uniform over the country, and there is in fact a considerable variety in Small House planning. It shows itself mainly in extension of plan (more rooms on each floor) and extension of section (more and more storeys brought into use), as well as in the varying relationships between entrance door, means of access between storeys and nature and location of the principal heat source.

As we have seen, possible variations of plan depend to a large extent on the relative positions of these three items; and this is particularly so in the Small Houses of the countryside, whose plans originated as simple rectangles and developed as variations *within* the rectangle and extensions *from* the rectangle.

There were three feasible positions for the main door: in the end or gable wall, at the corner of the main side wall and at or near the centre of the main wall. All have been used in the plans that follow. There were in practice four possible positions for the staircase in a multi-storey Small House: alongside the main fireplace, at the rear of the main living space, near the centre of that space and in an inner room opening off the main living space. Again, the use of all these positions will be noted, though as staircases become more generous in dimensions and easier in rise (as well as more prominent) the position alongside the fireplace fell out of favour. The nature of the principal heat source varied from open hearth through smoke bay or inglenook to fixed fireplace, and the position tended to vary in each stage of development.

The earliest Small Houses were heated by an open hearth in a hall or living room open to the roof. The fire of wood or peat was loosely located on a paved hearth and smoke rose to be absorbed into a thatched roof or evacuated through slates or tiles, or occasionally through a louvre. The small size of the living space of a Small House meant that a central position for the hearth was less convenient than in the lord's great hall and the absence of a separate kitchen meant that control of the fire for cooking purposes as well as room heating was very important. So the open hearth tended to migrate towards a fireback wall, based on an existing wall or built for the purpose, with smoke confined either in the partitioned section of roof which has been called a 'smoke bay' or in the funnel-shaped timber, wattle and daub chimney which has been called a 'smoke hood' or 'hooded chimney'. The smoke bay was ineffective and quickly superseded by what we would regard as a conventional brick or stone fireplace, flue and chimney-stack being placed in the former smoke bay, often blocking an earlier cross-passage. The smoke hood was rather more satisfactory in operation, and as it helped to create an inglenook, a room within a room, the peat fire against a fireback wall and beneath a smoke hood remained popular until the late 18th century in many parts of the country, and even later in some, before being superseded by fireplaces designed for burning coal and cooking food.

Although rooms became increasingly specialised in their uses, there were very long periods in which rooms served several purposes either simultaneously or in sequence. The parlour, for instance, was bedroom, dining room, drawing room, entertaining room, store room and workroom at one time or another. In the more advanced parts of the country the use of a first-floor chamber as a bedroom began at a very early period, but in the more conservative regions first-floor sleeping was reserved for servants, children and poultry, the bed of the master and mistress of the house being in the ground-floor parlour. Since sleeping was at that time the main function of the parlour, a heat source was not considered necessary, so that for a long time no hearth or fireplace was provided.

In most farmhouses, regular dining around the long table (supplemented on special occasions by the round table) was long confined to the living room; but in the more pretentious farming households the parlour came into use as a dining room, though for a long time such a heated parlour was also in occasional use as a bedroom. In the smaller and earlier of the houses the parlour acted as a store room for grain, fleeces or other valuable products of the farm and also for food for the household, but even in such houses it became common practice to partition an area from the parlour end of the house to serve as a pantry or dairy. Finally one should not ignore the use of the parlour as a workroom for spinning or weaving. The self-sufficient farming household needed space in which to store and use the simple machinery required, and during the boom years for hand-operated machinery at the end of the 18th and beginning of the 19th century virtually every space was conscripted to house the spinning jenny or the loom. Here again, the heated parlour would suit some activities and the unheated parlour others.

The plans that follow show variations according to time (and the improving standards demanded) and to place within the general hierarchy of the Small House dweller.

9 Wealden and other open-hall houses

As the name suggests, open-hall Small Houses are those in which the main room is a hall at ground level and open to the roof. The Wealden house is a special version of this plan.

In its basic form the open-hall house consists of the hall and a two-storey portion at one or both ends; entrance is by way of a cross-passage (sometimes called a cross-entry because it is induced by opposing doors but not precisely defined by parallel partitions) into one end of the hall. Where the hall has two-storey portions at both ends there are service rooms beneath a chamber at the entrance end of the hall, and a parlour beneath another chamber at the opposite end. The open-hall Small House resembled the double-ended hall among the Large Houses, but the two-storey portions are usually contained within a simple rectangular plan and

A Wealden house, but showing the developments usual in such buildings. The jettied upper floor of the two wings may be seen, but there is a bracket supporting the 'flying bressummer' at the intermediate truss of the hall. A bold dormer window announces the flooring of the hall while the prominent chimney-stacks mark the vastly improved heating provision.
(Peter Crawley)

do not project as wings, while the whole house is, of course, on a much smaller scale. The oldest examples of the open-hall plan retain a central open hearth (or evidence of its former existence), but the majority of surviving examples benefit from improved heating provision by way of a smoke bay locating the hearth at the service end of the hall, by way of a hearth, fireback wall and chimney-hood backing on to the cross-passage, or by way of a fireplace backing on to or inserted within the cross-passage.

This plan is old, and was widespread and enduring. The vast majority of houses originally erected according to this layout have been altered, especially by the insertion of an intermediate floor within the hall, but some few still remain without substantial alteration and may be dated as medieval in the south-east of England, late medieval or 16th-century in the west Midlands and the eastern counties of Wales, but probably of late 16th- or 17th-century date in the North, and even of 19th-century date and unsophisticated form in the western half of Wales.

The so-called 'Wealden houses' form a large and easily recognisable group within the general body of open-hall Small Houses. A Wealden house is one in which a central hall is open to the roof and flanked by two-storey bays, but in such a way that the upper part of each of the bays is jettied out at the front, or to one side, or even to front, sides and rear. On the ground floor the plan is rectangular, at first-floor level it tends to an H shape, but at the roof it reverts to a rectangle as the hipped or gablet roof covers the jettied plan, mastering the central part with the aid of deep eaves; in the most characteristic examples, the outer wall-plate is carried on brackets.

Entry was into a miniature screens passage or into a simple cross-entry space

7

15. Old Cloth Hall, Smarden, Kent
The complicated projections of the elevation betray the stages of development in this house.

taken off the hall, and doors led into the service rooms at one side. From the other end of the hall one, or usually two, doors led into one or two parlours at what might be considered the dais end of the hall. The first-floor chambers, though enhanced by their jettied floors, were reached by a pair of separate mean and unobtrusive stairs. The hall was heated by an open hearth, the smoke escaping (if at all) through a saddle-type louvre above.

Wealden houses are usually very well built, ample timbers of heavy section being used, and they were often decorated both on the roof-trusses and the external timberwork. The type emerged fully developed towards the middle of the 14th century and flourished until towards the middle of the 16th, maintaining a standard of design, construction and decoration to which other farmers in different parts of the country might aspire but hardly attain. Wealden houses were indeed the dwellings of yeoman farmers, not of gentlemen. Although concentrated in Kent, Sussex, Essex and Surrey, they may be seen in other parts of lowland England and an urban version is even more widespread. Although most were modernised 8

9 Wealden and other open-hall houses

a. Ground-floor plan showing hall (1), open hearth (2), cross-passage (3) and, opening off it, the buttery and pantry (4 and 5); at the opposite end of the hall are two unheated parlours (6).

b. First-floor plan with upper part of open hall (7) and a solar (8 and 9) on each side and reached by separate staircases.

c. Cross-section through the hall at the cross-passage showing doors to buttery and pantry and to staircase.

d. Cross-section showing the truss in the open hall and looking towards the parlours.

e. Sketch of Wealden house showing the entrance door that leads to the cross-passage and the tall window that lights the open hall; the upper floors are here shown jettied to the front at the left-hand end of the building and jettied to front and side at the right-hand end; the whole is covered by a hipped roof with gablets which would help in evacuation of smoke.

f. Ground-floor plan of a Wealden house as commonly transformed in the late 16th century; a fireplace has been inserted in the cross-passage.

g. Upper part of transformed Wealden house showing chimney-stack with fireplace serving the newly formed chamber over the hall.

h. Sketch of transformed Wealden house, showing chimney-stack and dormer window.

i. In some Wealden houses the entrance and cross-passage are incorporated in one of the 'wings'.

j. Often the hearth was moved towards the cross-passage and a partition in the roof-truss above created a smoke bay which served as a rudimentary chimney.

k. End-jetty house; chamber jettied over parlour.

16. Preston Cottage, Alderley Edge, Cheshire
Probably begun as a T-shaped Small House; the wing on the left was added shortly before an inventory was compiled in 1628. The prominent dormer window suggests that the room open to the roof was floored, probably in the late 17th century. The position of the brick chimney-breast suggests that a fireplace was inserted at this time, blocking the cross-passage.
(R. W. Brunskill)

54

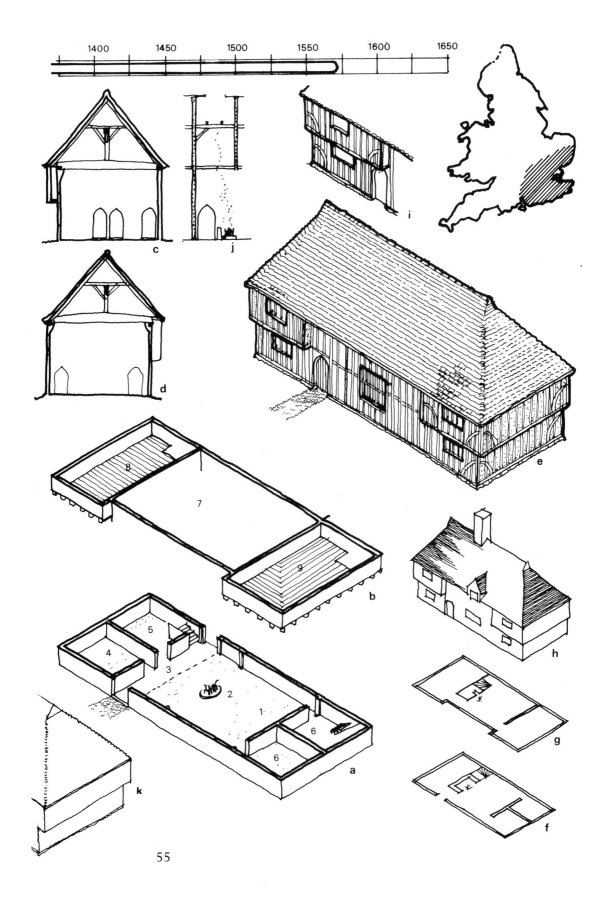

1400   1450   1500   1550   1600   1650

c

j

i

d

e

8

7

9

b

5

4

3

2

1

6

6

a

h

g

f

k

10 Small Houses with lateral chimneys

a. Ground-floor plan showing the living room (1), fireplace in front side wall (2), cross-passage or cross-entry between opposed doors (3) and two service rooms (4 and 5) opening off it; beyond the hall or living room there is a parlour (6), which in this case is heated by a gable fireplace (7).

b. Cross-section showing relationship of lateral chimney-stack to the main roof; at this stage the rooms on the upper floor might well be open to the roof.

c. Isometric sketch showing the relationship between lateral chimney-stack and entrance into cross-passage.

d. An alternative plan in which the heated parlour (8) is alongside the cross-passage.

e. A variation of the plan with a heated kitchen (9) alongside the cross-passage and a heated parlour at the opposite end of the house.

f. A smaller version in which there are no rooms beyond the cross-passage.

g. A larger version having parlour and service rooms placed together in a wing alongside the cross-passage and a multi-storey porch marking the entrance doorway.

h. Sometimes the lateral chimney was placed on the rear wall as in this plan.

---

in the second half of the 16th century by the insertion of an intermediate floor and the formation of a great chamber lit by a prominent dormer window, and although there were alterations to the hall fenestration, Wealden houses are still easily recognised.

10 Small Houses with lateral chimneys

We have seen that the central open hearth of the medieval Large House was usually replaced by a fireplace on a side wall. In the smaller hall of the medieval yeoman or peasant, the central position for an open hearth must have been far from convenient and a move to a side or end wall correspondingly welcome. There is a house-type in which the side-wall position was chosen. Examples are not numerous in relation to the country as a whole, but the type is definitely characteristic of certain areas.

The lateral-chimney house is similar to other successors of the late medieval open-hall houses in having three main units and a cross-passage. The entrance to the cross-passage usually lay near the projecting chimney-breast of the main fireplace and the passage (which may not have been precisely defined by partitions) ran across one end of the principal ground-floor room. Service rooms opened off the passage, and a parlour, often heated by a gable fireplace, opened off the other end of the main room. Such houses had chambers extending over the whole of the first floor, and often there were garret rooms in addition. In Small Houses the lateral fireplace was usually, though not invariably, located on the front wall alongside the front door, whereas such a fireplace was nearly always on the rear side wall of a Large House.

Small Houses with lateral chimneys were built between about 1570 and 1650. Examples may be seen on both sides of the Bristol Channel: in Monmouthshire, Glamorgan and Pembrokeshire and in the northern parts of Somerset and Devon.

1500   1550   1600   1650   1700   1750

17. House at Old Glasson, Lancashire The relative positions of door and chimney-stack indicate a hearth backing on to a cross-passage with accommodation for animals to the left and domestic accommodation (originally open to the roof) to the right.
(RCHME © Crown Copyright)

Some may be found in north Wales, but they are rare in other parts where Large Houses with lateral chimneys are common enough.

11 Longhouses

A longhouse is a Small House where farm animals and humans are housed within the same walls and under the same roof in an elongated rectangular building which has a cross-passage running behind the main hearth or fireplace in such a way that it is available for access by both humans and animals and for intercommunication between domestic and agricultural parts of the building. The longhouse plan may develop through subdivision or accretion.

Excavation has shown that the longhouse plan was used throughout the medieval period in many parts of England and Wales. Published results of excavation show the former existence of elongated rectangular buildings running either along a slope or across a slope and having stone foundation walls but a superstructure of some other material. A paved cross-passage may be detected with entrance at about the midpoint of the side walls; a hearth may be found fairly near this passage while an inner room was formed beyond the hearth at one end of the building. At the opposite end of the building the excavations indicate occupation by animals on the evidence of the bases of stone feeding troughs, of sockets for posts to which cattle could be tethered, or of drainage channels. Early examples of complete buildings that survive have such a plan enclosed within walls of stone, timber-frame or clay. They retain the two living spaces of the domestic half of the building, but with the hearth moved against a fireback wall that forms one side of the cross-passage. In such buildings cattle may be tethered either nose-on to the passage (which presumably served as a feeding passage) or nose-on to one or both of the side walls. In other examples there is a separate external entrance for cattle, but access to the cross-passage preserves intercommunication for the farmer between house and byre.

Generally, surviving longhouses have an intermediate floor to the house proper, with staircase access to the loft or chambers from the parlour or from the rear of the living kitchen or from alongside the hearth. A stage in which the inner room was lofted while the living kitchen remained open to the roof was presumably included in the development. Probably the most common staircase arrangement

58

is that in which the staircase rises from the rear wall of the living kitchen – either confined as a mural staircase or, in the later examples, as a double-flight staircase in a rearward projection. The most compact arrangement is that in which a winding staircase enters the fireback wall against the cross-passage and emerges alongside the chimney at first-floor level: such an arrangement was favoured in the southern half of Wales.

In essence, the domestic part of a longhouse contained the same accommodation as a two-unit Small House, and one can see how the rectangular building revealed in excavations could have been subdivided by partitions, inserted floors and added fireplaces until the fully developed longhouse emerged. Equally one can see how the longhouse was superseded by a set of distinct buildings, the domestic part becoming the two-unit house and the agricultural part becoming cowhouse, stable, barn, etc.

Certain longhouses, however, appear to have been formed by the addition of cowhouse, stable, barn, etc., to an existing two-unit Small House. When such a house had a gable entry and later farm buildings were attached, a cross-passage had to be formed to give access at least to the house, even if the farm buildings had separate entrances.

Understanding of the longhouse is complicated by the practice of alternate rebuilding, whereby the domestic part of the longhouse was rebuilt while the agricultural part remained and then the improved domestic part was retained while the agricultural part was rebuilt. In such a process, the overall dimensions of the original longhouse might remain unaltered. The cross-passage maintained its original position, perhaps even with its original doorway, but walls of the two

18. Houses at Porlock Weir, Somerset
The prominent side-wall fireplaces are typical of the south-western counties.
(Peter Crawley)

11 Longhouses

a. Ground-floor plan showing living kitchen (1) off which opens an unheated parlour (2) and also a pantry (3); the hearth in its inglenook (4) backs on to the cross-passage (5), which also gives an alternative access to the cowhouse (6). In this instance a winding staircase (7) leads to the upper floor.

b. Cross-section taken through the staircase and showing the chimney-hood above the inglenook.

c. Sketch to show the relationship between the two parts of the longhouse and the way in which the cross-passage is associated with the farming part.

d. An alternative plan with living kitchen (8) and parlour (9) all reached by a cross-passage (10) which also serves as a feeding passage for animals (11).

e. Plan based on excavations to show the true longhouse with its cross-passage between parts for humans (12) and animals (13) more clearly separated but with both using the same cross-passage.

f. The house (14) and byre (15) are part of the same structure.

g. Plan to show how cross-passage and farm buildings were added to an existing house of two units which had gable entry. The cross-passage leads to the original house (16) but also serves the cowhouse (17), which has a stable attached (18).

h. Sketch to show a stage of alternate rebuilding in which the farming part is later and of higher quality than the domestic.

i. Sketch to show a stage in which the domestic part is later than the farming part in its reconstruction.

---

parts could be in different materials, roofs of different height, pitch and covering material and the doors and windows might be of different periods.

Surviving longhouses (or longhouse derivatives) seem generally to be of the 17th or early 18th century. However, there are some examples, especially in the South-West and the west Midlands, which are much older, possibly late medieval, while in the North-West, at least, longhouses (or their derivatives) seem to have been under construction well into the 18th century, and in Wales were being formed by accretion throughout that century and much of the 19th. At all times one suspects that the surviving superstructures of such buildings may rise from much older foundations. Longhouses are characteristic of the western half of the country, but examples are also found in east Yorkshire and the former distribution may have been much more widespread.

12 Cross-passage Small Houses

The cross-passage type of Small House is that in which a purely domestic building, usually of three units, features entry by way of a cross-passage running behind the principal hearth or fireplace. Two of the three units consist of a parlour (or a parlour with a dairy partitioned off) opening off a living kitchen which in turn opens off a cross-passage. The third room is beyond the cross-passage and may be an unheated service room (such as a scullery or brew-house), a kitchen or another habitable room such as a heated parlour. The main hearth or fireplace

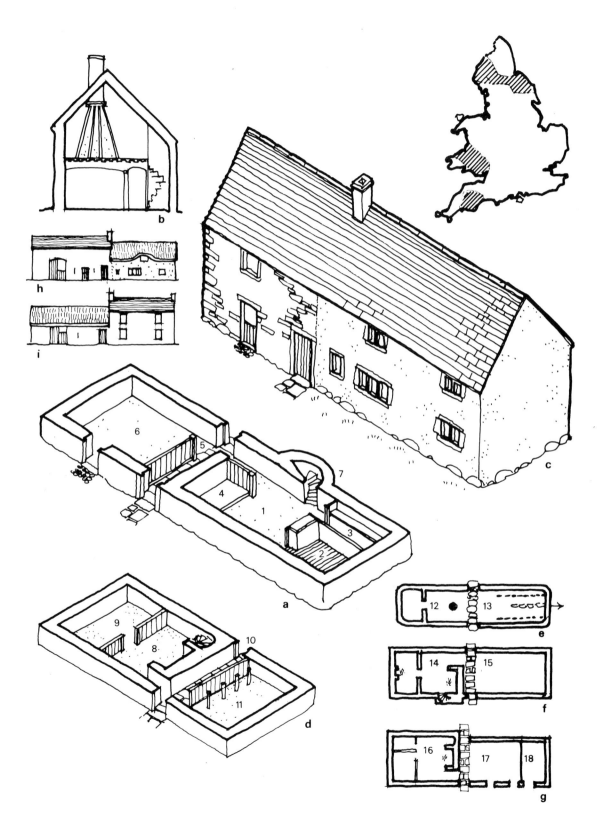

61

12 Cross-passage Small Houses

a. Ground-floor plan showing living room (1) with a hearth and inglenook (2) backing on to the cross-passage (3). At one end of the house there is a heated room (4) which is sometimes a kitchen and sometimes a parlour. At the other end of the house there is a heated parlour (5). The store room or pantry (6) and the staircase (7) project from the rear wall in this example.

b. Cross-section showing a full-height ground floor and a low upper floor which is partly in the roof space.

c. Isometric sketch which shows the relationship between the chimney-stack of the main fireplace and the door leading into the cross-passage.

d. Ground-floor plan of a smaller version of this house-type. Here a fireplace and adjacent staircase back on to the cross-passage, a heated parlour or kitchen opens off the passage, but there is no third room at the opposite end of the house.

e. Plan indicating the division of space by screens rather than full-height walls or partitions.

f. Plan showing entrance from passage to principal room coming between fireplace and staircase.

g. Plan showing the fireplace centrally placed under the ridge; the staircase projects from the rear wall.

h. Plan with no rooms beyond the cross-passage.

i. Elevation of plan (h).

---

was located in the body of the house since it backed on to the cross-passage, but increasingly as the type developed there was a subsidiary fireplace in one gable to serve the main parlour as well as another fireplace in the opposite gable. There were chambers on the first floor and sometimes lofts above.

Cross-passage houses may be seen in many parts of the country, with some concentration in the north of England but also many examples along the Limestone Belt. Dated examples of such Small Houses suggest a period of popularity extending from about 1660 to 1740, though in some parts of the North the plan remained in use throughout the 18th century.

There are some curious houses in Lancashire, and perhaps elsewhere, which have all the characteristics of this plan but no room beyond the cross-passage. This is not because of demolition or incomplete building; the masonry shows that the design was intentional, and in at least one case the landholding is such that no room could possibly have been built beyond the cross-passage. The reason for the design remains a mystery.

13 Lobby-entrance houses and houses with back-to-back fireplaces
A lobby- or baffle-entry house is one in which the front door opens into a lobby formed by the jamb wall of a fireplace or of two fireplaces back to back or of the equivalent in timber-walled inglenooks.

One group of house-plans widely used in the 17th and early 18th centuries had either a lobby entrance or a pair of fireplaces back to back or both. All the plans relate to multi-storey construction. Some were based on two main living rooms

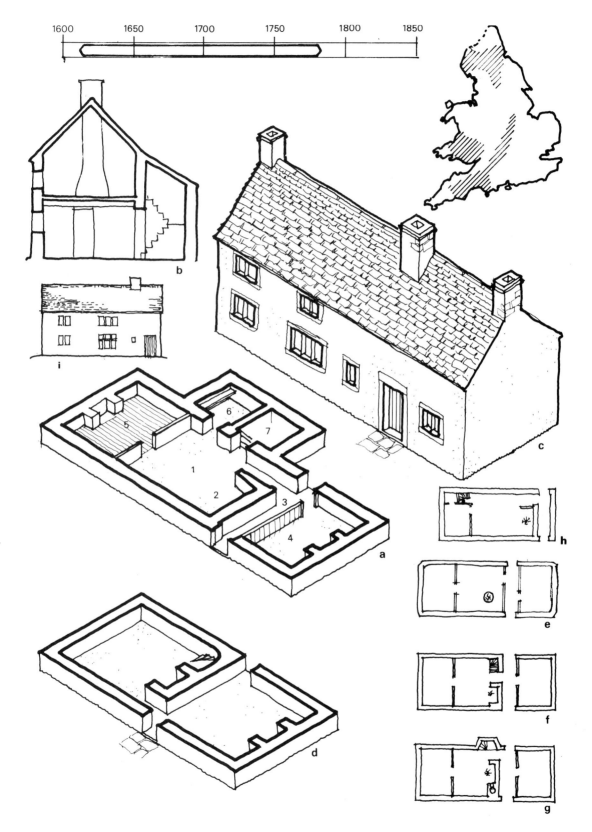

1600   1650   1700   1750   1800   1850

b

i

c

a

5
6
7
1
2
3
4

d

h

e

f

g

13a Lobby-entrance houses and houses with back-to-back fireplaces: two units

a. Ground-floor plan of a two-unit house with lobby entrance: the living kitchen (1) has a deep fireplace (2) and the parlour (3) has its own fireplace (4) placed back to back so that the two fireplaces and chimney-stacks make a compact central block; the entrance (5) is into a lobby against the staircase (6), which is squeezed against the jambs of the central fireplaces.

b. Cross-section showing the two full-height storeys and the fireplace in the upper floor joining with the stack from the ground-floor fireplaces.

c. Isometric sketch showing the relationship between chimney-stack and doorway.

d. An alternative ground-floor plan with living kitchen (5) and, in this case, an unheated parlour (6) and with staircase (7) located between fireplace and rear wall; the entrance (8) leads to a lobby against the fireplace jamb.

e. Another version of the plan with living kitchen and parlour and back-to-back fireplaces; projecting at the rear is a staircase (9) and at the front a multi-storey porch.

f. Sketch showing the cruciform arrangement dependent on the massive central chimney-stack.

g. An alternative plan with a service room projected at the rear.

h. Plan showing a third unit, a kitchen, added to the rear of the two basic units.

i. Hall and parlour with entrance by staircase.

j. Hall and parlour with entrance away from fireplaces.

k. Elevation showing entrance away from fireplaces, as (i).

---

and some on three, some had internal staircases while some had staircase projections, and all had internal fireplaces or hearths and so had chimney-stacks emerging through the roof.

a) Lobby-entrance plan with two units
In this plan-type two habitable rooms on each floor were served by back-to-back fireplaces helping to make a lobby or baffle entry. On the ground floor there were two rooms of somewhat unequal size, the larger being a living room (or rather a living kitchen) and the smaller a heated parlour. The fireplaces serving the two rooms being placed back to back, the lobby they created at the entrance gave privacy and protection from draughts to both rooms. On the first floor there were two chambers, and one or both might have a fireplace located over a ground-floor fireplace and with flues combined into a substantial common chimney-stack. There were often garret rooms above the chambers. Such a house was almost symmetrical in elevation, almost cubiform in mass and was dominated by the compact block of fireplaces and chimneys.

There were three possible positions for the staircase linking these various levels: in one the staircase was apparently considered as part of the double chimney-breast, a tight spiral tucked between fireplace and rear wall; in the second, which probably has the most numerous examples, the staircase was a wooden winding or newel staircase fitted into the lobby between the entrance door and the jambs of fireplaces which were pushed back to accommodate it; in the third position the

1550   1600   1650   1700   1750   1800

b

i

a

3

4

6

2

5

1

c

d

6

7

5

8

e

f

g

h

j

k

19. Home Farm House, near Devizes, Wiltshire
A two-unit lobby-entrance house, almost symmetrical in plan and elevation.
(Peter Crawley)

staircase was pushed out into a wing or turret at the rear. Where there was a porch in front of the door as well as a staircase at the rear, the plan became a miniature version of the cruciform Large House.

The two-unit lobby-entrance house-plan was in common use in the eastern half of the country from Lincolnshire to Essex, but is found elsewhere. Most examples appear to date from the first half of the 17th century, but some may be earlier and others were built later in that century. The plan was taken by settlers to North America and flourished especially in New England.

b) Lobby-entrance plan with three units
The other popular version of the lobby-entrance plan had three units instead of two in the main block, thus presenting an elongated elevation rather than a compact one.

On the ground floor there were two rooms (usually assumed to have been a living room and a kitchen) served by two back-to-back-fireplaces, but a third room opened off the larger of the two main rooms. Usually this third room seems to have been an unheated parlour but sometimes, and especially in later examples, it had its own fireplace in the end wall. However, it is possible that in some cases the third room was used as an unheated service room and the smaller heated room as a parlour. Entrance to the whole building was by way of the lobby against the back-to-back fireplaces, and it would have been easy to make a heated parlour and chamber above into separate accommodation to be occupied by, say, a widowed mother. There were variations in the position of the staircase similar to

66

20. House in Stoke-by-Nayland, Suffolk
Although later converted into three cottages, this appears to have been built as a three-unit lobby-entrance house with a kitchen to the left of the main room and an unheated parlour to the right. (Peter Crawley)

21. House at Fittleworth, Sussex
The relative positions of doorway and chimney-stack suggest that this is a three-unit lobby-entrance house with a small unheated parlour on the right. The timber-framing is exposed above, stone-clad below.
(Peter Crawley)

13b Lobby-entrance houses and houses with back-to-back fireplaces: three units

a. Ground-floor plan showing living room (1) with back-to-back fireplace block (2) serving also the kitchen (3); beyond the living room is an unheated parlour (4); the staircase lies between fireplaces and rear wall (5) and the entry (6) is a lobby entrance serving equally well the two main rooms.

b. Cross-section showing first-floor fireplaces added in the same stack that serves the ground-floor fireplaces.

c. Isometric sketch showing the relationship between door and chimney-stack.

d. An alternative ground-floor plan in which there are back-to-back fireplaces between a living room and a parlour (7 and 8) but with entrance by way of a cross-passage (10) which also gives access to a kitchen (9); the staircase (11) is associated with the fireplace.

e. A detail showing that back-to-back inglenooks lead to a similar arrangement as for back-to-back fireplaces.

f. Sketch plan showing baffle entry or lobby entry against a single fireplace.

g. A development from (f) with an extra fireplace added to the back of the original one – the door does not lie on the centre-line of the combined fireplaces; there is also shown here a fireplace for the inner room.

h. A three-unit plan with back-to-back fireplaces serving the two main rooms, a staircase in the lobby and a multi-storey porch marking the entrance.

i. A three-unit plan with lobby entrance but with the third unit developed as a wing.

j. Kitchen and small parlour reached through door in inglenook.

---

those found in the two-unit version, but also an additional one where the staircase was associated with the third room. Examples are widespread in lowland England and the eastern part of Wales and range in date from the early 17th century to well into the 18th century.

c) Fireplaces back to back, entrance away from the fireplace
It is perhaps paradoxical to include with this group of house-plans one type in which there is no lobby or baffle entry and yet the period and area of use coincide so closely with those of the others in the group that its inclusion actually seems appropriate.

In this version there are three heated rooms. Two are heated by back-to-back fireplaces and the third has its own fireplace in an end wall. The two main rooms may have been living room and heated parlour while the third was a kitchen, but the third room could equally have served as a separate heated parlour. These arrangements were quite feasible, as the entrance to the house was at the junction of the main and third rooms and there was often a cross-passage running from the entrance and separating these two rooms. The staircase position could vary as in the other versions, though a position at the rear between fireplaces was commonly used.

The plan occurs by no means as frequently as the other members of the group,

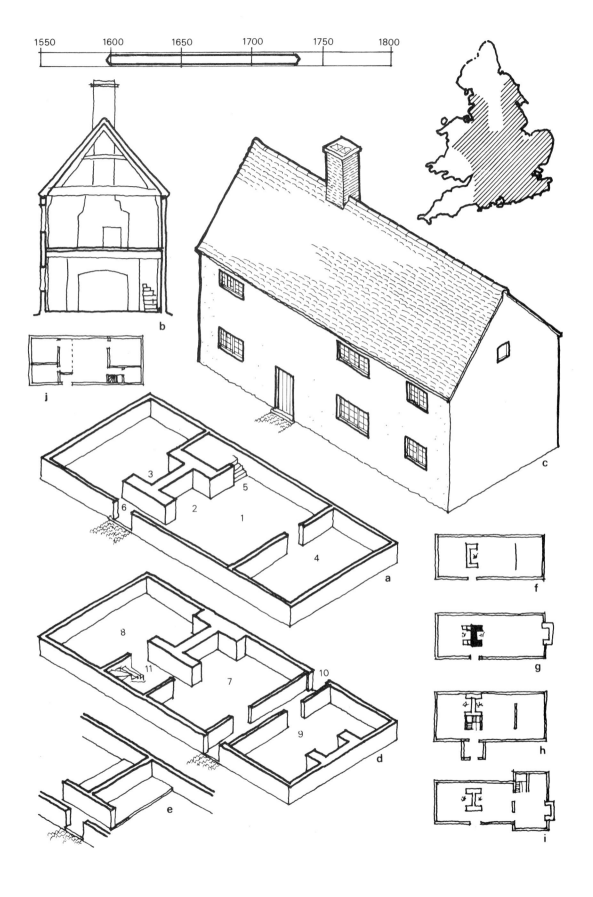

1550 1600 1650 1700 1750 1800

a b c d e f g h i j

1 2 3 4 5 6 7 8 9 10 11

22. Bryn-yr-Odin, Maentwrog, Merionethshire
This dour house of hard slatestone has an inside cross-passage with the main ground-floor room to the left and the main first-floor room to the right.
(British Crown Copyright: Royal Commission on the Ancient and Historical Monuments of Wales)

but examples are fairly numerous in Lincolnshire, Norfolk, Suffolk and Cambridge-shire and have from early 17th- to mid-18th-century dates.

14 Houses with central service rooms

There is a Small House plan which has not been discovered in many parts of the country but which seems to be fairly common in certain regions. In this plan there are three rooms on the ground floor: a living kitchen and a parlour (both heated) and an unheated service room placed between the other two. Since the two main rooms each have a gable fireplace, the arrangement tends towards a symmetrical plan and elevation, and in the most common version a central door-way strengthens the symmetry. When this door opens into a lobby from which all three rooms may be approached, quite an advanced plan emerges since no room opens off another room. However, early examples have a cross-passage which disturbs the symmetry and necessitates a further passage alongside the service room and some examples have a gable entry direct into the principal ground-floor room, again requiring a short passage alongside the service room. In a few early examples a central cross-passage has an unheated service room on each side as if the tradition of a cross-passage and the innovation of symmetry on plan and elevation were to be combined.

Staircases are usually to be found with the fireplaces, sometimes a staircase with each gable fireplace, one at each end of the building. Later examples tend to have a more spacious staircase conveniently placed alongside the service room, or between front door and service room, so producing a delightfully compact and convenient arrangement.

Examples appear to be mainly of mid- or late 17th-century date, but the range

12

70

of known dated buildings of this type extends from the late 16th to the early 18th century. At the moment the distribution gives some concentrations in the Cotswolds, Dorset and upland Monmouthshire, but examples are known from other parts of Wales, especially Denbighshire and Carmarthenshire. Further examples may await discovery in those many parts of England where gable fireplaces were commonly used.

15 Internal cross-passage houses

In this plan there are two main living spaces on the ground floor with a cross-passage between the two. Entry to the house was by way of a door placed near the centre of the main elevation and opening into a cross-passage which might be a true passage but more often was a cross-entry incorporated in the living kitchen though running alongside a partition. Beyond this partition was the second living space which was usually divided into two: parlour and service room, both unheated. A staircase rising beside the gable fireplace of the living room led to two chambers on the first floor. In the smaller examples both these rooms were unheated, but in the rather more pretentious examples the chamber over the parlour and service room was given a first-floor gable fireplace, was sometimes left open to a decorative roof and generally was made

23. House in Beaminster, Dorset
Although the house is of three units, back-to-back fireplaces serve the hall and parlour and are set away from the doorway. The kitchen at the lower end has a gable chimney. The continuous label mould running over all the windows suggests a late 17th-century date and that the porch has been added.
(Peter Crawley)

14 Houses with central service rooms

a. Ground-floor plan showing living kitchen (1) and parlour (2); an unheated service room (3) lies between the two and a cross-passage (4) gives access ultimately to all rooms.

b. Cross-section.

c. Isometric sketch; there may be no indication except for the width of wall on one or both sides of the door that there is a central service room inside.

d. Alternative ground-floor plan which has a living kitchen (5) and heated parlour (6) with unheated service room (7) between. Here entry is by way of a lobby (8), and the cramped staircase squeezed into the fireplace jamb has been replaced by a more spacious staircase opening off the lobby (9).

e. Sketch plan showing gable-entry version.

f. A variation in which there are two heated rooms and two unheated service rooms, one on each side of a cross-passage.

g. Plan showing the cross-passage eliminated; a central unheated service room has been introduced but staircases are retained beside the fireplaces.

h. A late development in which the lobby has become more of an entrance hall from which all rooms and the staircase may be reached.

---

into a miniature equivalent of the medieval solar.

Further variations include a rear lateral fireplace in the main ground-floor room and the provision of a third room, a heated kitchen, behind the main living room on the ground floor.

The plan was popular in the late 16th to early 18th-century period. Examples are most numerous in Snowdonia in north Wales, where this was the most distinctive Small House in use before the mid-18th century. However, there may be many examples still unrecognised in other parts of England and Wales, since the front elevation simply shows a door between two windows and a single gable-stack or two stacks, one at each gable – the child's picture of a house – and this elevation fits other plans.

16 Two-unit houses

Very many Small Houses built before the 19th century and not a few Cottages built during that century had two living spaces on the ground floor with a loft or chambers above but had no cross-passage. In such houses the principal room, occupying more than half the ground floor, contained the main hearth or fireplace in its gable wall and served as a combined living room and kitchen. The other space opened off the main room and was either divided into parlour and service room or was a single room serving both functions. In the earlier and smaller examples this space was unheated, but in later and larger examples the parlour had a fireplace in the end wall.

There were variations in the position of the entrance, the position of the staircase and the capacity of the upper floor. In some examples the main door was in the end wall (which was usually gabled) and so opened into a little lobby alongside the fireplace jamb or along the short partition which helped define an inglenook.

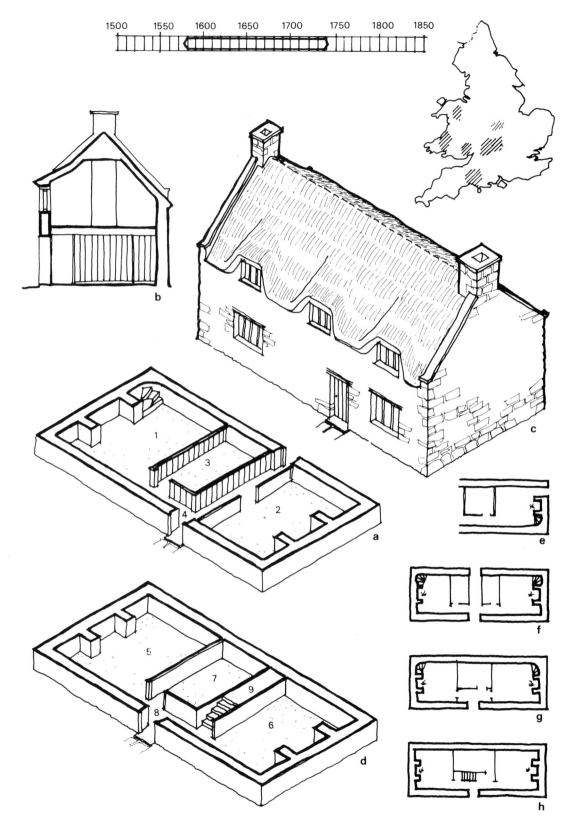

73

15 Internal cross-passage houses

a. Ground-floor plan which shows the main room and a living kitchen (1) reached by way of an internal cross-passage (2) which also serves the unheated parlour and service rooms (or two service rooms) at the opposite end of the house (3 and 4); the staircase (5) located at the corner of the chimney-breast rises directly into the chamber.

b. First-floor plan with an unheated chamber (6) off which opens a heated chamber (7) which is often decorated as a room of some importance.

c. Cross-section: the chambers are shown open to the roof.

d. Sketch showing the relationship of front door to chimney-stacks and especially the corbelled stack that serves the main chamber.

e. Internal cross-passage, but with rear lateral fireplace to the hall.

f. Cross-passage at end of hall opposite main fireplace.

g. Elevation of (f) showing relationship of doorway and chimney-stack.

In other examples the entrance was through the front wall but pushed into a corner so as to open against the fireplace jamb. The entrance finally settled into a position near the middle of the front elevation so as to open into one corner of the living kitchen and against the partition or wall that separated the two living spaces on the ground floor – the so-called 'direct entry' arrangement. This central doorway was in fact rarely placed exactly in the centre of the elevation as such a position would affect the proportions of the two rooms; in the smaller and later examples the door was pushed noticeably to one side, but in the majority of examples the offset was so slight that it usually passes unnoticed.

The staircase might rise from alongside the main fireplace, from within the parlour, by way of a projection from the rear wall, as a simple timber-framed, steeply inclined set of steps within one corner of the main room, or as a steep straight-flight staircase between the two rooms. The first type was probably the oldest and survived long in the stone-walled houses of the upland districts; it was compact and took up little space on either ground floor or first floor, but such a narrow winding staircase had its limitations. The second type was more convenient: housed in a projection, the staircase intruded on neither floor; being central it conveniently served the first-floor rooms while the rear projection made a start which was followed by other extensions to the plan. The third type was used less often than the others. The fourth was an arrangement which was used extensively when smaller Cottage versions of the two-unit plan were built. The various staircase arrangements became more significant as the upper floor developed from a mere loft lit by tiny gable windows or low dormers into a storey of full height lit by windows at the front.

The two-unit house belongs to the 18th century even though examples in the late 17th century are quite common and even though smaller versions, merging into Cottage scale, were built throughout the 19th century. Examples may be seen in virtually every part of the country, but the two-unit plan was the dominant plan-type for its period in many upland regions such as the southern half of Cumbria.

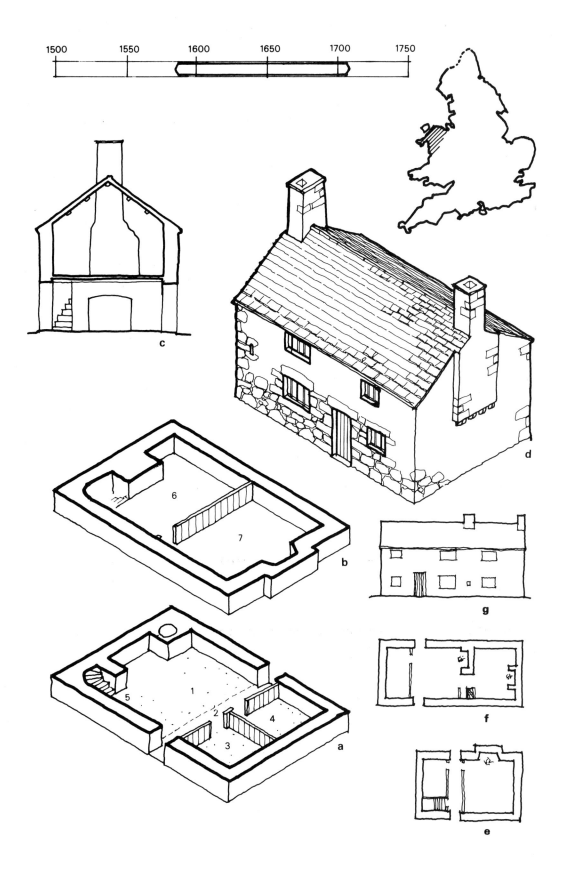

1500   1550   1600   1650   1700   1750

c

d

b

6

7

g

a

5

1

2

4

3

f

e

16 Two-unit houses

a. Ground-floor plan of a gable-entry two-unit house showing the living kitchen (1) and a second unit here divided between parlour (2) and buttery/pantry (3), both unheated.

b. Sketch to show gable entry.

c. Ground-floor plan of a two-unit house with front entry alongside the fireplace and leading into the living kitchen (4); again the second unit is divided into parlour (5) and buttery/pantry (6).

d. Cross-section showing an upper floor lit by a dormer window.

e. Isometric sketch showing relationship between door and chimney-stack.

f. Third version of ground-floor plan with front entry into living kitchen (7) off which opens a parlour (8) which is heated in this case, and from which a staircase rises to the upper floor (9).

g. Sketch to show the central doorway and flanking chimney-stacks; this elevation is common to several plan-types.

h. Cross-section showing fireplace and tapering flue.

i. A further type of two-unit plan in which entry is into a living kitchen (10) off which opens a heated parlour (11); there is no cross-passage nor does the door make a lobby entrance against a chimney-stack.

j. Two units of living kitchen (12) and parlour (13) with staircase (14) rising in between. This is an earlier and larger version of a Cottage plan.

k. Sketch to show chimney-breast and stack projecting from the gable wall.

24. House at Over Kellett, Lancashire
Located on the fringe of the Lake District, this two-unit house has a large heated living kitchen to the right of the doorway and a smaller heated parlour to the left. There are full-height bedrooms on the first floor. The continuous label mould rises over the door lintel which bears the date 1684. The windows have lost their intermediate mullions.
(Peter Crawley)

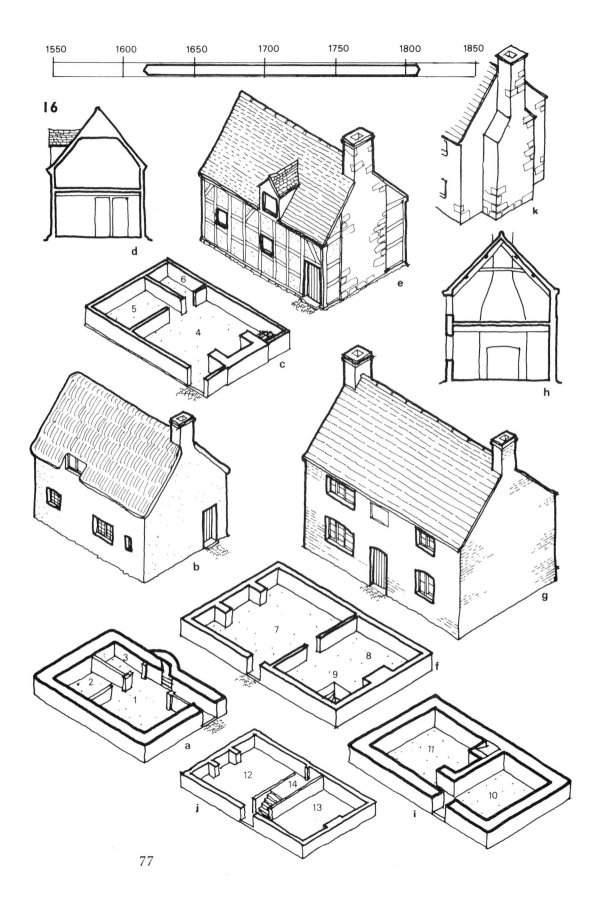

16

1550 1600 1650 1700 1750 1800 1850

77

17 T-shaped and L-shaped houses

The general arrangement of the two-unit house plan suited the Renaissance ideal of a balanced elevation but could not provide the greater amount of accommodation that was required as living standards improved. A house which is one room deep and two rooms wide can, up to a point, provide extra floor area but it cannot readily provide extra and easily accessible rooms. Various efforts were therefore made to increase accommodation without affecting the appearance of the main elevation.

One way of increasing floor area was to extend at the rear with a wing that produced an L-shaped or T-shaped plan. The main block retained living room and parlour with entrance in between, the extension contained a kitchen with its fireplace in a gable wall, possibly a scullery or pantry, and a staircase near the junction of main block and wing and so in a convenient position to serve three bedrooms on the first floor.

Such an arrangement was quite widely employed in the 18th century, especially in the brick farmhouses serving the lowland counties of the Midlands.

25. House near Earl Soham, Suffolk
A lobby-entrance house, basically of three units but extended by a wing which, unusually, projects towards the front to give an L-shape.
(Peter Crawley)

26. House at Walton, Cumberland

The change of pitch of the roof at the rear of this building distinguishes the outshut from the main block, though both parts seem to have been built at the same time. Window positions indicate the lower room-heights in the outshut.
(Peter Crawley)

18 Two-unit houses with an extra bay

Another way of extending the two-unit house was to add an extra bay to the end of the main block. This meant that the roofing problems involved in the L-shaped or T-shaped plan were avoided, and also that a more imposing elevation was produced. Of course it was no longer a symmetrical elevation, but the symmetry

27. House near Banks, Cumberland

This imposing farmhouse is two rooms deep, but with the eaves at the rear level with the eaves at the front. Even in this carefully composed front elevation the front door and window above are slightly offset.
(Peter Crawley)

79

17 and 18 T-shaped and L-shaped houses and houses with an extra bay

a. L-shaped plan with living room and parlour (1 and 2) and a kitchen (3) at the rear making the leg of the L.

b. T-shaped plan with living room (4), parlour (5) and the extra room (6) a kitchen, making extra accommodation without affecting the elevation.

c. Sketch of house with L-shaped plan.

d. Ground-floor plan of house with extra bay; the entrance leads to a living kitchen (7) and parlour (8), making a two-unit plan, but the extra bay contains the 'men's end' (9) with its own access to a separate bedroom above.

e. Isometric sketch showing the relationship of the extra bay to the main block.

f. Another plan in which the house is two rooms deep and two rooms wide; the extra bay is also two rooms deep.

g. Plan consisting of hall (10), parlour (11) and kitchen (12), but with entrance in the gable and staircase (13) beside the parlour fireplace.

h. Hall (14), parlour (15) and kitchen (16), but with a staircase in the angle between main block and wing.

i. Extra bay containing a second (unheated) parlour.

---

and significance of the two main living units were marked by devices such as the provision of false quoins or corner-stones at the junction of main block and extension.

The extra bay could conveniently serve as a kitchen or as an additional parlour but, in east Yorkshire at least, and probably in other lowland counties, the extra bay became a 'men's end', i.e., the room on the ground floor was a mess room for the unmarried labourers while the room above, reached by its own staircase, was their bedroom. Access to the 'men's end' was usually from the farmyard, at the side or back of the farmhouse, and this distinguishes the provision from the separately occupied cottage, which was sometimes attached to a farmhouse as an extra bay but which had a doorway at the front.

14

19 Continuous-outshut houses

In terms of the development of Small House planning the most significant type of extension was the continuous outshut running along the rear of the two-unit plan. The addition of ground-floor rooms or extensions to increase accommodation had been common enough in many of the plans already considered: an end extension to a two-room lobby-entrance house, for instance, might contain a pantry or scullery, and a rear extension behind a cross-passage house might equally provide for pantry or dairy or scullery; but it was the staircase extension which began the trend that culminated in the continuous-outshut plan.

In the early 18th century the narrow, steeply rising mural staircase tucked into the rear of a two-unit plan was succeeded by the provision of a dogleg or open-well newel staircase rising in a projection from the rear wall which was covered by an extension of the main roof. The sweep of such a 'catslide' roof down from the

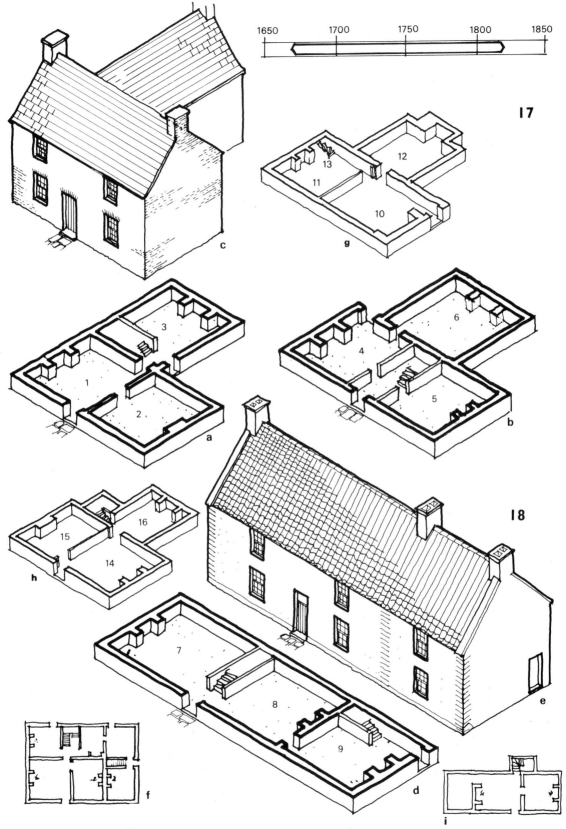

17

18

f

i

81

19 Continuous-outshut houses

a. Ground-floor plan showing living kitchen (1) and parlour (2); behind are the dairy (3) and the scullery (4) with staircase between.

b. Cross-section showing the main roof swept down to cover the outshut.

c. Sketch showing the asymmetrical lines of the gable ends.

d. and e. Plans showing how the outshut develops from a rear staircase projection, adding rooms first on one side and then on both.

f. Ground-floor plan: back-to-back fireplaces and heated outshut.

g. Partial outshut containing staircase (3), scullery and dairy (4).

h. Partial outshut with staircase and scullery: entry against inglenook jamb.

i. Cross-section showing lower-height rooms in outshut.

j. Rear view showing outshut roof and staircase window.

---

ridge of the main roof could also cover a scullery or back kitchen behind the living room and a dairy behind the parlour, one on each side of the staircase. At first these rooms were open to the roof, but later it was customary to insert a ceiling which also acted as the floor to a couple of cramped little store rooms or servants' bedrooms on the first floor. Store rooms were often lit only by borrowed light from the staircase; bedrooms were lit by narrow windows confined between the eaves and the floor. The floor level of these rear upper rooms was normally a foot or so below that of the front rooms. The actual depth of the extension depended partly on the form of the staircase and partly on the pitch of the roof: a steep staircase and a steeply pitched roof meant a narrow outshut whereas a more gradual staircase and a roof of shallower pitch meant that a generous outshut could be built. Indeed this plan was popular in the northern, western and Midland counties where slates or stone flags were the covering of the 18th century and, being laid to a low pitch, allowed a deep outshut. The intermediate wall between main block and outshut was considered a structural wall and the simple forms of roof structure used for the two-unit plan could equally well be used in this developed version.

This house-plan was in use throughout the country from the early 18th century until well into the 19th. It may easily be recognised from the asymmetrical end elevation of high eaves at the front and low eaves at the back.

20 Double-pile houses

The culmination of Small House planning was the double-pile house which had four rooms of equal height on each of the two principal floors. Here, as at the Large House level, the Renaissance ideal of the compact cubiform building matched the functional convenience of well-lit, easily heated rooms based on a central communications core of staircase and lobby, taking the least possible space from the living and service rooms.

The double-pile plan may be considered as the farmhouse diminutive of the double-pile Large House, or it may be considered as the final development of the continuous outshut plan wherein the level of the rear eaves was raised to match

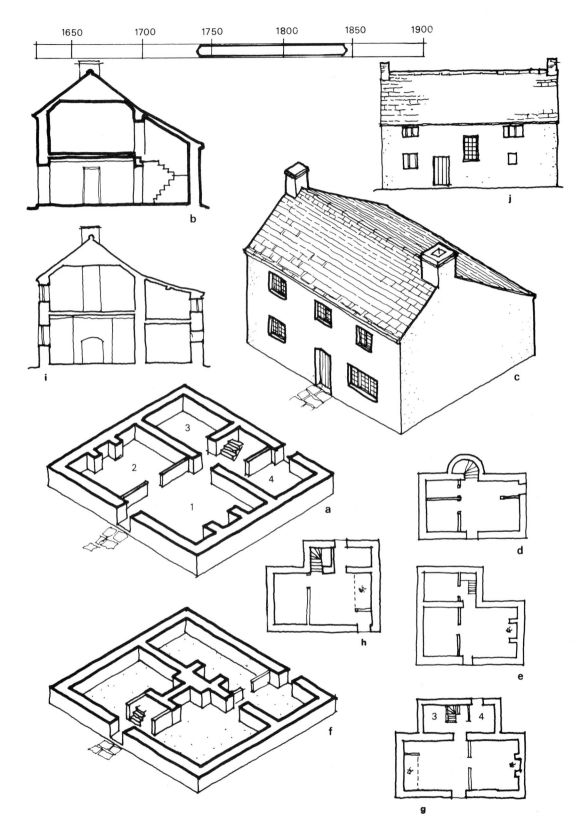

20 Double-pile houses

a. Ground-floor plan showing the living room (1), parlour (2), scullery or kitchen (3) and dairy (4) with staircase (5) in between.

b. First-floor plan showing four bedrooms (6).

c. Cross-section showing eaves at same level front and back; sometimes a cellar at the rear adds to the service accommodation.

d. The sketch shows the symmetrical gables with eaves at the same level.

e. Alternative plan with fireplaces back to back on the spine wall rather than on the gable walls.

f. Later examples have entrance into a lobby rather than directly into the living room.

g. An alternative position for the staircase, lit from a gable wall rather than from the rear.

h. An alternative position for fireplaces across the spine of the building.

i. End elevation sometimes found with plan (g) allowing a tall staircase window.

---

that of the front and the asymmetrical end elevation was abandoned; but it is probably more accurate to consider it as a happy combination of the two influences.

Dimensions were more critical than with Large Houses, and so a slightly off-centre placing of the front door was maintained, and in the older and smaller examples the door led into the main living room rather than into a passage between the two main ground-floor rooms. Often a partition has been added to create such a passage leading from the front door to the staircase, but the construction of the partition and the details of the necessary door leading into the truncated living room show that the partition is an insertion. Upstairs, smaller houses had space for only two bedrooms at the front, and so a central first-floor window was omitted or was included in the elevation as a blind window; larger houses could include a small third bedroom on the front, lit by a third window over the door. Fireplaces were usually located in the end walls whether the roof was gabled or hipped, but sometimes they were more centrally placed in the dividing wall between front and back rooms. Staircases were usually placed on the rear but sometimes were placed on one end wall; in either instance a tall staircase window anticipating the tall, narrow windows popular in the 1930s was often used.

Extra accommodation for storage or secondary bedrooms was quite often placed in a garret, or simply in the roof space where it was lit by small windows in the gable walls. Quite a number of these houses have a cellar, sometimes only under the parlour where it was probably more for ventilating the newly fashionable suspended timber floor than for increasing service accommodation.

The double-pile plan may be found in all parts of the country. Examples are most plentiful from the late 18th until the mid-19th century, but the plan was probably introduced about 1725. At first classical detailing was used on these houses (including Greek Revival details in the early 19th century), with Gothic Revival later.

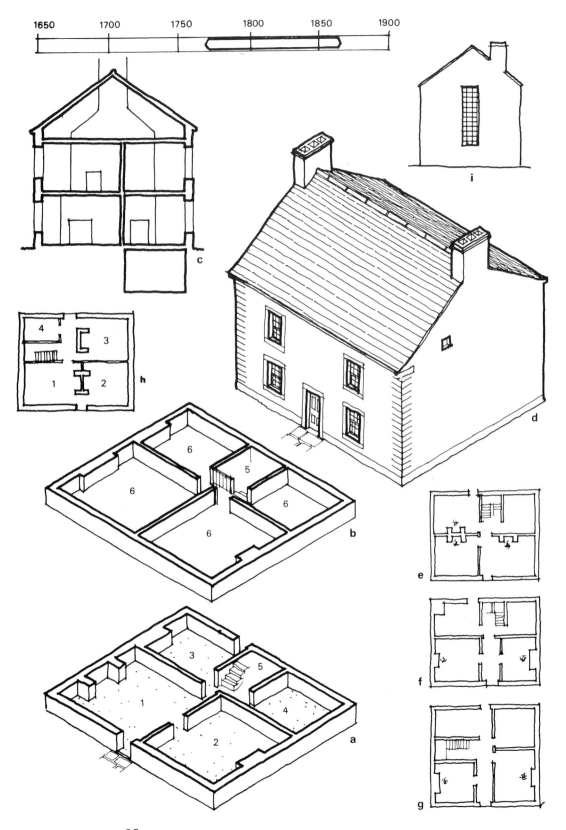

Rural Cottages

The design of cottages generally

Nowadays the term 'cottage' is rather loosely used. It is often applied to any rural property which is clearly below manorial status and is given as a house-name to suburban dwellings occupied by families who would be very distressed to be classed as cottagers. In the past the term was used much more precisely, a cottage being the dwelling of a member of the lower levels of society who lacked the position which comes from having a secure stake in a substantial amount of farmland. Cottages were inhabited by those who might have a couple of pigs or even 'four acres and a cow', but were labourers on other men's land rather than full-time farmers on their own account; they were occupied by miners, quarrymen or industrial workers who laboured or plied their trade as circumstances allowed but who might take advantage of grazing rights on the common land when seasonal or cyclical fluctuations meant the loss of their main employment; they were occupied by craftsmen, tradesmen, widows, the elderly and the poor generally. Cottages have probably always existed but they became numerous and proportionately more significant during the 18th and 19th centuries. Relatively few cottages survive in villages and the countryside from before about 1700, and the vast majority are of late 18th-century and 19th-century date.

Some cottages incorporate the remains of those built by squatters on waste land, including the *ty-unnos* dwellings of Wales where the custom existed of building a cottage overnight to establish squatter's rights.

The simplest sort of cottage had one room which served public and private needs, service and storage; but most cottages came to be designed, like examples of other size-types, around two spaces: one for more public activities, the other for more private. The two-room cottage emerged relatively early as a type and, even in the simple one-room cottage, furniture or partitions usually denoted one part as being distinct from the rest. The two spaces thus consisted of one unit with another, smaller unit added in some way, or a single unit subdivided as when the roof space was lofted to form a bedroom. Once cottages came to be built in materials permanent enough to survive or to be incorporated in a later dwelling, the various stages of improvement followed rapidly until little more than a century later the cottager could reasonably expect his dwelling to have four rooms – small rooms certainly, but twice the number and at least doubling the size of the accommodation that had been considered adequate for so long.

The housing revolution for the cottage dweller occurred practically simultaneously in town and country. The cottager moving to the town was attracted not only by employment but also by accommodation that was at least as good and probably better than that which he was leaving in the countryside; the cottager who stayed on the land could expect in most areas (and certainly in those where industry was competing for labour) that newly built cottages of improved standard would help to encourage him to stay. In some respects the drift or stampede to the towns has been exaggerated. Much of the early Industrial Revolution took place in the countryside: dependent on hand, horse or water power, many of the newly developing industries, especially in textiles and metal-working, were rural rather than urban in basis. Extractive industries such as coal-mining, quarrying for iron, tin or lead ore, etc., were necessarily based in the countryside. There was also the uncertainty of the revolution itself. We marvel at the enterprise and

28. Cottage at Corfe Castle, Dorset
Basically a one-room cottage; there is nevertheless some accommodation in the roof space.
(Peter Crawley)

86

optimism of those concerned, but we tend to underestimate the caution of those in vulnerable but still viable traditional industries and the pessimism that accompanied business failures and fluctuations in trade. These and other factors make it difficult and a little unrealistic to divide the developments in cottage design between urban and rural. Nevertheless we can see now that towns were to attract an ever-increasing proportion of investment and that cottages designed or adapted for the needs of town dwellers on urban sites should be considered separately from cottages that continued to serve rural needs.

21 One-unit cottage

The one-unit cottage consists of a single room about 12 ft or 14 ft (3.66 m or 4.27 m) square, usually with a further space in a loft above. The single room contained the only hearth or fireplace and this was sometimes located on the rear wall but more customarily on the end or gable wall. Entry was normally from the front wall either into a lobby against the fireplace or directly into the single room, though sometimes entry was through the gable alongside the fireplace jamb.

The loft space, which served as a bedroom, was lit through the gable or under a half-hip, or from the front wall by way of a dormer or a small low window tucked between floorboards and eaves. Access was by a ladder, either left open or encased in a sort of cupboard, in one corner of the ground-floor room.

Such a one-unit cottage came to give the two-part accommodation that was needed even at the most humble level of domestic arrangement, but the two parts were disposed vertically rather than horizontally.

These cottages were sometimes built singly, but were more often arranged in pairs or short rows or attached to other buildings. They may be found in practically any part of the country, though their numbers are drastically cut year by year as they are abandoned as dwellings, lost in later extensions or destroyed as useless reminders of standards accepted until recently.

They were built in more or less permanent materials during the 18th century, and the one-unit form was still being proposed for model cottages late in that century. 15

22 One-and-a-half-unit cottages

So small was a one-unit cottage that in absolute terms even a 50 per cent increase in floor area represented only a small gain in usable accommodation; and yet even that gain must have seemed a welcome improvement. The one-and-a-half-unit plan consists of a single living kitchen off which opens a narrow pantry; a ladder or very steep staircase gives access to a small bedroom over the living kitchen and often partly in the roof space, with a still smaller room, barely a cubicle, above the pantry. The pantry was only a few feet wide and yet it confined some of the activities and contained some of the storage that would otherwise have intruded on to the floor space of the single room. Where the ladder or staircase was squeezed into the back of the half-room, a further intrusion on to the living kitchen floor was eliminated.

The one-and-a-half-room cottage may easily be recognised. Like its smaller counterpart it is only one room deep, but the extra space gives an elongated plan rather than a square one, and the window lighting the pantry adds a little more incident to the elevation. Examples are found quite widely but the plan was especially popular in the west Midlands. 16

23 Single-storey and croglofft cottages

Here accommodation was contained within a single structural cell divided to form a larger and a smaller part of a rectangular building. Entrance was sometimes through the end wall but was usually from the front directly into the larger room which contained the only hearth or fireplace. Off this room opened the bedroom/store which was usually unheated. The whole was open to the roof, except that

29. Plas Bach, Rhoscolyn, Anglesey
The cottage appears to consist of one room open to the roof, but possibly with one part separated from the other by means of furniture such as a dresser.
(British Crown Copyright: Royal Commission on the Ancient and Historical Monuments of Wales)

30. Cottage at Muchelney, Somerset
This cottage may also consist of one room open to the roof, but the half-hip at one end may equally indicate the presence of a loft over a small room to the right of the door.
(Peter Crawley)

21 and 22 One-unit and one-and-a-half-unit cottages

a. Ground-floor plan of a one-unit cottage with front entry into a room with fireplace and ladder leading to a loft above.

b. Ground-floor plan with gable entry.

c. Ground-floor plan with entry away from the fireplace.

d. Ground-floor plan with tight winding staircase squeezed against the fireplace jambs rather than a ladder set in one corner of the room.

e. Isometric sketch to indicate one-unit cottage with a loft which is lit by a dormer window.

f. Ground-floor plan of a one-and-a-half-unit cottage showing the half-unit at one end of the main room and the steep staircase in one corner giving access to the loft above.

g. An alternative plan with the entrance near the centre of the main elevation.

h. Sketch showing the extra width that comes from use of this plan.

i. Sketch showing the use of a roof-light to serve the loft space.

j. Sketch showing the use of a double-pitch or gambrel roof to permit greater headroom in the loft space (which is lit from the gable).

k. Cottages as a semi-detached pair with doors together.

l. Cottages as a semi-detached pair with doors apart; here the lofts are lit at the half-hips.

m. Terrace or row of cottages, pairs not reflected.

n. Baffle-entry version of (f).

o. Plan showing gable entry opposite the fireplace.

---

sometimes there was a loose floor above the inner room giving extra storage space or even a subsidiary bedroom; in Wales this is called a 'croglofft' cottage. There were slightly more elaborate versions in which the inner room was divided into two, making a small parlour bedroom and an even smaller pantry. There were also larger versions in which a central inglenook or fireplace served the living kitchen; there was a parlour beyond, but there was also a third room behind the hearth which could either be for domestic use, or could accommodate a loom or similar piece of craftsman's equipment, or could house a cow, horse or pig. The larger and later examples of this version approached in size the smaller and earlier of the two-unit Small Houses. 17

Single-storey cottages survive in relatively small numbers. They were associated with mining and quarrying and with the brief occupation of marginal land. They may be found in practically any building material: stone or brick, timber-frame or clay; they may be found practically anywhere but mostly in remote moorland areas, especially near the Scottish border, on the moors now incorporated in the Yorkshire textile areas, and in Wales around Cardigan Bay. They are difficult to date but were probably under construction throughout the 18th century and, in Wales at least, well into the 19th century. They are generally too small and low to adapt to modern housing standards, and indeed some may have been occupied for a comparatively short time. However, the long low proportions appeal to the contemporary eye and such cottages are an important element in the rural scene. 18

90

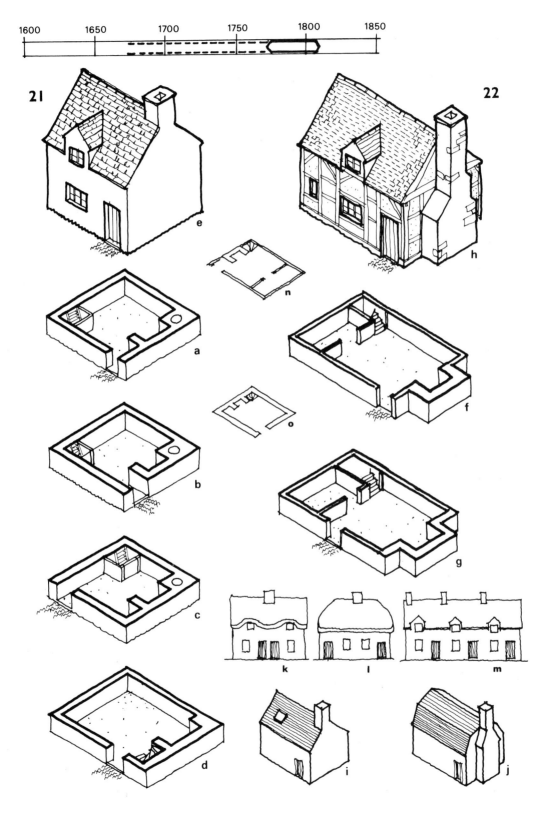

23 Single-storey and croglofft cottages

a. Ground-floor plan with living kitchen (1) and unheated parlour/store (2).

b. Cross-section showing living kitchen open to the roof.

c. Isometric sketch showing low eaves and relative positions of central doorway and single chimney-stack.

d. Ground-floor plan with gable entry to living kitchen (3) off which opens the inner room, the parlour/store (4).

e. Cross-section showing the partition that divides off the parlour/store and the ladder giving access to the 'croglofft' or space within the roof over the parlour/store.

f. Ground-floor plan with baffle entry into a living kitchen (5), off which open a bedroom (6) and store (7).

g. Isometric sketch showing the relationship between door and chimney-stack.

h. Ground-floor plan of a baffle-entry or lobby-entry cottage: the entrance against the jamb of the fireplace leads into a living kitchen (8) with parlour (9) beyond; a scullery (10) is here shown behind the fireplace.

i. Sketch to show the relationship between doorway and chimney-stack.

---

24 Double-pile single-fronted cottages

Often called the 'two-up and two-down', this cottage-type provided a living kitchen and a service room on the ground floor and two bedrooms above. The plan may be considered as a contraction of the double-pile Small House plan or as an expansion of the one-unit Cottage plan. In the former sense such dwellings shared the two-room depth and rear staircase of the double-pile plan but lacked the extra pair of rooms that lent symmetry to such a house. In the latter sense they represented the culmination of a process of addition and improvement to the simpler cottages. For as the loft space of the cottage was improved to become a bedroom, so the ladder, which was inconvenient and encroached on the main living space, was replaced by a winding or a double-flight staircase extending from the rear; and as an additional larder or wash-house or other service room was placed alongside the staircase, so a small extra bedroom was added above.

Such cottages were rarely built singly. Most commonly they were built in reflected pairs, symmetrical about a chimney-stack that grouped together flues from all the living room and bedroom fireplaces. Sometimes they were built in villages in short rows of three or four, and sometimes in mining or quarrying districts they occur in long rows to give an incongruously urban effect.

Single cottages were, however, attached to larger farmhouses or to farm buildings, and some of the smaller and later 'laithe houses' of the Pennines were really cottages attached to barns.

Cottages of the double-pile single-fronted type date mainly from the late 18th, 19th or even early 20th century, and may be found in villages or on farms in any part of the country.

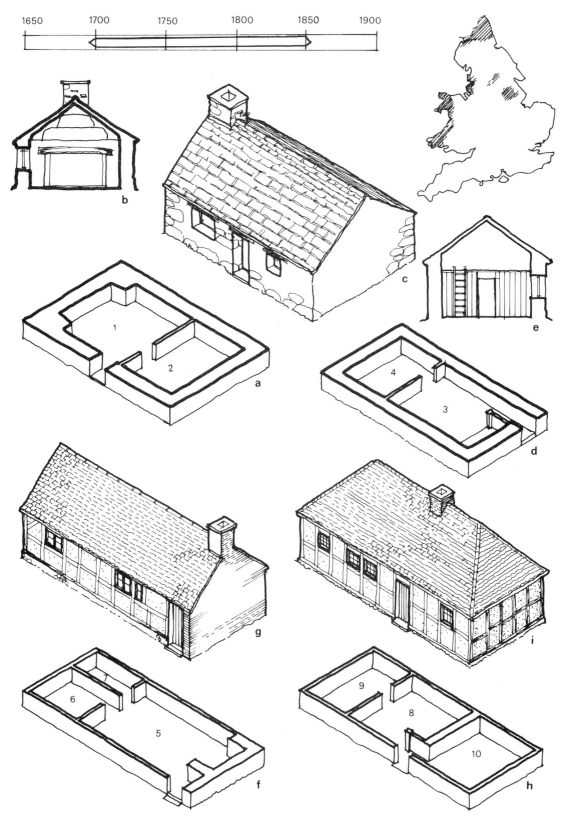

24 Double-pile single-fronted cottages; 25 Other multi-storey cottages

a. Ground-floor plan of a reflected pair of single-fronted double-pile cottages: entrance from the front is directly into a living kitchen (1) with a pantry or scullery (2); one cottage shows a rear staircase (3), the other a staircase alongside the fireplace (4).

b. Cross-section showing the same eaves height at front and back.

c. Cross-section showing the earlier and humbler version in which the rooms at the rear are even lower than those at the front.

d. Plan of a version in which the straight-flight staircase rises from the front and only door.

e. Plan of a version in which the staircase rises from close to a back door.

f. A common form of multi-storey cottage is one room in depth and double-fronted or two rooms in width. The plan shows a central door, a central staircase, and living kitchen and parlour (5 and 6) on each side.

g. The cross-section shows that the cottage is one room deep.

h. Sketch showing that the cottage looks like a miniature version of the two-unit Small House plan.

i. An alternative plan with the staircase associated with the fireplace: only one room is heated in this cottage, but the other room is larger than in the one-and-a-half-unit cottage.

j. Sketch of (a).

31. Cottages at Hatfield Broad Oak, Essex
This reflected pair of early 19th-century cottages illustrates the double-pile single-fronted cottage plan with minimum dimensions. The decayed rendering reveals clay-lump construction.
(J. McCann)

94

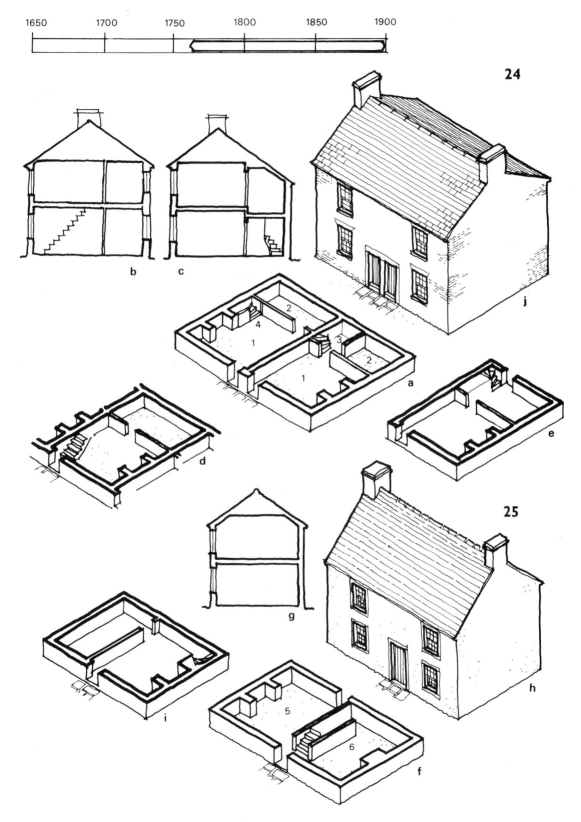

32. Cottages at Ware, Hertfordshire

This row of cottages is arranged mostly in reflected pairs but with some variations. Although single-fronted, the cottages have quite a lot of accommodation in their two and a half storeys.
(Peter Crawley)

33. Cottages at Crayke, Yorkshire, NR

These cottages are like Small Houses in miniature. The chimney-stack and window positions suggest that there is a living room and a heated parlour on the ground floor and two bedrooms above.
(Peter Crawley)

34. Cottage at Bampton, Oxfordshire

This cottage has a two-unit plan in miniature with two tiny rooms, both heated, on the ground floor and two equally tiny rooms on the first floor.
(Peter Crawley)

25 Other multi-storey cottages

Just as the one-unit cottage developed into the double-pile single-fronted cottage-plan, so the single-storey cottage had its own development. A common cottage-plan had a central door leading to a small lobby off which opened a living kitchen to one side, a small parlour or service room to the other, and a straight-flight staircase to two bedrooms above. Such a dwelling was like the single-storey cottage in being one room deep and more or less symmetrical but, having a second storey reached by a convenient staircase, it was much improved. An alternative arrangement placed the staircase alongside the fireplace, but then the layout had all the characteristics of the two-unit plan as used in Small Houses; where the staircase rose between the two ground-floor rooms, the plan was similar to one that was popular in urban Small Houses and cottages. Generally the dimensions of cottages are minimal, but it is sometimes difficult to distinguish externally between a large double-fronted cottage and a modest two-unit Small House.

Special-purpose houses

26 Laithe houses

A laithe house consists of a dwelling and farm buildings erected simultaneously, under the same roof and usually to a simple rectangular plan. A laithe house differs from a longhouse in that there is no cross-passage, there is always separate access for humans and animals, and there is not necessarily any intercommunication between the parts of the building. Also, in practice, the agricultural part of a laithe house always includes a barn, whereas in a longhouse there is always accommodation for cattle but not necessarily a barn. The term was coined by C. F. Stell following his research in the Halifax area during the 1950s and makes use of the Yorkshire dialect word 'laithe', meaning a barn. The term 'coit' had been used by S. O. Addy to include what we now call laithe houses. [19]

Both domestic and agricultural parts of the laithe house are small and unpretentious, though there was sometimes a little architectural embellishment of either one or both parts. There was a tendency for the proportions of the two to change during the period in which the laithe houses were built. The earliest recorded example – Bank House, Luddendon, West Riding of Yorkshire, of 1650 – is nearly two-thirds domestic and the next earliest – Barrack Fold, Hepworth, nearby, of 1691 – has similar proportions. The latest recorded example – Catherine Slack, Hebden Royd, of 1880 – is nearly three-quarters agricultural and the farmhouse part is no more than a cottage in size and layout. Indeed, generally, the smaller and later examples have cottage-type accommodation – a kitchen living room and scullery on the ground floor and one or two bedrooms above – whereas the larger and earlier examples have Small House accommodation – kitchen living room, parlour, scullery and dairy on the ground floor and four bedrooms above. The agricultural part consists, as a rule, only of barn and cowhouse (though there may be a tiny stable also) and these are combined in one space. Typically there is a conventional threshing floor with tall double doors to the front and a small winnowing door to the rear. The threshing floor often acted as a feeding passage for the cattle tethered longitudinally: sometimes one row of cattle with a storage [20] bay opposite, sometimes two rows facing each other across the floor. In either case there would be storage lofts above the cow tyings. The laithe house, built of gritstone, generally presents a rather austere elevation, dominated by the tall barn door, but enlivened by the miniature Palladian windows often found above.

There is some doubt as to whether the barns were intended for corn or hay. Those remaining in use until recently stored hay, the production of grain crops on the bleak and sour moorland being long abandoned. The absence of winnowing doors in the later examples might imply that hay storage only was anticipated, but the majority were built after the winnowing machine had been invented and possibly with its use in mind. The tall barn doors, leading to a floor that one can hardly avoid calling a threshing floor, make no sense if hay storage was intended, as hay could have been pitched perfectly well through upper-level access doors or pitching eyes on to the loft. The use of the threshing floor as a feeding passage suggests that it was kept empty during the winter rather than treated as a hay mow or a storage bay for hay. To clinch the matter, the Palladian window over the barn door was not solely decorative but allowed daylight to fall deep on to the floor where it would be helpful to the threshers.

The laithe house as a building type seems to have responded to the circumstances in which enclosure of common and waste land made small parcels of land available to men who could combine farming and domestic industry, the one hopefully balancing the fluctuations of the other – the happy state of the integral family and economic unit so enthusiastically described by Defoe. Laithe houses are very numerous in the Yorkshire Pennines between Skipton and Sheffield; they may be seen singly, dotted over the square fields of the late 18th-century enclosure, and in little groups, sometimes huddled together, sometimes stretched out in an irregular line. They also stray over into Lancashire, into the valleys to the north and east of Manchester, the moorland areas of the Forests of Bowland and Rossendale, and occasionally even further afield such as the Parbold area north of Wigan.

27 Almshouses

One of the ways in which the medieval church ministered to the body as well as the spirit was in the provision of special accommodation for the elderly, the infirm and the sick. The medieval 'hospital' serving the sick and injured, the frail and the senile was the ancestor not only of the modern medical hospitals but also of almshouses and so of the modern old persons' accommodation. Provision originally made for religious reasons by benefactors was later made out of a sense of social duty by rich individuals or out of mutual self-interest by guilds and companies, until eventually it became accepted as a social responsibility to be faced by the whole community. Almshouses are found in most towns and many villages; as a special type of domestic building their layout and planning deserve a brief note.

The earliest examples have a hall open to the roof with a chapel on the long axis at the east end, as may be seen at Chichester and Glastonbury. There was provision for communal living, including eating and sleeping, in the hall as well as for communal worship in that extension of the hall which was the chapel. There were obvious disadvantages in the hall-and-chapel arrangement – lack of comfort, lack of privacy, difficulties in lighting and heating, waste of space in the huge draughty upper levels of the hall – and these were presumably among the factors that led to the abandonment of this arrangement.

Its successors in the late medieval period followed the precedent of the college rather than of the hall: they had the combination of chapel, hall, kitchen and individual rooms that we recognise in the old English universities. Before the Reformation some almshouses were arranged as colleges: Ewelme, founded in 1437, is the best surviving example. The ancient Hospital of St Cross at Winchester,

26 Laithe houses

a. Ground-floor plan with a house part consisting of a kitchen living room (1), a parlour (2), scullery (3) and pantry (4), and a farming part consisting of a threshing floor (5) and cattle stalls facing.
b. First-floor plan with bedrooms (6), and lofts (7) over the cattle stalls.
c. Cross-section through the threshing floor.
d. Sketch showing the two parts under the one roof and the Palladian window over the barn doors.
e. A variation with farming space small in proportion to domestic space.
f. Equal proportions of farming and domestic accommodation but on a smaller scale, the house being only one room deep.
g. A variation with domestic space small in proportion to farming space.

35. Laithe house at Calderbrook, Lancashire
Set in a characteristically bleak moorland location, this laithe house combined domestic and farming accommodation in approximately equal proportions. In the house, some mullions have been removed and modern window frames inserted.
(G. D. Bold)

reorganised in 1445, includes cottages for the brethren arranged with the earlier church and the refectory to make a self-contained collegiate community.

The foundations of medieval almshouses, like those of chantries, usually required prayers to be said for the souls of the benefactors, and so during the Reformation, from 1547, they became liable to dissolution. Some were spared, some were refounded, others were superseded by new almshouses based on existing buildings or on virgin sites. Dwellings for elderly couples or single people were arranged around a courtyard that also included a chapel, as at Leycester's Hospital at Warwick, or simply a hall, as at Cobham College, Kent. The dwellings looked inwards on to the courtyard which was entered by a narrow passage and so was cut off from the noise and bustle of the street. Other examples included Whitgift Hospital, Croydon, of 1596–9, and on a much smaller scale there was the little Hospital of St Mary Magdalen at King's Lynn, rebuilt in 1649. The pattern of enclosed quadrangle with or without a chapel remained in use for many almshouses founded during the 17th century.

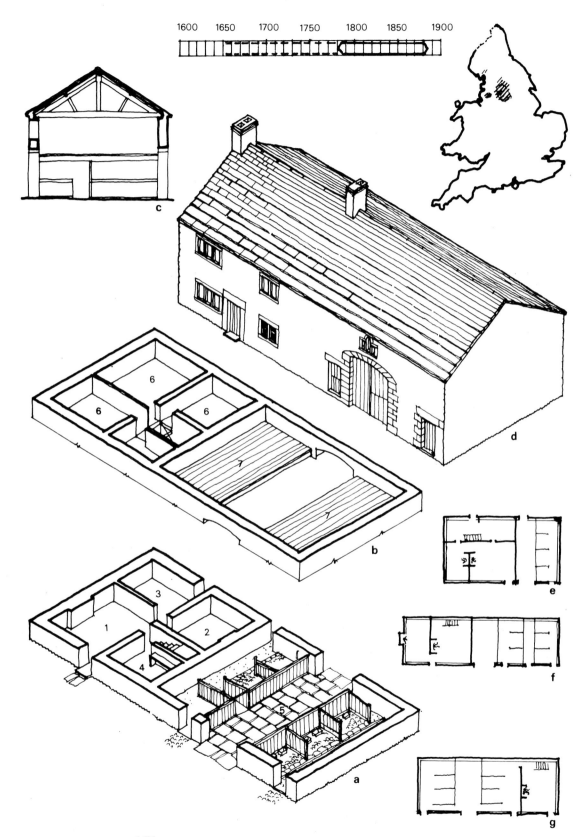

1600 1650 1700 1750 1800 1850 1900

c

d

6
6
6
7
7
b

3
1
2
4
5
a

e

f

g

101

36. Farmstead near Lowick, Lancashire
Here a small farmstead is contained within a single range of buildings. The farmhouse is of continuous-outshut plan; attached is a barn, whose tall doors to the threshing floor are protected by a canopy, incorporating a stable or cowhouse with a loft over. A further extension contains a cartshed and hayloft.
(R. W. Brunskill)

Towards the end of that century, the quadrangular plan was opened out to give a three-sided composition, probably under the influence of the great royal foundations of Greenwich and Chelsea, and this modification may be seen at the quite palatial Turner's Hospital of 1742 at Kirkleatham in the North Riding of Yorkshire. The Geffrye Almshouses of 1710 at Shoreditch in London provide a large-scale example; Ward's Hospital at Buntingford, Hertfordshire, endowed in 1684, and the Marlborough Almshouses at St Albans are on the more usual scale. All are on three sides with a fourth side open to the street and with a pediment or some other architectural emphasis at the centre.

Another arrangement popular from the early 18th century onwards consisted of an elongated courtyard, with one end giving on to the street and the other occupied by a chapel or hall so that the dwellings faced each other in two parallel rows across a paved, cobbled or grassed courtyard. Tomkins' Almshouses of 1733 at Abingdon, Berkshire, Penny's Almshouses of 1720 at Lancaster are examples..

Throughout the period in which these substantial ranges were built there were many small sets of almshouses consisting simply of a row of cottages: two, three or four as a rule, sometimes rather more. These rows usually had some sort of architectural emphasis in the centre, and less often the 18th- and early 19th-century examples were arranged in a three-part composition with the ends of the row marked as well as the centre. Almost always they can be distinguished from other cottages in the village by signs of conscious composition, however elementary, by the use of rather more up-to-date architectural details, and by the careful architectural setting provided for the plaque commemorating the founder.

Except for the hall-and-chapel foundations, almshouses were usually designed as groups of cottages with fairly conventional plans. No doubt in the earliest halls there were no fixed divisions to define accommodation for the residents; life was communal. At Chichester, however, there are cubicles, and at Glastonbury the 14th-century hall was divided rather awkwardly in the 16th century into separate dwellings. Some of the later almshouses, succeeding the hall-and-chapel arrangement, provided each resident with only a single room with door, window and fireplace. Much the most common arrangement, however, consisted of a single room with a loft or bedroom above. The position of the fireplace varied: alongside the door, opposite the door, on a party wall between dwellings or, in the early 18th century, in a corner. The position of the staircase also varied: close to the fireplace or close to a party wall. Later and superior almshouses had a larder alongside the living room and under the loft or bedroom. Most almshouses of the

102

37. Almshouses at Machynlleth, Montgomeryshire
This timber-framed range bears the date 1628 on the central bay window.
(Peter Crawley)

38. Sackville College Almshouses, East Grinstead, Sussex
Built in 1619 the almshouses include a hall and chapel and are set around a quadrangle.
(Peter Crawley)

17th and early 18th centuries were one and a half storeys in height, the upper room being lit by a dormer window, but late 18th- and 19th-century almshouses were two storeys in height.

Almshouses were really special types of cottage. Since they were normally intended for single people or elderly couples they did not require family accommodation. Nevertheless the similarity of individual almshouse dwellings to cottages of the 18th and early 19th centuries is as striking as the difference between the more formal, large-scale, open- or closed-courtyard layout and the less formal, small-scale, more haphazard one. Almshouses are vulnerable to change. To meet modern standards almshouse units have to be combined or extensions added. At best, the external appearance is maintained and fireplaces and staircases are preserved even if not used. At worst, all sense of the interior and exterior is lost.

28 Priests' houses (rectories, vicarages, parsonages)

The village rectory has become an easily recognised house-type, and as familiar a part of the village as the manor house or even the parish church itself. However, most of the rectories that are now eagerly sought by all except the clergy themselves were constructed or extended and reordered in the late 18th or 19th centuries and do not exemplify priests' houses as a historical building type.

Before the Reformation parish clergy were celibate (or at least nominally so), and evidence suggests that their houses consisted of a hall and chamber for the priest and additional accommodation for his housekeeper. However, even in medieval times, parish clergy were a stratified body with wide variations in status and income, so that surviving examples are probably not typical of the general run of priests' houses. At the same time parochial revenues were due to the rector, [22] who might be a resident priest but was as likely to be a layman, an institution such as an Oxford or Cambridge college or, in pre-Reformation times, a monastic establishment, and this situation continued until comparatively recently. Thus in size and design a priest's house both before the Reformation and after would depend on the stipend; it could approximate to a Large House or even a Cottage, but would be likely to correspond to that of a farmer of yeoman status.

Until well into the 19th century, indeed, most parish clergy were farmers cultivating the glebe land, so the parsonage complex would include some farm buildings such as a barn and cowhouse as well as the dwelling itself.

Few studies of pre-Reformation priests' houses have been published, but the pioneering work by Pantin and the Royal Commission's Inventory for Glamorgan suggest that on both sides of the Bristol Channel priests' houses – at least those sufficiently well built to survive – were of two storeys, in whole or in part, with a hall and parlour, or upper hall and chamber, for the priest with the parlour or chamber also serving as his study. Accommodation for a resident housekeeper or servant was either below or alongside that of the priest. [23]

After the Reformation, and by canons of 1571 and 1604, terriers of information about the holdings and possessions of a parish were prepared at intervals, chiefly for the benefit of the archdeacons. From the early 17th century in many parts of England and Wales they included useful information about the parsonage house, at least about its construction and state of repair if not about its design and layout. They are especially useful for the period of roughly 1620–1820. During this period there are references to the provision of a study for the use of the parson (who was by now usually a family man). Barley quotes an example from Leicestershire in [24] 1638 and another from Devon in 1674. Some increase in the parson's comfort is

39. Howard Hospital Almshouses, Castle Rising, Norfolk
This set of almshouses, founded by Henry Howard, Earl of Northampton, who died in 1614, is of brick and tile and ranged around a courtyard.
(Peter Crawley)

40. Almshouses at Poole, Dorset
These cottages are arranged in reflected pairs with one main room on the ground floor and another in the roof space, lit by dormer windows.
(Peter Crawley)

27 Almshouses

a. Medieval arrangement of hall and chapel.
b. Late medieval collegiate layout.
c. The closed quadrangle derived from the collegiate layout.
d. The open-fronted wide quadrangle: centre block and short flanking wings.
e. Narrow courtyard, long ranges facing each other, chapel or hall at the end.
f. A simple range of village almshouses.
g. Communal living in the medieval hall.
h. The one-roomed almshouse cottage: one unit is shown with a rear fireplace, another with a side-wall fireplace.
i. One-room-and-a-loft almshouse unit: one is shown with a fireplace near the entrance and winding staircase beside the fireplace, the other with a fireplace away from the entrance and with a steep straight-flight staircase.
j. One room and a pantry in an interlocking arrangement with bedrooms above; corner fireplaces are shown.

---

indicated by the laying of boarded floors in parlour and study in a house in Lincolnshire in 1707, while reroofing or complete rebuilding of the parsonage is mentioned quite often during the 18th century.

Although a special-purpose house, a priest's house would not have been distinguishable from the general run of farmhouses in a village until greater wealth and higher status for some clergy in the late 18th and 19th centuries led to the design and construction of the rectories so cherished in our time.

29 Inns (alehouses, public houses)

Nowadays the village inn has become an easily recognised building type, but one in which the public accommodation exceeds that for the innkeeper and his family. Similarly the hotel or coaching inn built in the town or along the turnpike road has become a building type far removed from the domestic. Although the village inn may now be a special-purpose house, this distinction is quite new.

Until recently most village inns were houses distinguished from others only by having one or two rooms given over to the public. Even that distinction was not universal, since within living memory the innkeeper's parlour was often shared with the customers and sometimes his kitchen living room also.   25

Similarly bedrooms were let to visitors just as they would have been made available to members of the family. As the beer or cider was kept in the dairy, even a beer-cellar was not necessary to distinguish an inn from a house.

The regulations operating from time to time to govern innkeepers suggest that, again until fairly recently, it was the character of the person rather than the arrangement of his house that was important. Farmers or tradesmen or their wives took up and discarded the victualler's trade as they felt inclined. Like most other members of the village community, the innkeeper had land to farm and so would have farm buildings; and while the innkeeper would make his own beer or cider in brew-house, malt-kiln or cider press, so would most of his neighbours.

The inn, therefore, was not traditionally a house-type whose special purpose was indicated by anything other than the bush or sign by which public houses are known at the present day; in towns the inn did acquire some special accommodation and architectural distinction, but mainly no earlier than the 18th century.   26

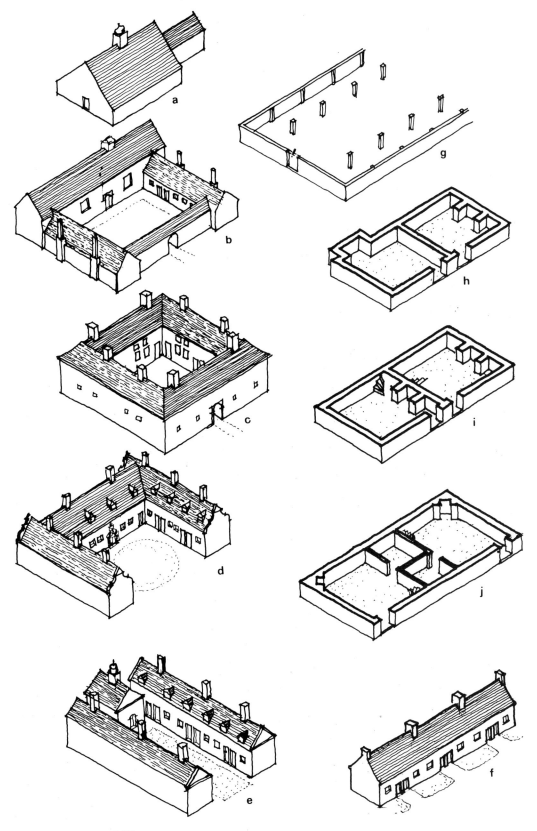

a

g

b

h

c

i

d

j

e

f

107

Chapter 3

Urban Houses and Cottages

The evolution of urban house-plans

Broadly speaking, the town house was intended to serve different needs from the house in the countryside, it was subject to greater restriction on design, and surviving examples have suffered more alterations; so it is hardly surprising that town houses usually differ materially in appearance from those of the countryside and that they deserve separate study.

Town houses were not farmhouses. They might have a stable and carriage house, perhaps even a pigsty or a stall for a cow in the outbuildings, but they were not designed as integral parts of working farmsteads. On the other hand many town houses were not exclusively residential, being designed to incorporate workshops, retail shops, warehouses, space for cottage industry, accommodation for lodgers, etc., and each non-domestic use brought its own architectural requirements.

Most town houses were built on restricted sites subject to the particular legal restraints of the urban system of land tenure. The classic medieval urban site consisted of a narrow strip fronting onto a market place or shopping street and stretching back into gardens and so on to a river, perhaps, or a piece of common land. Plots were usually about 20 or 30 ft (6.10 m or 9.14 m) wide and stretched back 250 or 300 ft (76.2 m or 91.4 m). In Taunton and Oxford about 30 ft was a standard width, though some plots were subdivided into as little as 10 ft (3.05 m) widths; in Totnes and York by the mid-15th century the characteristic width was 20 ft but again there was some subdivision and some amalgamation. The narrow width meant that houses built on a single plot could only be one room wide, while the great length meant that from the narrow width a passage had to be taken in order to give access to the greater part of the plot. Because the shape available for building was so awkward, town houses were built several storeys high at a time when houses in the countryside were commonly only one or two storeys in height; but this multi-storey construction was limited through the need to provide light to the rooms at the rear of the building by way of courts or light-wells that might themselves be overshadowed by adjacent property. Multi-storey construction was also limited by the need for staircases and chimney-stacks, required at each level but taking up valuable floor space.

Like houses in the countryside, most of the older town houses have been rebuilt or refaced, extended and reroofed several times during their period of existence, but town sites have generally been much more subject to over-building than those in village or open country. Pressure on space – either because of the physical limits of a city wall or, more commonly, because of the legal difficulties in expanding into the collar of common land that encircled many towns – meant that the orchards and gardens, paddocks and cesspits along the length of the urban plot became building land, especially during the late 18th and early 19th centuries when expansion of urban population was so rapid. These developments intensified the difficulties of designing houses for convenience and privacy.

At the same time, not all town houses were subject to these restrictions. Powerful landowners acquired large plots on which they could build houses similar to conventional types in the countryside. The church owned large, compact tracts of land in every town and a religious establishment might develop the fringe of one of its properties to provide shallow plots of relatively wide frontage for fairly spacious cottages or small houses: examples occur in York and Tewkesbury for instance. After the Reformation many pieces of church land became available for building. While all towns were developed to high density in the prime commercial areas, in few towns was there a high overall density. Even in cities such as York and Chester whose medieval walls still survive, the overcrowded zones were limited and many streets outside the commercially desirable area were available for relatively unfettered domestic construction. Then again, suburban development along the roads extending from the town gates was practised whenever conditions were safe and frontage of ample width was available. The effects may be seen on streets such as Blossom Street in York or North Bar Without in Beverley. So the conditions of the 18th and 19th centuries that led to intensive development of the medieval urban core also led to the more extensive ribbon development of at least part of the periphery.

Up to about 1700 two principal methods of extending down the length of a medieval plot were developed: a continuous range along one side of the plot and a series of buildings alternating with courts along the length of the plot. The first

41. Dedham, Essex
The curving street of this small town has a mixture of older houses of timber-frame construction with gables facing the street and later houses of brick with eaves along the street frontage – though some of the brickwork may conceal earlier timber-framing.
(Peter Crawley)

42. Nayland, Suffolk
The street curves to reveal different views of houses, mainly timber-framed, and mainly with eaves along the street frontage but with one narrow-frontage house with gable facing the street. Most of the half-timbered houses have jettied upper storeys while the plastered houses have uniform surfaces (probably concealing underbuilt jetties in some cases).
(Peter Crawley)

43. Chipping Campden, Gloucestershire
Houses of narrow frontage, two and three storeys high and in several cases with prominent dormers.
(Peter Crawley)

method allowed easy access from one room to another by means of internal corridor or open-fronted gallery, but the width of the rooms was limited by the width of the plot and the need for penetration of light, especially into the ground floor. The second method gave limited space for ground-floor rooms, since part of the width of the plot had to be reserved for continuous corridors linking court with court; but at first-floor level the whole width could be used unless, as was often the case, a gallery was provided. There was no restriction on the depth of the rooms, the only limitation being the area of court needed to provide useful daylight, especially for the ground-floor rooms. Since medieval houses in the countryside often consisted of several buildings only loosely associated on the site and without covered access from part to part, the use of separate buildings along the length of the medieval urban plot would hardly have been considered a great handicap to domestic life.

The influence of the Renaissance during the 17th and 18th centuries led to a different concept of what was appropriate for the urban site. The terrace, with its variations in square and crescent, represented by examples to be found in practically every town, reflected new attitudes to the siting of urban houses. Long rows of houses built to regular design and with classical details were erected in Great Queen Street and Lincoln's Inn Fields in London during the 1630s. The layout of Covent Garden at the same time transformed the terrace into a formal square. The idea of making each house in the terrace part of a grand palatial composition, reducing its individuality but enhancing its share in the greater whole, was

110

44. Godmanchester, Huntingdon
Gables and jettying indicate medieval origins but the three-storey double-pile brick inn is from a later period.
(Peter Crawley)

developed during the late 17th and early 18th centuries in examples such as Bloomsbury Square and Grosvenor Square in London. The Woods of Bath, in the Circus and especially in the Royal Crescent of 1767–75, developed the flat terrace into the livelier crescent to the great benefit of urban design in Britain. Indeed, well into the 19th century, many humble cottages were given dignity as part of a terrace or vitality as part of a circus or crescent.

Town-house plans may be divided into three main groups with subdivisions within each group. The general sequence will be considered here, and then each type will be separately described.

The first group consists of medieval houses in which at least one room is a hall open to the roof. Some examples, of very narrow frontage, have the hall running at right angles to the street, others of rather wider frontage have the hall running parallel to the street. There are also a few surviving first-floor halls. Many of the medieval houses included workshops or retail stores opening off the street and capable of separate access and separate letting, and plans were varied to allow this and to permit upper-level domestic rooms to extend over these shops.

The second group consists of multi-storey houses: dwellings that lacked open halls but had several storeys of rooms conveniently reached by a single staircase and adequately served by fireplaces and flues. Again there was a distinction between narrow-frontage and wider-frontage properties, in the first case leading to rooms one behind the other and in the second to rooms side by side. Fireplaces were either back to back, giving a compact stack which kept the heat within the house, or were arranged separately in the party wall. Staircases were either compact and within the house or extended and at the rear. The group ranges from the large, many-storeyed houses of London, Bristol and Bath to the humbler two-storey houses of the smaller provincial towns.

The third group consists of the urban cottages, generally of quite late date, comprising developments from the simple cottage of one room and a loft, which filled so many spaces in medieval towns, to the comparatively spacious and well-equipped narrow-frontage cottage of the 19th century.

45. Ruthin, Denbighshire
Although one associates Wales with stone construction, many of the older towns, such as Ruthin, retain timber-framed houses with decorative black-and-white work. Here the elaborate Nantclwyd House with its prominent porch dominates but does not overwhelm the street.
(R. W. Brunskill)

Urban houses: summary of the main plan-types

A. *Earlier houses including an open hall*

    1. Narrow frontage, internal hall, undercroft.

    2. Wide frontage, first-floor hall.

    3. Wide frontage, lateral hall behind shops.

    4. Wide frontage, cross-passage, single-ended ground-floor hall.

    5. Narrow frontage, cross-passage in hall.

    5a. As 5, but with wider frontage.

    6. Narrow frontage, long passage incorporated in house.

    7. Narrow frontage, small hall.

B. *Later houses, multi-storey throughout*

    8. Wide frontage, back-to-back fireplaces.

    9. Wide frontage, L- or T-shaped plan.

    10. Wide frontage, double pile, end-wall fireplaces.

    10a. As 10, but with central fireplaces.

    11. Narrow frontage, longitudinal passage, back-to-back fireplaces.

    12. Narrow frontage, longitudinal passage, party-wall fireplaces.

    13. Wide frontage, central stair, party-wall fireplaces.

    14. Universal terrace houses.

    15. London terrace houses, rear stairs.

    16. London terrace houses, central stairs.

    17. Narrow frontage, central stairs between fireplaces.

C. *Cottages*

    18. One-room cottages, longitudinal passage within.

    19. One-room cottages, no passage within.

    20. Back-to-back cottages.

    21. Houses for cottage industry.

    22. Two-up-and-two-down cottages, rear stair (along plan).

    23. Two-up-and-two-down cottages, central stair (across plan).

    24. Tunnel-back cottages.

EARLIER URBAN HOUSES

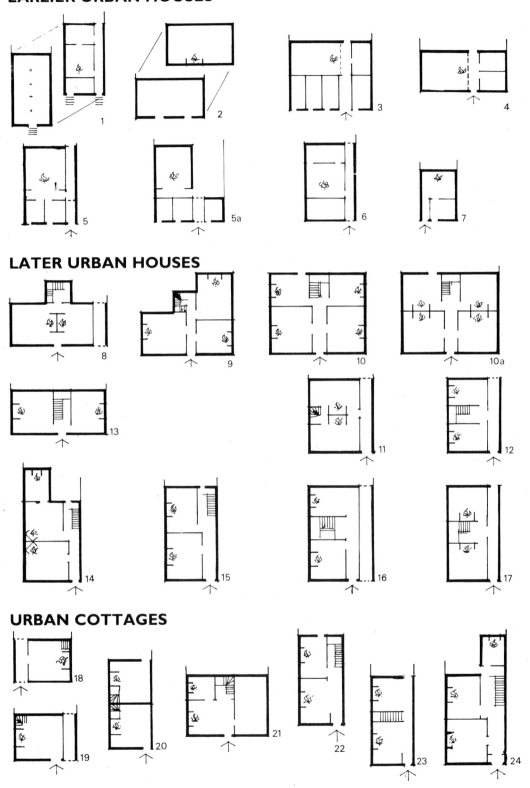

LATER URBAN HOUSES

URBAN COTTAGES

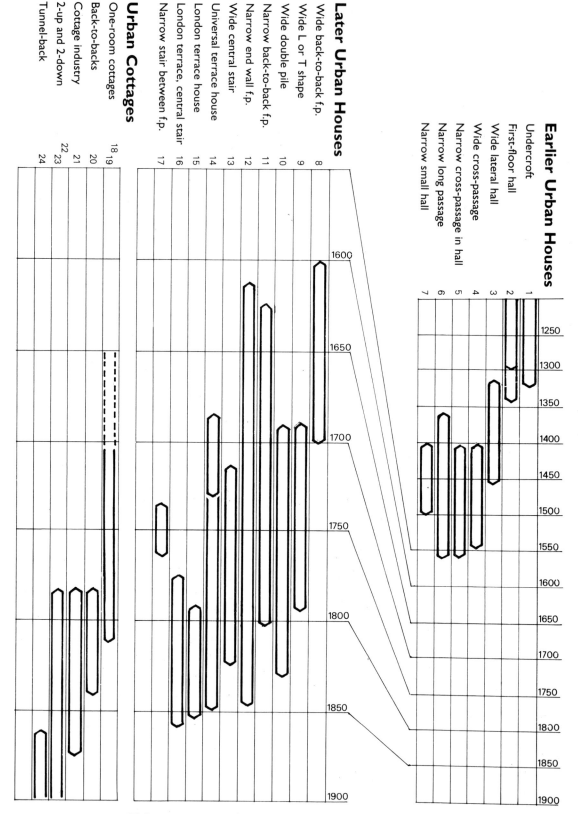

Earlier Urban Houses

1 Undercroft
2 First-floor hall
3 Wide lateral hall
4 Wide cross-passage
5 Narrow cross-passage in hall
6 Narrow long passage
7 Narrow small hall

Later Urban Houses

8 Wide back-to-back f.p.
9 Wide L or T shape
10 Wide double pile
11 Narrow back-to-back f.p.
12 Narrow end wall f.p.
13 Wide central stair
14 Universal terrace house
15 London terrace house
16 London terrace, central stair
17 Narrow stair between f.p.

Urban Cottages

18 One-room cottages
19
20 Back-to-backs
21 Cottage industry
22 2-up and 2-down
23
24 Tunnel-back

Earlier urban houses including an open hall

1 Narrow frontage, internal hall, undercroft

Amongst the earliest types of town house is that in which an open hall and its attendant rooms are raised over a vaulted undercroft. Such houses were usually built on narrow plots of 20 ft (6.10 m) or so in width. At the street front, one flight of stairs led down to a half-basement that extended the whole length of the main building and was used as a workshop, warehouse, retail shop, etc., according to the occupation of the householder or tenant; another flight of stairs led up from the street to the main entrance, giving access often to a smaller shop and through it to the hall, parlour and chambers. The hall, like the other rooms, was raised over the cellar on a stone vault and was of conventional medieval type, open to the roof and presumably with a central open hearth to provide heat in the winter-time; where the site permitted, it had a cross-passage at one end. Off the hall opened a parlour, and above parlour and shop there were chambers reached by narrow internal staircases and sometimes linked by a gallery running along the upper part of one wall of the hall. Beyond the parlour there would be a courtyard leading to the detached kitchen and other service rooms.

In this plan the provision of daylight was difficult: it was impossible to light the undercroft except by what little daylight could penetrate the low front wall, and the hall could only be lit by borrowed light from any convenient courtyard provided by an adjacent owner. The houses usually presented a gable to the street, and there was no problem in lighting chambers and garrets.

This building type has been most thoroughly studied in Southampton, but [3] examples are also known from Exeter and Stamford. The 'rows' of Chester may have been developed from some version of the type. The general period of use is believed to be the 13th and early 14th centuries. [4]

2 Wide frontage, first-floor hall

The hall raised to first-floor level was employed contemporaneously with the ground-floor hall in early medieval towns as well as in the countryside, though few examples actually survive. Probably the best-known are the two 'Jew's Houses' in Lincoln, but other generally similar houses may be found here and there – at Southampton, for instance. [5]

The first-floor hall was a room open to the roof and running in effect through two upper storeys; it was heated by a side-wall fireplace and well illuminated by windows which, being at a safe upper level, were quite large for the period. One end of the hall was probably partitioned off to form a solar. The use of the ground floor is not clear; as in rural versions of the first-floor hall, its principal use was to raise the hall to its required position; but in a town the space could presumably be used as a warehouse or let off for shops. The surviving first-floor halls are all built of stone and must have been impressive, perhaps formidable, when all other houses in the towns were built of timber. Although none of the surviving examples are securely dated, they are generally ascribed to the end of the 12th century or the early part of the 13th.

3 Wide frontage, lateral hall behind shops

The principal feature of this type is the ground-floor open hall running across the width of a fairly generous plot but hidden from the street behind a line of shops.

117

1 Narrow frontage, internal hall, undercroft

a. General view showing two examples together, one cut away on the long axis; entrance to long passage (1), to shop (2), hall (3), parlour (4), chambers (5).

b. Cross-section showing undercroft (6), shop (7), passage to hall (8), chamber (9).

c. Undercroft with steps down from street (10), piers supporting floor above (11).

d. Ground-floor plan with long passage (12), shop (13), hall (14), parlour (15), kitchen (16), steps up from street (17).

e. Upper-floor plan showing chambers (18) and upper part of hall (19).

Note Heating provision, fenestration and position of internal staircases not determined.

The hall was reached by way of a passage running through the shops and becoming a cross-passage as it entered the hall, whence it continued in order to give access to the yard or court. One end of the hall was partitioned to make a parlour with solar above; chambers occupied the space above the shops. At the rear there was a kitchen wing including further chambers and garrets and linked to the main building by a covered gallery.

Examples are fairly widespread and have a range of dates. Pantin cites Tackley's Inn, Oxford, of *c.*1291–1300 as of this type but with half-basement cellars under the shops; S. R. Jones describes an example in Coventry as 'at least 14th-century'; Faulkner ascribes a building in Market Square, Faversham, to the mid-15th century. All known examples are timber-framed and might have either double gables or a continuous jettied range to the street front. ₆

4 Wide frontage, cross-passage, ground-floor hall single-ended or double-ended
This plan-type is also characterised by an open hall running across the site, but here the hall opened straight off the street. The hall was single-ended in the sense that subsidiary rooms opened off the cross-passage at the lower end of the hall with no corresponding rooms at the upper end. The subsidiary rooms could be for private or service use, but the small room facing on to the street could have its own door and be used or let as a shop. The chamber was placed above the two smaller rooms and jettied over the street, giving the effect of a truncated Wealden house. The kitchen and other service rooms were placed further into the site and reached by way of the cross-passage. Sometimes there was a line of shops along the street front with an entry giving access to a courtyard which in turn contained the main house. Sometimes the solar extended beyond the service rooms, over the passage and into the hall. Sometimes the full width of the plot was given to hall and cross-passage, and the service rooms and solar were placed behind the hall.

The type was widespread, used over a fairly long period, and had many variations. It has been recorded in York, Stamford, Burford, Coventry, Oxford and Exeter, and from the late 14th century through the 15th and even into the 16th. The houses were not usually very large, though needing a wide frontage of between 30 and 50 ft (9.14 and 15.24 m), houses with this plan are to be found in the side streets of larger towns or on the less valuable sites in the smaller towns, and not in the prime commercial areas where every foot of frontage to the street or

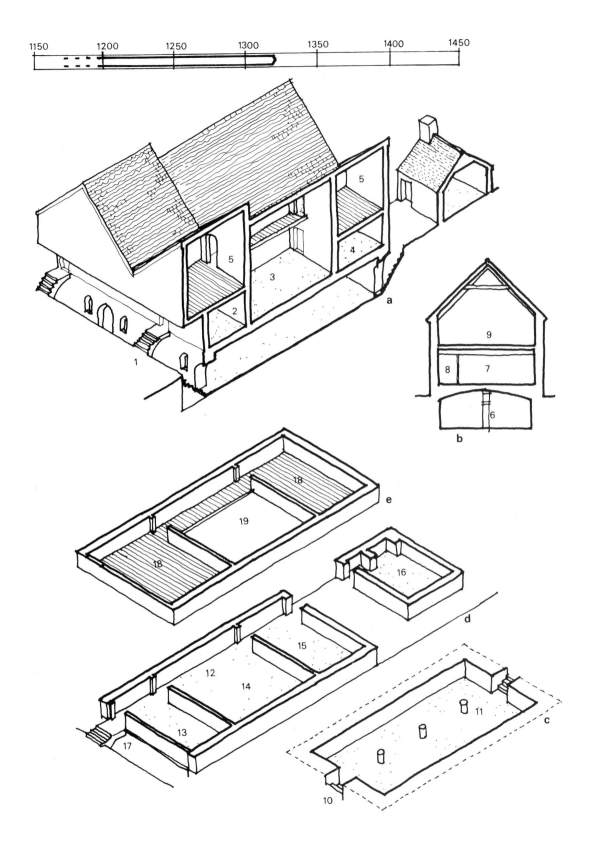

2 Wide frontage, first-floor hall

a. General view.

b. Section showing hall (1) raised to first-floor level over vaulted undercroft (2).

c. Ground-floor plan (staircase positions varied).

d. First-floor plan showing hall with side-wall fireplace (3).

3 Wide frontage, lateral hall behind shops

e. General view.

f. Ground-floor plan showing shops (4), entrance to cross-passage (5), hall (6), parlour (7), courtyard (8), kitchen (9).

g. Arrangement at upper-floor level showing chambers (10) and upper part of hall (11) (staircase positions varied).

Note Heating provision and position of internal staircase not determined.

46. Jew's House, Lincoln
This well-known house has a first-floor hall raised over an undercroft. The stone construction and the double-depth of the plan, as well as its late 12th-century date, are all unusual.
(Peter Crawley)

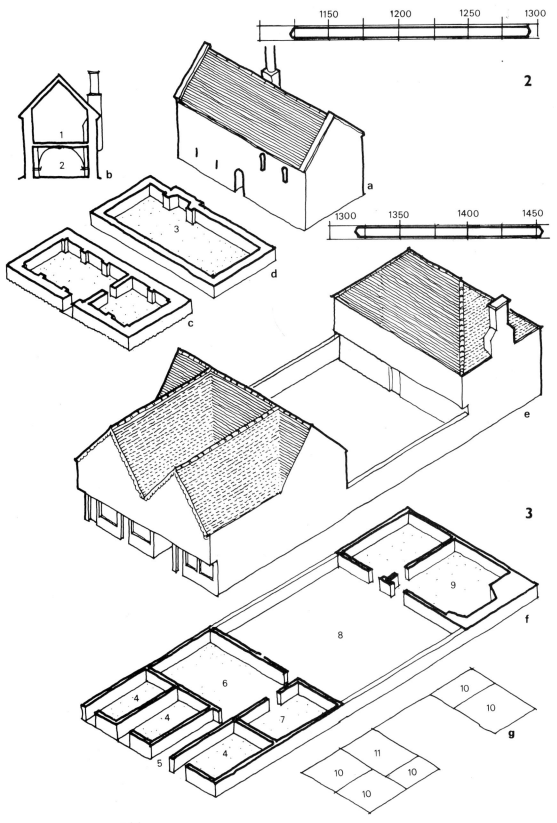

4 Wide frontage, cross-passage, ground-floor hall single- or double-ended

a. General view showing shop and hall entrances and jettied upper storey.

b. Cross-section through hall, open to the roof.

c. Cross-section through two-storey portion, chamber open to the roof.

d. Ground-floor plan showing hall (1), shop (2), parlour or service room (3) and cross-passage (4) also giving access to rear of plot.

e. Part upper-floor plan showing chamber (5) and upper part of hall (6).

f. Plan showing double-ended hall on wider frontage; as in the Wealden houses of the countryside there is a parlour (7) and chamber above located at one end of the hall (8), with chamber over service room (9) and shop (10) at the other.

g. Diagram to show a chamber occupying part of the hall.

h. Chambers (11) over parlour, shop and service room.

Note Position of staircases not determined everywhere.

---

market place was of great value. They were well lit, and quite attractive in appearance. Clearly they share some features with the Wealden houses of the countryside, and they extend this general house-type far to the north and west of its rural heartland.

5 Narrow frontage, cross-passage in hall

Although the narrower medieval plots did not allow the conventional medieval house-plan of the double-ended hall to be placed across the frontage, it was possible to use this plan placed along the depth of the site with one end fronting on to the street. The double-ended hall was that which had an open hall with a cross-passage at the socially inferior end, giving access to service rooms under a solar, and at the superior end a parlour or private room of some sort with another solar above. When the type was adapted to urban use, one of the service rooms could be used as a shop and access to the cross-passage came from a longitudinal passageway already giving access to parts of the plot further from the street.

In some examples the gable end of a single range of buildings overlooked the street or market place, in others the service room, shop and solar were arranged as a separate wing – as they would have been in the countryside – but with the eaves-line along the street. In either case the hall had little natural light.

Examples of this type of house have been noted in Norwich, King's Lynn, Chester and Exeter. In Oxford, Pantin recorded a variation in which the hall overlooked a courtyard on a fairly wide site; the valuable frontage was given to shops and the less valuable inner parts of the plot used to improve conditions within the hall. Generally, these houses are assumed to belong to the 15th century, though the demolished Oxford example was ascribed to the early 14th century and Exeter examples have been dated to the early 16th century.

7

122

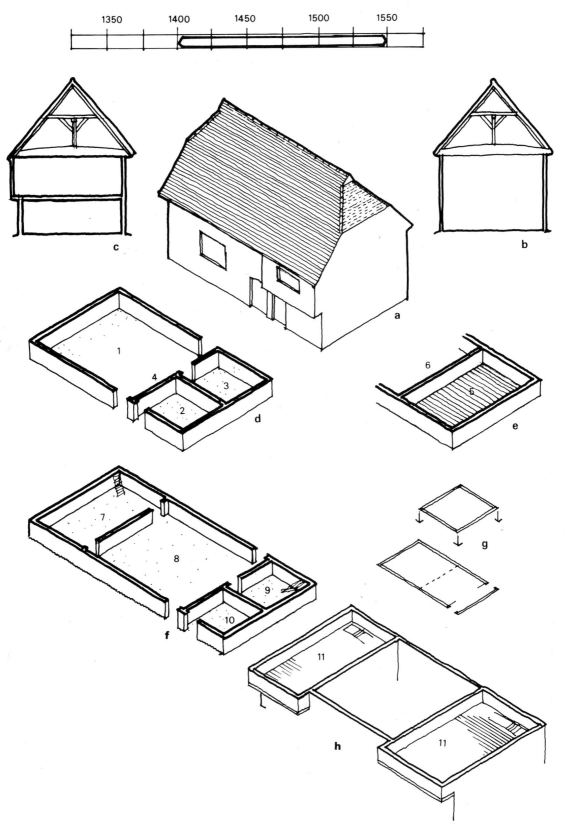

123

5 Narrow frontage, cross-passage in hall

a. General view showing shops and chambers roofed separately from hall.

b. Ground-floor plan with entrance to longitudinal passage (1), cross-passage (2), shop (3), parlour (4), hall (5) and service room (6) with chamber over; the alleyway (7) provides little light for the hall.

5a Wider frontage, cross-passage in hall

c. Sketch showing a range of shops in front of the hall but with chambers over.

d. Plan showing the shops (8), hall (9) and the wider yard (10) with service or lodging accommodation (11).

Note Heating and staircase positions not determined.

---

6 Narrow frontage, long passage incorporated in house
Superficially similar to the previous type, these houses in fact differ in having the longitudinal passage built into the house. In the basic version there is a central open hall with a two-storey parlour wing at the front and a two-storey service wing at the back; the parlour wing might actually function as a shop. The longitudinal passageway serves as both an internal corridor on the ground floor and as the means of access to the full depth of the site – the 'casual attitude to privacy' that

47. House in Tenterden, Kent
This house is an urban Wealden house but with the recessed portion of the upper storey jettied, probably at the time that a floor was inserted in the hall.
(Peter Crawley)

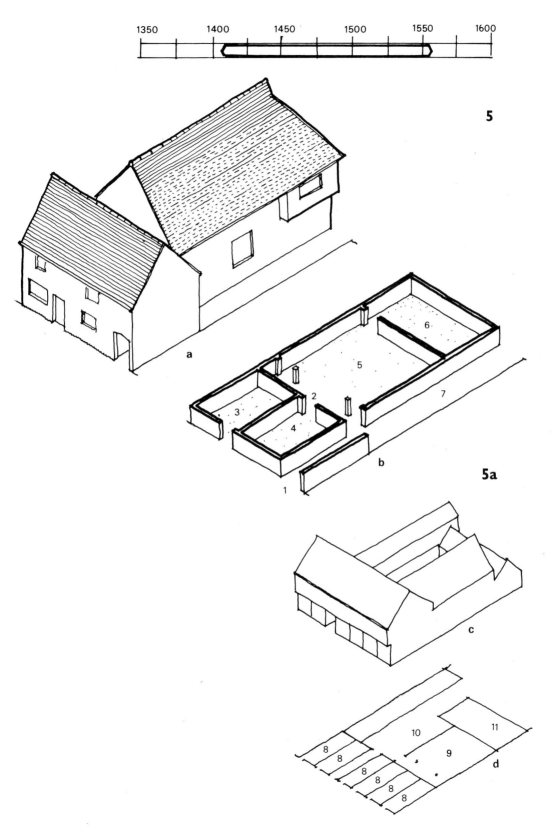

1350 1400 1450 1500 1550 1600

5

a

b

5a

5

6

7

3

2

4

1

c

d

8
8
8
8
8
8

10

11

9

125

6 Narrow frontage, long passage incorporated in house

a. General view with entrance to longitudinal passage (1).

b. Ground-floor plan showing longitudinal passage (1), parlour or shop (2), hall (3) and service room (4).

c. First-floor plan with chambers (5) and upper part of hall between (6).

7 Narrow frontage, small hall

d. Sketch showing house door (7), shop door (8) and lean-to service room at the rear.

e. Ground-floor plan with longitudinal passage (9), shop (10), hall (11) and service room (12).

f. Sketch of alternative without the service room.

g. Plan of alternative.

h. Upper floor showing the chamber (13) and the upper part of the tiny hall (14).

i. Smoke from the open hearth rose into the upper part of the hall as if in a smoke bay.

Note Heating and staircase positions not determined.

---

has been noted as characteristic of medieval house planning.

This house-type made full use of a narrow site (indeed one example recorded in Sandwich has a site as narrow as 14 ft (4.27 m)) but at the expense of difficulty in lighting the central hall. Indeed, except for the use in some circumstances of dormer windows, the hall could only be lit by courtesy of an open space in adjoining properties. But as an economical use of limited site area it was quite widely used in the 15th century, examples being in Taunton, Exeter, Chester and Sandwich.

7 Narrow frontage, small hall

A smaller version of the preceding type was recognised as a result of work in Tewkesbury. Here a row of twenty-four shops with living accommodation was erected during the 15th century, each unit having a shop at the front with a short passage running alongside to a shallow hall. There was a kitchen in a lean-to building off one side of the hall, and a solar over the shop and entrance passage opposite. To call the main room a hall would be generous, since the awkwardly proportioned space had a minimal floor area (much of which was presumably occupied by the hearth) but was very tall, rising as a sort of smoke bay up to the ridge. Apart from Tewkesbury, examples have only been recognised in Exeter, but they may once have been quite common.

Summary

All these plan-types of the medieval urban house, ranging from the late 12th to the early 17th century, had an open hall and open hearth as their main character-istics. Other portions might be multi-storey and have fireplaces, but they were subservient to the open hall. The principal rooms were deep in the site, while valuable street frontage was given over to shops on the ground floor. A utilitarian doorway gave access to the series of rooms or courts within the depth of the site, and jettied upper-storey construction announced the status of the occupants.

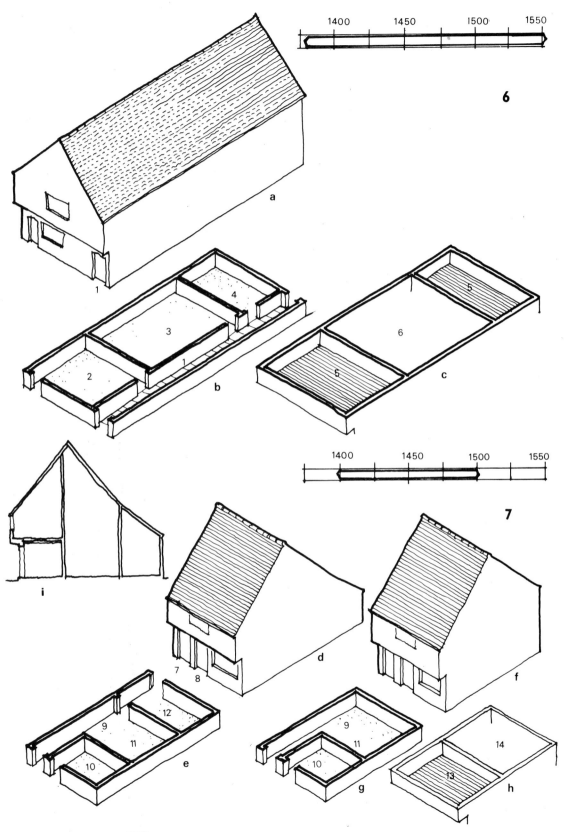

6

1400 1450 1500 1550

a

4
3
2
1
b

5
6
5
c

7
1400 1450 1500 1550

i

7
8
9
12
11
10
e

d

9
11
10
g

14
13
h

f

127

Later urban houses, multi-storey throughout

8 Wide frontage, back-to-back fireplaces

By about 1500 the open hall had fallen completely out of favour. Houses built during the 16th century and later were of several storeys connected by staircases (which were given steadily greater architectural importance) and heated by fireplaces that gained increasing significance in house planning. Since the narrow plots of the medieval urban core in each town were already occupied, the newer houses of the 16th and 17th centuries were built on wider plots on the fringes and this tendency continued through succeeding centuries; but some houses were built as replacements on existing narrow plots, and some plots were even subdivided when pressure on the most favoured sites made such land ever more valuable.

The basic multi-storey town house consisted of two rooms on each floor heated by fireplaces that were placed back to back and whose flues rose to a huge central chimney-stack. The rooms were served by a staircase which either projected from the rear or was tucked into the baffle-entry lobby against the chimneys. There were usually two main floors and an attic or garret storey lit by dormer windows. This house-plan was certainly introduced into Oxford and Stamford, and possibly elsewhere, at least during the early 17th century. Adopted for houses built either in brick or stone, it remained a popular plan especially for smaller dwellings until well into the 19th century.

As an alternative, houses were designed for a wide frontage but with the central entrance giving on to a staircase hall and the two principal rooms on each floor having gable fireplaces (see type 14 below).

9 Wide-frontage, L- or T-shaped plan

Since the plot-width of a town site was limited, extra accommodation could only be provided by increasing the height or depth of the house. One way was to add a third heated room on each floor in a wing projecting from the rear to give an L- or T-shape on plan. The three rooms on each floor were connected by a staircase, usually of quite generous size, located in the angle between the wing and main block.

10 Wide frontage, double pile

The end of the 17th century and the early years of the 18th saw the introduction of the double-pile house-plan, an event as significant in the development of urban house planning as it was in the planning of houses in the countryside. The essential feature of the plan was that there were four rooms on each floor, two at the front and two at the back. Double-pile houses were two rooms in width, two in depth and usually two in height if one discounts garret and cellar spaces.

Variations on the double-pile plan lay in the position of staircase and fireplaces and, to some extent, in the method of roofing. The type that was probably commonest had the staircase at the rear between the two back rooms and rising in two flights or about a narrow well from floor to floor, but the larger and rather later houses sometimes had a staircase at one side, lit from above and giving more space to the rooms at the rear; this variation was introduced about the middle of the 18th century and remained in use into the 19th. Probably the commonest location for fireplaces was the gable wall (or party wall as it would so often be in the

48. The Old Vicarage, Burford, Oxfordshire
Dated 1672, the house presents a formal elevation to the street, with emphasis on the first floor and enlivened by three false dormers.
(Peter Crawley)

128

129

8 Wide frontage, back-to-back fireplaces

a. General view showing how central fireplaces rise to a compact grouped chimney-stack half-way along the ridge. In the sketch there are deep dormer windows lighting the topmost storey.

b. Plan showing the back-to-back fireplaces serving hall (1) and parlour (2), with newel or dog-leg staircase at the rear (3).

c. Alternative plan with the back-to-back fireplaces serving hall and parlour but with newel staircase (4) tucked between front door and fireplace jambs.

9 Wide frontage, L- or T-shaped plan

d. Sketch showing a house one room deep with gable fireplaces and chimney-stacks and a rear projection making an L-shaped plan.

e. Plan with entrance passage between hall (5) and parlour (6) and with a projecting kitchen (7) and newel staircase (8) in the angle.

f. Plan with staircase projection at rear making a T-shape.

g. Cross-section showing staircase as in plan c.

49. House at Marshfield, Gloucestershire
This house, the former Catherine Wheel Inn, is unusual among town houses in having what appears to be a chimney-breast backing on to a cross-passage giving an asymmetrical elevation. In cross-section the garret rooms have dormer windows hidden behind a balustrade, but the gambrel or double-pitched roof is prominent.
(Peter Crawley)

130

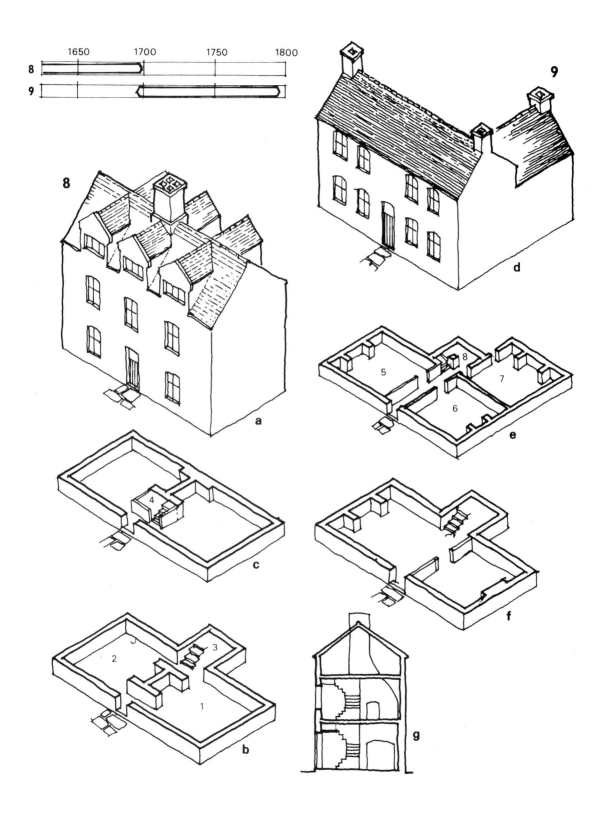

8

9

1650   1700   1750   1800

8

9

a

b

c

d

e

f

g

1

2

3

4

5

6

7

8

131

10 Wide frontage, double pile

a. General view of a double-pile town house showing the depth of two rooms in this instance covered by two parallel roofs drained by a valley gutter.

b. Plan showing entrance and staircase between hall (1) and parlour (2) and kitchen (3) and rear parlour (4); the fireplaces are on the end or party walls.

c. Plan showing a similar general arrangement but with fireplaces on the internal or spine walls.

50. House in St Mary's Place, Stamford, Lincolnshire
An early 18th-century elevation with (according to RCHME) rear portions rebuilt in 1833. The ground-floor window on the right has been made into a door.
(Peter Crawley)

132

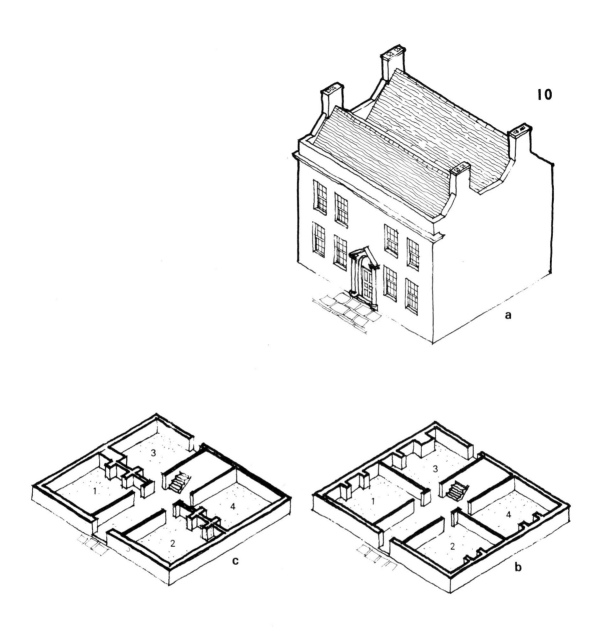

10

a

c

b

133

51. House in St Andrew Street, Hertford, Hertfordshire
This is a typical double-pile house with parallel roofs covering the two halves of the plan, giving an M-shaped effect. The house is unusual in having a rendered timber-frame side elevation, though there is a brick front to the street.
(Peter Crawley)

town house). Flues for the four fireplaces in each wall would rise directly to four chimney-stacks or be combined into two stacks according to the roofing system employed. During the late 17th century there was a vogue for using corner fireplaces, and such sources of heat were located side by side in corners of adjacent rooms, allowing the chimney-stacks to be combined. The other method of heating was to have fireplaces back to back in the heart of the house; this practice was fairly common in the late 17th and early 18th centuries but tended to fall out of favour. Gable-wall fireplaces were especially suitable for the all-embracing gabled roof but were also used with the M-shaped roof (two parallel gabled or hipped roofs and a central gutter). Internal fireplaces were especially appropriate for hipped roofs rising to a central flat area.

This plan was so versatile that it could serve for a large, pretentious house as well as for a smaller tradesman's house and for houses incorporating shops, but it was also capable of such variety in architectural detail within its strong architectural form that it was universally used: practically every town can show examples in its late 17th- or 18th-century streets.

11 Narrow frontage, longitudinal passage, back-to-back fireplaces

The problems facing the designer of a house for a narrow urban plot during the 17th and 18th centuries were similar to those that had confronted his medieval predecessor. He still had to provide access through his narrow frontage from the street to the rear of the plot; he still had to contrive to bring daylight into the rooms; but in addition the rooms on several storeys had to be heated from fixed fireplaces and connected by staircases as commodious as possible. Access and daylight entailed longitudinal corridors and rear courtyards; fireplaces and staircases gave opportunity for more variety in arrangement. ·

Many houses built in towns after the early part of the 17th century had two fireplaces set back to back on each floor with a spiral staircase or very tight newel staircase rising alongside. On the ground floor there was a longitudinal corridor or passageway giving access from street to yard, as well as providing internal communication, and the staircase was confined between passageway and fireplace jambs. Where two rooms on each floor would suffice, the plan was neat and compact and gave no serious problems in daylighting. There were some problems in roofing, however: the obvious method was to present a gable to the street and have a ridge running along the depth of the house, but this was a medieval type of roof and unfashionable in the 17th century and more commonly a hipped roof was provided, partly concealed behind a front parapet. An alternative solution was to run a ridge across the house, the deep roof being used for attic rooms and a gambrel section giving more headroom to these attics. A more complex roof had an eaves to the front with a ridge running across the site (i.e., parallel to the eaves and street) and a gable to the rear terminating a longitudinal ridge. Where more than two rooms were required on each floor the plan was not satisfactory; extra rooms had to be built as pavilions along the length of the site, leaving small courtyards or light-wells to allow daylight into the rear rooms of the main building.

After its introduction early in the 17th century this plan remained popular for nearly two hundred years, and examples may be found in the smaller towns well into the 19th century. The plan was found mainly in the southern half of England, examples having been recorded from Oxford, Harwich, Taunton, Blandford, Exeter and Totnes. The variation in which a staircase splits the fireplaces, as found in York, for example, is noted as type 17 (p. 146).

12 Narrow frontage, longitudinal passage, end- or party-wall fireplaces

The association of staircases with fireplaces was never very convenient. This tightly packed block within the centre of the house dominated each floor and gave little freedom in floor or room planning. The staircase tended to be narrow, tightly turning, and generally cramped. As the fashion developed for taller and taller rooms, it became ever more important to allow space for the staircase, to take the fireplaces away, and to place them where they could be in proportion to more spacious rooms. Since front and back walls were required for windows, the only other location for the fireplace was the end or party wall. The advantages of the central staircase conveniently serving rooms on each floor and reached from a longitudinal corridor were retained and the disadvantages minimised when fireplaces, flues and chimney-stacks migrated to the party walls.

Such a plan was introduced into Exeter and Totnes during the late 16th and early 17th centuries, known in Stamford in the early 18th century and in York rather later, and used in these and other towns right through the 18th century and well into the 19th. Earlier examples had a gabled roof, but from the end of

11 Narrow frontage, longitudinal passage, back-to-back fireplaces

a. Ground-floor plan showing a parlour or shop (1) and living room (2), then an open space (3) that allows light into living room and outside kitchen (4); access is by means of a passage through the front part of the house and so along an alleyway (5) that leads to the rear part of the site.

b. Isometric sketch showing the whole frontage of the site occupied by the front part of the building; there is an eaves-line along the street and dormer windows light an attic storey. The remaining part of the site has buildings roofed at right angles to the street.

c. Ground-floor plan of a smaller house with parlour (6) and living room (7) having fireplaces back to back; there is a staircase against the fireplace jambs (8); the passage (9) is incorporated within the house but also gives access to the rear of the plot.

d. Isometric sketch of plan c: a front parapet partly conceals the low-pitched roof.

e. An alternative ground-floor plan, less common, in which the staircase is located *between* the back-to-back fireplaces: this is noted as type 17 on the general summary.

---

the 17th century the use of a hip or a complex roof with ridge parallel to the street may be observed.

Even in central areas of ancient towns, not all urban plots were of the long medieval type; some were short because they were extensions to existing streets or because they were carved from the depth of some narrow frontage. Consequently many 18th- and early 19th-century town houses were only one room in depth, had a short passage running from front to back between the straight-flight staircase and single room on each floor and rose up two or three storeys, often with additional rooms in the roof space. It was virtually inevitable in such a plan that the fireplace should be on a gable or party wall.

13 Wide frontage, central stair, end- or party-wall fireplaces

While the earlier way of handling a wide frontage was to employ fireplaces back to back, another way, and ultimately the one that was preferred, was to arrange a central entrance opening on to a staircase hall and to provide two principal rooms, with fireplaces in the end or party walls, on each floor. The compactness of the central common stack was lost but better proportions were gained for the various rooms, and a better approach: it can hardly have been comfortable or satisfying to enter from the street against the blank wall of a fireplace jamb. Such a house was less spacious and compact than a double-pile house, but it was just as imposing when set within an urban terrace and gave an adequate amount of well-lit, well-heated and well-served accommodation on each floor.

The plan was introduced during the early part of the 17th century but was not in general use until a century later. Examples may be seen in what were then the newly developing suburbs such as those outside the walls of York, Beverley or Chester.

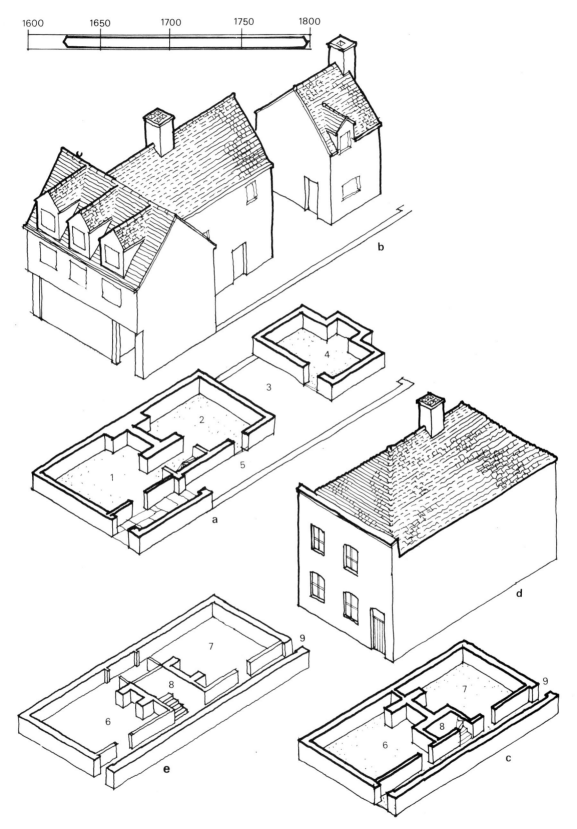

1600   1650   1700   1750   1800

137

52. House at Feckenham, Worcestershire
A double-fronted house with bow windows, a central dormer window and a semi-basement below.
(Peter Crawley)

14 Universal terrace houses

An urban house-plan that came to dominate domestic design for more than two centuries was first seen in London in the houses built by Nicholas Barbon between 1670 and 1700 and has continued in use virtually to the present day. It was so convenient for domestic life, and so economical for the development of new housing areas on land free from earlier site restrictions, that few variations of any significance were ever introduced.

The universal terrace-house plan provides two rooms on the ground floor, one at the front and a slightly narrower one at the rear. Alongside the front room is the entrance lobby; alongside the back room is the staircase rising in one long

10

53. Houses at Bradford-on-Avon, Wiltshire
A row of narrow-frontage houses, two and a half storeys high with prominent dormer windows.
(Peter Crawley)

54. The Promenade, Cheltenham, Gloucestershire
This terrace of narrow-frontage houses has an elevation built as a single composition and enlivened by iron balconies.
(Peter Crawley)

12 Narrow frontage, longitudinal passage, end- or party-wall fireplaces

a. Ground-floor plan showing a parlour or shop (1), living room (2) and detached kitchen (3) with a courtyard (4) lighting kitchen and living room; the fireplaces are on the end or party walls and the staircase (5) is between the main rooms. The passage (6) leading from the street is incorporated in the ground floor of the house.

b. Isometric sketch showing a gable to the street and, in this instance, jettied storeys as from a timber-framed front wall.

c. Ground-floor plan of a house which is on a similarly narrow frontage but is only one room in depth. The fireplaces (7) are on the end or party wall and the entrance lobby (8) also serves as a passage to the rear.

d. Sketch showing, in this example, an eaves-line along the street and dormer windows lighting the attic rooms.

13 Wide frontage, central stair, end- or party-wall fireplaces

e. Plan showing the house turned through 90 degrees as permitted by the wide plot. There is a living room (9), a parlour (10) and a staircase between (11); the fireplaces are on the end or party walls. A short passage (12) serves the rear of the plot and the bedrooms would be built over this passage.

f. Plan of a wide-frontage house with stairs winding alongside the main fireplace. Access to the rear is through the house.

---

flight to the half-landing and then in a shorter return flight to the first floor, and so on up the full height of the house. On the first floor the front room usually ran the whole width of the house, but on the second floor there might be two rooms at the front to give three rooms on that floor. The earliest examples had a small single-storey 'closet' or heated study opening off the rear ground-floor room. Fireplaces were usually placed along the end or party wall except that at the turn of the 17th century into the 18th there was a fashion for corner fireplaces.

The rear staircase worked well in that the foot was prominent and conveniently located in relation to the main entrance, and the head emerged near the centre of the plan, requiring little landing space at each floor level. The staircase was well lit from windows at each half-landing; it was adequately supported in the angle between the rear and party walls and could be narrow enough to leave plenty of width for the rear room. Eventually it permitted the development of a projecting wing at the rear to increase accommodation at each floor level.

The plan also presented no serious constructional or roofing problems: front, back and party walls were well braced, and some partition walls could be raised through the full height of the building to help with roofing and yet were properly restrained at each floor level. The roof could be arranged to run in one span across the width of the building, it could be carried by purlins which were supported if necessary on the partition walls, or it could be run in a series of valleys between party walls. It could even be organised as an M-section roof with a valley gutter at the junction between front and back rooms.

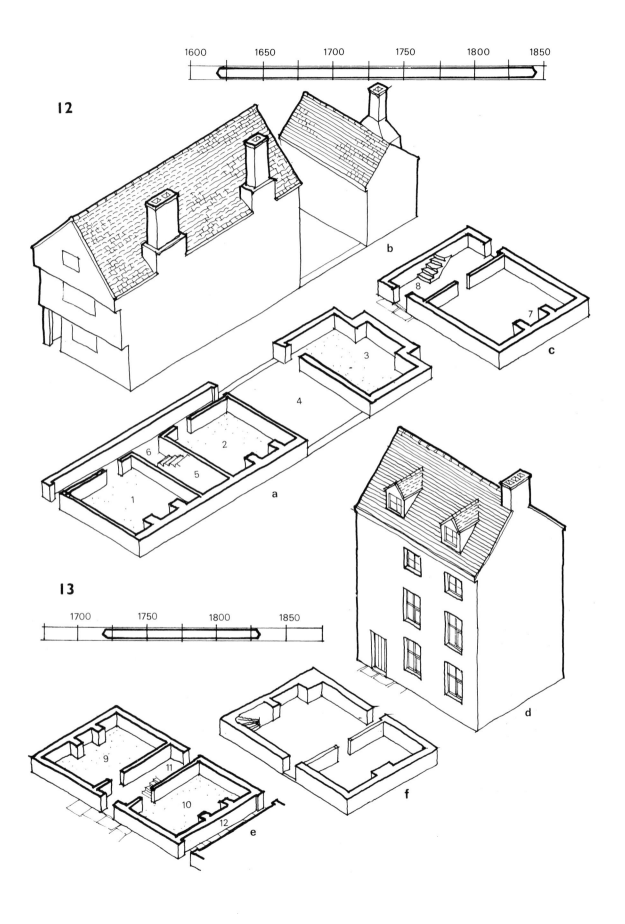

1600 1650 1700 1750 1800 1850

12

1700 1750 1800 1850

13

1

2

3

4

5

6

7

8

9

10

11

12

a

b

c

d

e

f

14 Universal terrace houses

a. Ground-floor plan with parlour (1) and dining room (2) and a closet (3) which was sometimes heated in order to serve as a study; the staircase (4) is at the rear of the building; fireplaces are in the gable or party walls.

b. First-floor plan showing the room (5) that extended over the whole front of the house and came to be used as the drawing room or principal living room. One bedroom (6) is on this floor, others are above.

c. An alternative ground-floor plan with similar accommodation but with corner fireplaces.

d. Sketch showing one house in a terrace.

e. Plan showing fireplaces back to back.

f. Elevation of a terrace with houses in reflected pairs.

g. Elevation of a terrace with houses not arranged in pairs.

Many variations could be played on the basic pattern of windows and door on the main elevation, and most country towns and such large cities as have been spared redevelopment can show a range of elevational details, from the stone dressings and prominent wooden cornice of the Wren period to the hard brickwork and cast-iron ornament of the Greek Revival.

15 London terrace houses, rear stairs

One version of the universal terrace house flourished in London during the late 18th and early 19th centuries and enclosed a large amount of domestic accommodation within a compact and relatively convenient building. There were usually three principal floors.

The dining room and study were on the ground floor, drawing rooms and parlour (or main bedroom) on the first floor and bedrooms on the second floor. The ground floor was usually raised two or three feet (0.69 to 0.91 m) above street level; in the basement were the kitchen, wash-house and servants' day-room, while at the top of the house, within the roof space, were the servants' bedrooms. The basement rooms at the front of the house were lit from an 'area', i.e., an open light-well within the curtilage of the house that also gave access to coal cellars under the footpath. Servants and tradesmen reached the area by way of steps from the pavement for, in the absence of any means of access at the rear, the area stairs provided the tradesmen's entrance and the only means of servicing. Since the artificial road level was often several feet above the natural ground level, the back basement rooms might open directly on to a garden at the rear of the site. The rooms within the roof were true attic bedrooms in that the double-pitch gambrel roof which was so often included was above the cornice-line and behind the parapet. Since every room from basement to attic had a fireplace, the party walls were a honeycomb of flues and the simple, even austere, lines of the elevation were relieved by the dozens of chimney-pots that once contributed so much to the visitor's impression of London.

The side staircase was usually lit from a window or series of windows at each landing level, and light penetrated down the well between the two flights that

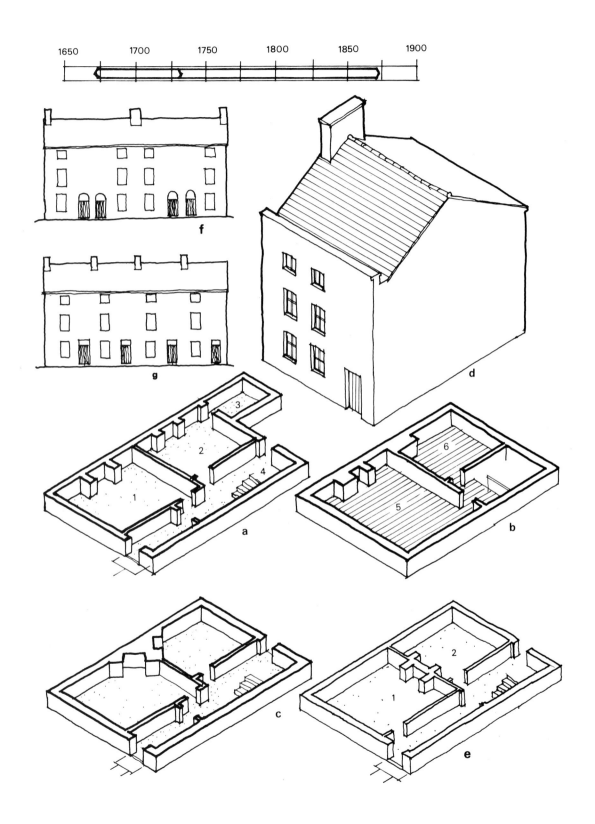

15 London terrace houses, rear stairs

a. Ground-floor plan showing the entrance lobby (1), parlour (2) and dining room (3) with a double-flight staircase (4) at the rear; there is a service room (5) projecting into the main yard. At the front of the house an area (6) gives light and access to basement rooms; in this instance another area (7) has been provided to light basement rooms at the rear.

b. Basement plan showing kitchen and staff rooms (8 and 9) lit from the front and rear areas; the front area also gives access to coal bunkers under the footpath (10).

c. First-floor plan with the drawing room (11) stretching across the front and a bedroom (12) beside the staircase.

d. Sketch showing the building as a tall narrow slice from a terrace. Here there are front parapets with attic storeys and a collection of chimneys in a huge stack in a party wall.

---

formed each stretch of the staircase and along the short corridors serving each floor.

16 London terrace houses, central stairs

The central-staircase plans of the 17th century were never entirely superseded by the rear-staircase or universal terrace-house plans. The central-staircase plan had a renewed period of use in the late 18th and early 19th centuries, but with fireplaces on the party wall; in London especially, it was employed for some of the most magnificent town houses of the late Georgian and Regency periods.

The distribution of rooms by floor was similar to that of the London terrace house with side stair already described, but the central staircase, top-lit from a lantern in the roof, wound gently around a generous open well to give light and movement in a part of the plan that would otherwise have been dark and rigid. The whole of the rear wall was available for lighting an important room on each floor, and by interposing an ante-room behind the stairs and between the principal rooms, an attractive architectural sequence of spaces on each floor could be contrived.

The very generosity of the space allocated to the staircase meant that this plan was not as economical as its counterpart with the rear staircase. For the larger houses, however, the architectural gains were presumably considered worth the slight reduction in economy.

As in other terrace houses, there was the problem of access to the rear of the plot to be solved. In smaller examples the only access might be through the house, though usually an open corridor was provided between houses; in larger examples access was by way of the basement.

Where there was a rear service road or alleyway, access was readily available. For larger houses so favoured there was often a mews consisting of a coach house and stable with a coachman's quarter above.

The London terrace-house plans were convenient and economical, but only up to a point. Their many fireplaces, several reception rooms and many bedrooms were on a number of floors. This made for economy of construction and compactness at each floor level, but the family, for some of the time, and the servants, for much of the time, must have found flight after flight of staircase something less than a

144

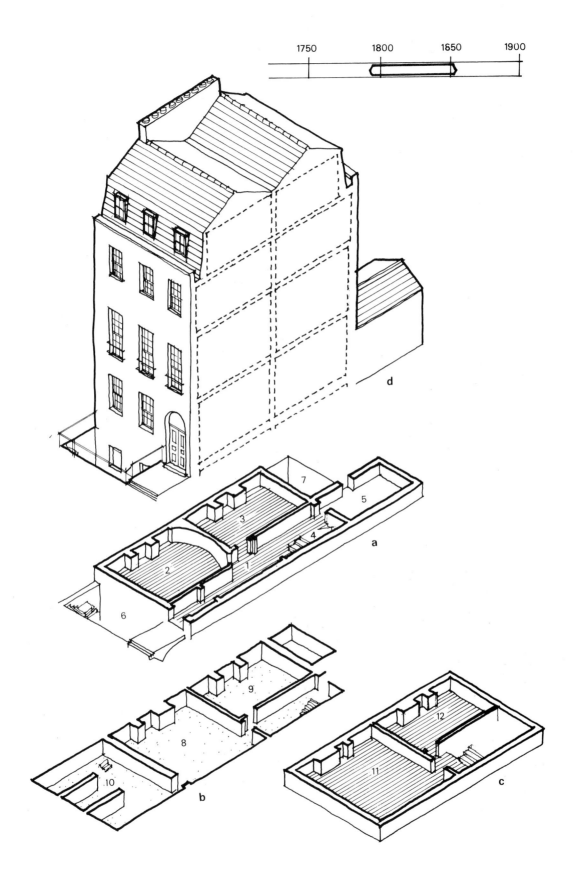

1750 1800 1850 1900

d

7

5

3

4

a

2

1

6

9

8

10

b

12

11

c

16 London terrace houses, central stairs

a. Ground-floor plan showing the two main entertaining rooms (1 and 2) with the staircase (3) in between; fireplaces are in the party wall.

b. Alternative ground-floor plan found in some smaller houses with parlour and living room (4 and 5) and a service room (6); the staircase (7) lies between the two main rooms. The passage (8) acts as an internal corridor and also gives access to the rear of the site.

c. A ground-floor plan as found in some larger houses and indicating a spacious staircase (9) lit from a lantern above.

d. Cross-section showing how the lantern lights the staircase. A subsidiary staircase would give access to servants' bedrooms in the attics and another to the kitchens etc., in the basement.

e. Sketch to show the full depth of the house, the narrow double-pitched roofs often used and the lead flat roof between.

17 Narrow frontage, central stairs between fireplaces

f. Ground-floor plan showing the two main entertaining rooms (10 and 11) heated by fireplaces split by the central staircase.

---

convenience. It was an arrangement that often drew comment from continental travellers more accustomed to the wide and spacious 'hotel' or the flat all on one level.

17 Narrow frontage, central stairs between fireplaces

This plan, which has been particularly noted in York, has a room at the front and a room at the back on each floor. It has a staircase between the rooms, and a longitudinal passage linking rooms and staircase and sometimes serving also as the means of access from the street to the rear of the plot. It is unusual, however, in having fireplaces backing on to the staircase walls. The arrangement gives rooms that are well proportioned, well lit and as spacious as restricted sites of narrow frontage will allow. It also gives a staircase rising easily and graciously about two equal flights to a landing that serves the rooms on the upper floors with the minimum of wasted floor space. The central staircase, as in all similar plans, frees the front and back walls for windows to the principal rooms, but in the darkest part of the plan can itself be lit only from a lantern. The split back-to-back fireplaces require two separate but closely adjacent chimney-stacks or a complicated gathering of flues in the roof space, so it is hardly surprising that the plan did not enjoy very widespread favour.

11

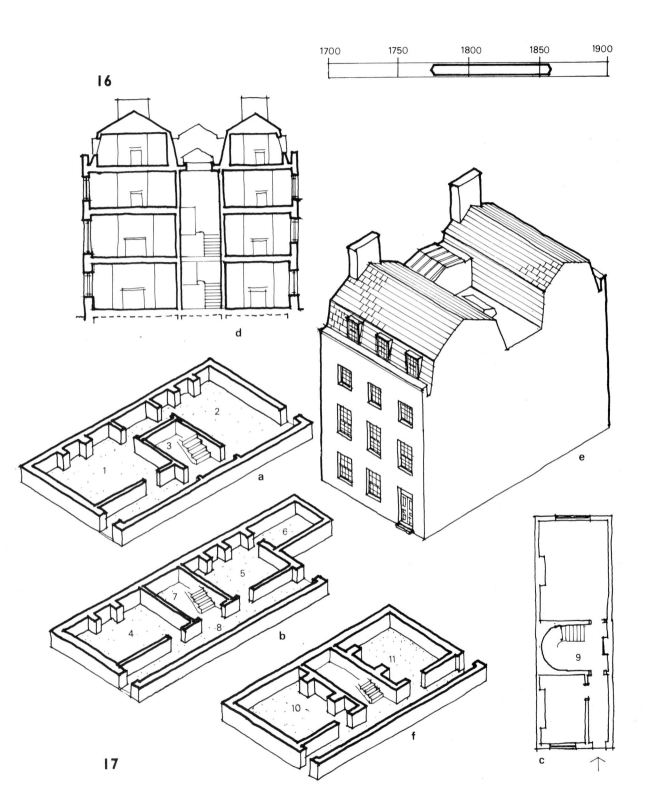

16

1700   1750   1800   1850   1900

d

a
1
2
3

b
4
5
6
7
8

e

f
10
11

c
9

17

147

Urban cottages

Documentary evidence suggests that medieval towns were full of independent families of relatively poor people – labourers, minor tradesmen, artisans and the elderly – who lived in dwellings that were basically of a single cell. Virtually nothing remains of these dwellings, though their foundations are being revealed in excavations in sites in towns such as Winchester, York and Carlisle. Only occasionally, as with cottages in Goodramgate, York, have they been preserved by special circumstances; otherwise they have been demolished or incorporated in later structures, because in neither size nor construction did they meet the standards of the 17th and 18th centuries, let alone of the 19th.

12

As towns expanded during those years, so more and more cottages were needed. They were built initially on such plots as were available within the gardens or yards of older houses. Later they were built on small virgin plots as new land became available to be incorporated in the towns. Until recently virtually every small town or large city of medieval foundation had its crowded section of cottages tightly packed along narrow alleyways hidden from the streets and reached by way of narrow and often low passages through the buildings on the street frontage. But central-area development, combined with campaigns to clear slums that may have been full of history but lacked adequate light and ventilation, has left few such areas to be seen and appreciated.

Standards of accommodation rose swiftly during the late 18th and 19th centuries and have risen even more swiftly during the 20th. The urban cottage dweller in the 17th century would have had one room and about 150 sq. ft (13.93 sq. m) of floor space, whereas his counterpart at the end of the 19th century could expect six rooms on two floors (and often a cellar and attic in addition) amounting to more than 1,000 sq. ft (92.9 sq. m), not counting cellar or attic. The arrangement and siting of urban cottages was increasingly dominated by the perceived requirements of health and sanitation, as ill-health and epidemics were put down to overcrowding and lack of light and air as well as to faults in water supply and sewage disposal. Until waterborne sanitation became quite widely available in the early 20th century, access was needed for the night-soil men as well as the dustbin men. Such access was provided by means of entries between houses, by cart access to common yards behind sets of dwellings, and eventually by alleyways between streets. To secure light and air, the width of streets and the distance between rows of cottages was regulated by local acts or by-laws that also required ever greater room heights. The overall improvement in the housing of the working classes during the 19th century was really quite remarkable.

18 One-room cottages, longitudinal passage within
Among the very few surviving early cottages are those in which a passage runs from the street to the back yard and gives access to a single ground-floor room. This passage is incorporated within the single-cell structure of the cottage: the door on the street is really the entry to the site, for the front (and only) door to the cottage opens off the passage. In the very smallest examples, single-storey though often with a loft, the one room, plus the loft if there was one, comprised the whole dwelling.

148

19 One-room cottages, no passage within

When small cottages were built in a more permanent form than their predecessors, from about 1700, they still consisted basically of a single cell. The principal room was about 12 ft or 14 ft (3.66 or 4.27 m) square with a door near one corner, a fireplace on one wall, and a steep narrow staircase leading to any remaining accommodation in the form of a loft (or later a bedroom) in the roof space. This plan remained in use throughout the 18th century and into the early part of the 19th.

Cottages had to be sited on the least valuable pieces of land: on roadsides at the extremities of the town, or within the former gardens and yards of other properties near the town centre. The single-cell plan of these cottages made them suitable for infilling narrow medieval burgage plots: a plot 20 ft (6.09 m) wide could take a row of cottages having a 12-ft (3.66-m) room-depth and still leave 6 ft (1.83 m) or so for access and a certain amount of daylight. Unlike other house-plans there was no possibility of through ventilation, but few houses and cottages even of shallow depth had such ventilation, and it was not until the association of disease with lack of ventilation was assumed that this absence was considered important. In Yorkshire such cottages were called 'blind-back cottages'.

Improvements to the single-cell cottage took the form of greater floor area, greater floor-to-ceiling heights (including a full-height first floor instead of a loft in the roof space), slightly easier staircases and more fireplaces and chimneys. Eventually the improving one-room cottage merged with the smaller versions of the universal terrace-house plan to produce the standard single-fronted double-depth cottage of the 19th century.

There were few urban equivalents of the one-and-a-half-room or two-room single-storey cottages of the countryside. Where found, single-storey cottages tend to be associated with certain occupations – the fishermen's cottages of Cullercoats, Northumberland, or the miners' cottages of other towns in that county come to mind – or they survive from villages that have been engulfed by the 19th-century spread of towns such as Bradford. 13

20 Back-to-back cottages

As well as the very narrow backlands behind existing houses, the newly expanding towns had plots that were empty or could be cleared. Many were long and narrow, reflecting the shape of the fields. The only feasible way of filling such sites with single-family dwellings was to place rows of single-cell dwellings back to back. Sites were developed to high density because of the need, in the absence of a cheap local transport system, to house workers close to their work-places. When they were built, such cottages were not in themselves inferior, either in size or construction, to those inhabited by workmen generally. High-density development spread land costs over many dwellings, which could then be let at rents that workmen could afford. 14

Later generations condemned such cottages for size, lack of through ventilation and inadequate sanitation and water supply, but at the time they were so superior to the flimsy hovels of Ireland and the more remote parts of Britain that they may well have encouraged the drift from the countryside to the towns.

The standard back-to-back urban cottage had a kitchen living room on the ground floor (sometimes with a pantry in addition) and a bedroom on the first floor. Often there was a cellar below and sometimes there was an attic above.

149

18 One-room cottages, longitudinal passage within

a. Plan showing the one-room cottage reached from a passage that also serves the rear of the site; a ladder in one corner of the room rises to the loft above.

b. Sketch showing the door that serves passage and cottage; the dormer lights the loft.

19 One-room cottages, no passage within

c. Ground-floor plan showing the cottage opening directly off a street or alleyway; access to the rear of the plot would be from a separate back lane or by way of a passage alongside the cottage.

d. Sketch of the cottage; in this instance the gable facing the street allows a window to light the loft space.

e. Plan showing ladder-like staircase in a cupboard opposite the door and also a passage giving access to the rear of the plot.

f. Sketch showing the eaves running along the street elevation and a dormer serving the loft space.

g. Plan with a winding staircase projecting from the rear.

h. Plan with fireplace in the rear wall.

i. Plan with access through the cottage to the rear of the plot.

j. Plan showing development to a one-and-a-half-unit cottage.

k. Elevation showing entry giving access to rear, and development to three storeys.

Cottages such as this were being built by the building clubs of Leeds and surrounding areas from about 1787.

The improved back-to-back cottage, found particularly in the West Riding of Yorkshire, was usually built on a wide frontage giving two rooms to each floor. Entrance was still directly into the kitchen living room, but the provision of a separate scullery and staircase lobby meant that this room was more convenient to use than in earlier cottages. There were two bedrooms on the first floor, further bedrooms on a second floor or in the roof space. There might also be a cellar. In the later, most improved versions there was a through passage between each pair of sculleries. This meant that there was some corner ventilation on the ground floor; it also meant that each cottage could have a back door or at least a side door, space for an individual privy, access for night-soil collection, and, indeed, many advantages of the conventional cottage of the time except access to a private yard.

Back-to-back cottages were almost unknown in the south of England but were once common in most of the big industrial cities such as Manchester and Birmingham. They fell out of favour because of overcrowding or sanitary defects and were either demolished or converted in pairs into single 'through' houses. They were commonest of all in Yorkshire and especially in Leeds, Bradford and the surrounding towns. The improved versions were still being built well into the 20th century. In the same areas there were also experiments at the turn of the 19th century with the 'through by lights' plan, whereby interlocking dwellings on an L-plan

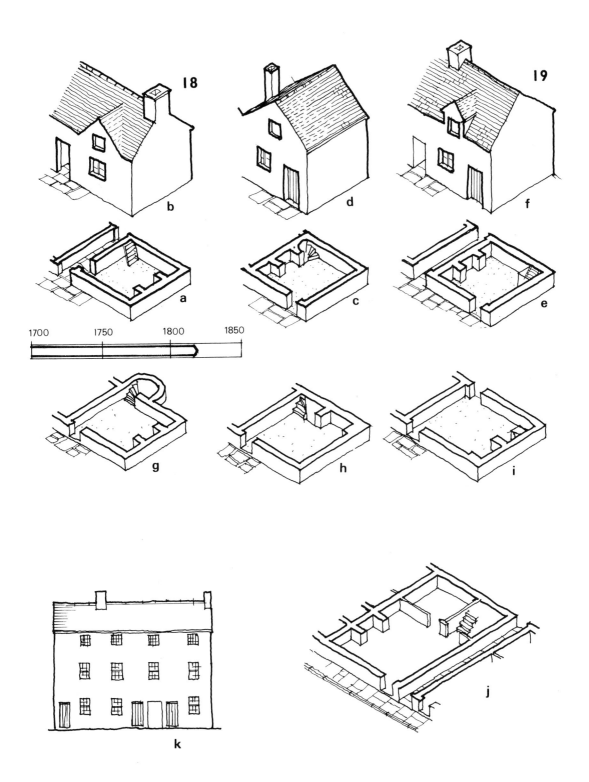

18

19

b

d

f

a

c

e

1700   1750   1800   1850

g

h

i

k

j

151

20 Back-to-back cottages

a. Ground-floor plan showing two cottages placed back to back: each has a single exposure to the outside air; fireplaces are in the longitudinal party wall. One cottage is shown with a staircase fireplace, the other has a staircase running alongside the lateral party wall.

b. Sketch to show the deep plan covered by a roof of shallow pitch.

c. An alternative plan with the staircases rising alongside the longitudinal party walls and the fireplaces back to back on the lateral party walls.

d. Here the plan shows the urban equivalent of the one-and-a-half-unit cottage of the countryside, but organised as back-to-back cottages. Living kitchen (1), pantry (2).

e. In this plan, corner ventilation is shown by way of a passageway between pairs of houses. Each one has a living kitchen (1) and pantry (2).

f. Ground-floor plan of interlocking cottages with through ventilation but no back or front yards; living room (3) and kitchen (4).

---

maintained the high density and consequent economy of land of the back-to-back plan but gave every cottage the chance of through ventilation.

21 Houses for cottage industry

Before considering what became the standard plan for the late 18th-century and 19th-century urban cottage, it is important to glance at the plans devised in connection with cottage industry. These layouts were developed in the towns as well as the countryside towards the end of the 18th century, and their representatives survive, though now in purely domestic use, in many parts of the Midlands and north of England.

The greatest demands on design for cottage industry were made by various branches of the textile trade: silk in Manchester, Stockport, Macclesfield, Leek and Congleton, cotton-spinning and -weaving in Manchester and east Lancashire, work in the woollen trades in the West Riding of Yorkshire, lace-making in Nottingham, hosiery in Nottingham and Leicester. Metal trades also made their demands on cottage design: jewellery in Birmingham, lock-making in Willenhall, horse tackle in Walsall and so on. In the Midlands some of these activities required a separate building in the yard, but elsewhere workshop and dwelling were one.

The workshop might be above, below or alongside the dwelling. It might be used by the cottager or let separately to a craftsman who had to reach the workshop without intruding too seriously on the privacy of the family. The buildings were erected in twos and threes, in short terraces, or in great numbers so as to dominate a whole quarter of an industrial town.

Probably the most characteristic arrangement is that in which the workroom was placed above the domestic accommodation. This arrangement is easily recognised by the elongated 'weavers' windows' of archaic pattern contrasting with the more up-to-date windows of the house – though sometimes the weavers' windows were confined to the back of the building, the front of the workroom being lit by domestic windows matching those below. The workroom (or 'loomshop') usually ran without interruption from front to back of the building, the roof being carried on purlins that spanned from party wall to party wall. For many textile operations

15

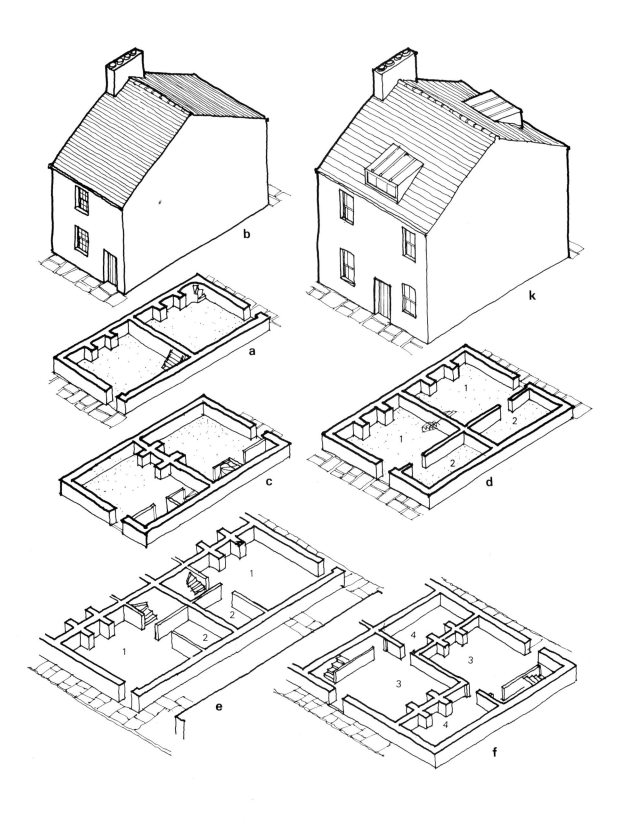

b

k

a

c

d

e

f

153

21 Houses for cottage industry

a. Ground-floor plan of a cottage which has a loomshop above: entrance from the street is directly into the living kitchen (1) and there is a scullery/wash-house (2) at the rear; the staircase (3) leading to the bedroom floor is adjacent to the back door.

b. Plan of the loomshop which was generally on the second floor: working space (4) was reached by a ladder or steep staircase that rose from the first-floor landing into the darkest part of the room.

c. Cross-section showing the loomshop lit by windows at front and back and with a storage space (the cockloft) within the roof.

d. Sketch showing the 'weavers' windows' lighting the loomshop floor just beneath the eaves; many such cottages have conventional windows lighting the front of the loomshop and the special horizontal windows lighting the rear.

e. Ground-floor plan of a cottage that incorporates a loomshop at ground level: entrance is directly into the living kitchen (5) from which is entered the (often unheated) loomshop (7), lit from front and rear. There is a small scullery (6) and a staircase at the rear of the cottage.

f. Sketch to show the domestic and industrial parts of the elevation – though room uses would vary with fluctuations in trade.

g. Ground-floor plan of a cottage with basement workshop: entrance is made over an area into the living kitchen (8) and scullery (9); separate steps lead down to the area (10), from which the workshop is entered.

h. Sketch showing the cottage above the workshop: there was usually no intercommunication between the two parts of the building.

(weaving and frame knitting, for example), adequate headroom was important and this could be most conveniently obtained on the top floor. Within the roof space, the 'cockloft' immediately under the ridge was used for storage. As the machinery of the period was light in weight and made of wood and wrought iron, no heavy loads were imposed on the floor; and as assembly within the loomshop was practicable there was usually no difficulty in taking the parts up a domestic staircase. In the standard arrangement each workroom ran over a separate cottage and between party walls. In later examples, however, several rooms were run together along the length of a terrace, roofs were carried on trusses and a single access point was provided at the end of the terrace. In some instances at least, power was transmitted from a steam engine to be tapped for the looms or other machines of individual workers.

Another convenient arrangement was that in which a workshop was included with domestic accommodation within a two-storey structure. One common practice was to have a single ground-floor workroom running the whole depth of the building with kitchen living room and scullery alongside and bedrooms above. This meant that separate access to the workroom was easily provided for any craftsman tenant and the second bedroom could be let to lodgers – an important consideration during the swift urban expansion – or used temporarily as a loomshop if volume of trade so required.

Sometimes workrooms could be recognised as such through the use of archaic

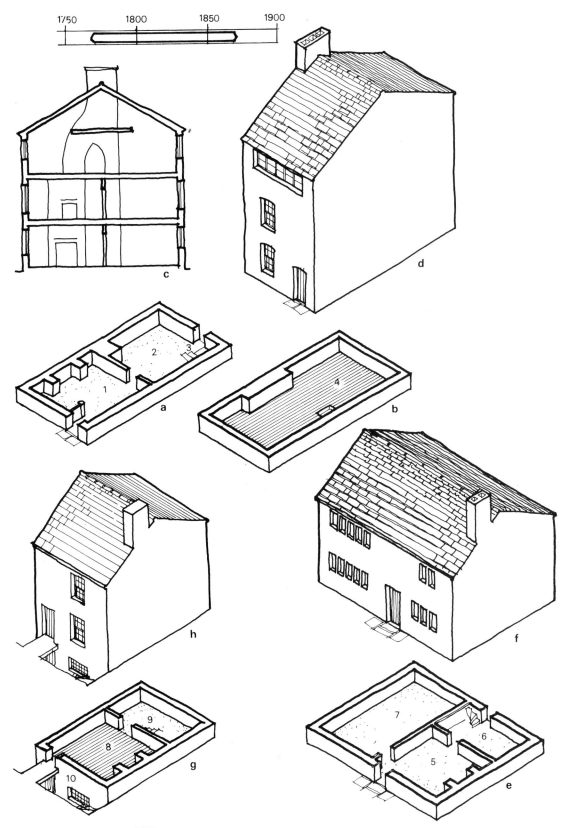

1/50   1800   1850   1900

c

d

a

1

2

3

b

4

h

f

g

8

9

10

e

7

6

5

155

55. House or cottage at Littleborough, Lancashire

This building has been designed to adapt to changing fortunes in the textile industry. At one extreme domestic accommodation could be confined to the ground floor with a loomshop occupying the whole of the first floor; at the other extreme, as now, the first floor could be used as bedrooms with many window lights blocked.
(G. D. Bold)

details or through the particular provisions for certain processes (some silk-weaving, for instance, demanded large windows but no ventilation), though special windows might be confined to sides or rear with conventional domestic windows at the front. Windows were often altered when workrooms were converted into parlours or other domestic rooms after hand-based craftworking had been abandoned.

The cellar workshop was most convenient for the heavier metal-working trades, but it was found in textile areas also, especially where the process required a damp atmosphere. The cellar was usually only half underground and was approached by steps from an area while other steps led to the cottage above. Separate access for a tenant was available and internal access was often not provided, so it is not always easy to distinguish cellar workshops from cellar dwellings, which were an unpopular feature of the early years of the Industrial Revolution.

Industry, and in particular the textile trades, developed through the alternation of shortage and surplus as the inadequate capacity of one sector led to inventions that turned shortage into surplus, leading in turn to relative shortage in some other sector. The alternation of improved methods in spinning and weaving is a case in point. For the handloom weaver or other domestic operative there was no certainty that a period of great activity would last indefinitely or that enforced idleness was necessarily permanent. There was considerable investment in property suitable for handloom weaving especially between about 1770 and 1840. Even after factory processes appeared to have triumphed, the more optimistic builders erected cottages that could be adapted to part-industrial use; not all the blocked weavers' windows of the Pennine terraces represent conversion to domestic use — some were built blocked and have never been opened.

In the hatting districts, terraces of cottages were built as factories but complete with half-formed doors and windows in case millinery fashions changed and cot-

56. House and cottage at Thurlstone, Yorkshire, WR
A double-fronted house and a single-fronted cottage, both two rooms deep, are combined with a second-floor loomshop or weaving loft illuminated by a fine range of mullioned windows.
(Peter Crawley)

tages rather than workshops were needed. Gradually, however, as the 19th century wore on it became clear that few opportunities for independent working would remain. Although cottages in Macclesfield were still being built with weavers' windows into the 1870s, integrated workrooms were generally abandoned. Only occasionally, as in the back yard workshops of Leicestershire and the Black Country, did domestic industry survive until recent times.

157

Urban cottages of the late 18th and early 19th centuries were vulnerable to the fashion of the 1960s and 1970s for large-scale redevelopment. Although actually quite spacious when the workroom was added to the domestic accommodation, they lacked modern sanitation and were in some cases neglected or poorly built. Many such buildings have been demolished but here and there, in pockets both in smaller towns and big cities, the tell-tale features of design for cottage industry may still attract the observant eye.

22, 23 Two-up-and-two-down cottages

Just as the double-pile house developed from its 17th-century origins to become first a standard Large House plan of the early 18th century and then the standard plan for Small Houses of the late 18th century and much of the 19th, so its reduced counterpart, the universal terrace house, may well have influenced the design of the single-fronted 'two-up-and-two-down' urban cottage which was similarly ubiquitous and even more numerous. This plan-type consists of four rooms, a kitchen/living room and a scullery/wash-house on the ground floor and two bedrooms on the first floor; it had a staircase which ran either along or across the plan.

It is likely that one line of development leading to this plan originated in the single-cell cottage. Just as Small Houses one room in depth had been extended and made more convenient by adding a staircase and scullery at the rear, so the single-cell cottage gained better access to a full-height bedroom through the introduction of a dog-leg or winding staircase alongside a small pantry or other service room at the rear, The cottages were further improved when the first floor accommodated two bedrooms and the ground-floor service room became nearly as big as the main room. Another line of development may have been represented by the universal terrace-house plan, with its staircase in one long flight and another shorter flight at the rear alongside the secondary living room, 'filtering down' the social scale. However, a third possible ancestor of the two-up-and-two-

16

57. Cottages at Lewes, Sussex
A reflected pair of cottages with doorways together. There is probably one main room on each floor with a small garret room. The timber-frame is weather-boarded.
(RCHME © Crown Copyright)

158

58. Cottages at Styal, Cheshire
In this terrace of 'two-up-and-two-down' cottages there is also accommodation in the half-basement with separate access. These cottages are part of the industrial hamlet serving Styal Mill.
(G. Wheeler)

down plan is the urban house two rooms deep with a central staircase: early 19th-century pairs of cottages in Stamford, for instance, have central staircases of two return flights in small-scale imitation of those introduced for superior dwellings nearly two hundred years before. For the smallest cottages, the easy double-flight staircase was evidently considered an extravagance and a steep single-flight staircase running across the plan between the two ground-floor rooms was generally used instead. Such a staircase could be accepted within the smallest cottages while room-heights were comparatively modest, but became uncomfortably steep as room-heights increased.

Where the staircase ran along the plan, adjacent to a party wall, it normally rose from just inside the front door, reaching the first floor in a single straight flight and not usually partitioned from the kitchen living room. There was one

159

59. Rear of cottages at Styal, Cheshire

The privies, coalsheds and small back yards behind the cottages are reached by a cobbled alleyway.
(G. Wheeler)

60. Cottages at Cromford, Derbyshire

These two- and three-storey cottages are part of the early industrial complex at Cromford. Their substantial coursed-masonry walls indicate the faith of the mill-owners in their water-powered mills and also the strength of the stone-walling tradition in this part of the county.
(Peter Crawley)

variation, however, in which the staircase rose from inside the back door, inside the scullery, beginning with three or four winders. This variation was first noticed in connection with houses having workrooms on the second floor, and it was assumed to be a means of maintaining some privacy when the workroom was separately let. However, as it has since been recorded in cottages with solely domestic accommodation, there must be some additional explanation – maybe the maximising of the usable floor area in the main room of a small cottage. At any rate the longitudinal position rising from the front door was standardised; as cottages improved in size and quality, the staircase and passage were set in a partitioned lobby and, with increasing room-heights, rose in two flights to the first floor.

Once adopted, the two-up-and-two-down cottage-plan, in either of its variations, remained without fundamental change except where it developed into the tunnel-back plan. Architectural fashion and enthusiasm for hygiene led to ever increasing

22 Two-up-and-two-down cottages with rear stairs

a. Ground-floor plan showing the living room (1) and kitchen (2) with the staircase (3) alongside.

b. Alternative ground-floor plan with living room (4) and dining room (5); the staircase (6) which is at the rear is approached by a lobby leading from the front door. In such a cottage there would be a kitchen in the basement or as a lean-to at the rear.

c. Sketch showing the parapet and hipped roofs that were much used in the smaller London terrace houses and cottages.

d. 'House over house' with the house at the lower level built into the slope.

e. Ground-floor plan with staircase beside the back door. Here a heated copper is shown in the corner of the scullery.

f. Elevation showing entry to the yards.

23 Two-up-and-two-down cottages with central stairs

g. Ground-floor plan with kitchen living room (7) and scullery/wash-house (8) and a steep staircase in between.

h. Cross-section showing the tall floor-to-ceiling heights of the rooms.

i. Sketch of the cottage with the characteristic arrangement of door and windows.

---

room-heights, however: many otherwise unpretentious late 19th-century cottages have ground-floor rooms as much as 12 ft (3.66 m) tall as against the 7 ft 6 ins. (2.29 m) often found nowadays. Cheap coal and improved living standards led to the provision of three or four fireplaces in the meanest cottages. Demands for greater privacy led to the formation of a lobby or passage running from the front door and alongside the staircase. These were simply refinements to the basic plan.

Urban cottages of this type are often misnamed 'back-to-back' from the common and reasonable layout of terraces facing on to a street for public access and backing on to an alley for service and sanitary access. Such cottages have two exposures, however, and so are fundamentally different from the true back-to-back dwellings with their single exposure.

A curious variation on the layout of front streets and back alleys occurs in certain of the Pennine towns such as Hebden Bridge and Holmfirth. The only available sites for building were on steep valley sides, and so cottages were built on top of cottages: one row of conventional two-up-and-two-down cottages reached by a footpath or gallery at the upper part of the slope was superimposed on another row of similar cottages reached from a road or path lower down the slope. In a variation of this arrangement, the upper cottage was superimposed on a flat or single-storey cottage.

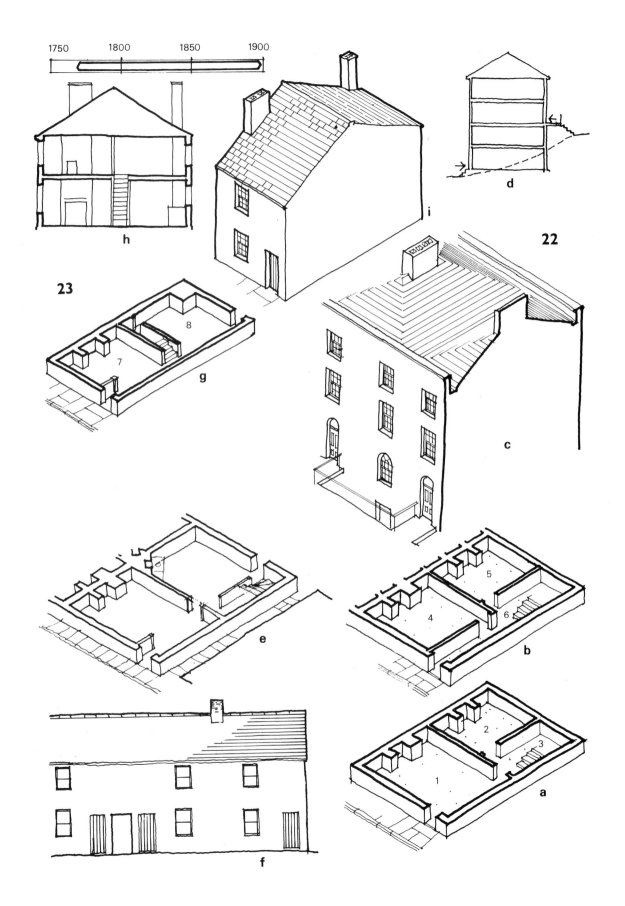

1750   1800   1850   1900

22

23

h

i

d

g

c

e

b

f

a

1

2

3

4

5

6

7

8

24 Tunnel-back cottages

a. Ground-floor plan showing the living room (1) and parlour (2) with a rear projection housing the kitchen or scullery (3), privy (4) and coal house (5). Here the staircase runs across the house.

b. The sketch shows the rear projection and the way in which the living-room windows are lit by a tunnel-like recess between the adjacent projecting scullery blocks.

c. Ground-floor plan with rear stairs and showing kitchen (6), parlour (7), scullery (8), accessible from a back yard, pantry (9) and coal house (10).

d. Sketch indicating rear wing.

e. Plan at first-floor level showing bedrooms (11, 12, 13).

---

24 Tunnel-back cottages

The culmination of urban cottage-plan development was the tunnel-back plan. An extension, usually of two storeys, was added to the rear of the two-up-and-two-down plan so as to provide an extra service room on the ground floor and an extra bedroom (and even a bathroom) on the first floor. In this plan the front door, set back from the footpath, opened by way of an internal porch into a lobby with a parlour to the front and a kitchen living room to the rear. The lobby gave on to a staircase which usually had two flights, one long flight and a short return flight. Under the staircase landing, a passage led to the scullery and so out to the back yard with its coal store, ashpit, privy and, in the better examples, separate wash-house. From the staircase landing there was access to the small bedroom over the scullery, and to the bathroom where one was provided. The short second flight then led to the two principal bedrooms. The most extensive versions of this plan included attic bedrooms and a full-height cellar, and such a cottage might well have six or seven fireplaces. The buildings were imposing at the front, especially when arranged in pairs or terraces, but the backs were much less attractive and the deep projections cut off light from the rear kitchen living room to give the tunnel effect that gives the plan its name.

17

25 Tyneside flatted cottages

There remains one further variation: a dwelling containing the usual accommodation for an urban cottage of its period but arranged as a flat in a two-storey block in which each flat has its own front door to the street and its own access to a yard at the rear. Such cottages are found in the north-east of England and principally on Tyneside. Muthesius has brought this house-type to general attention and places the period of its use to the second half of the 19th century, with the main period after about 1870.

Externally it is difficult to distinguish streets of these dwellings from those of two-up-and-two-down or tunnel-back plans, except that often the front doors are grouped together in fours serving reflected pairs of flats, two to the ground-floor flats and two to the first-floor flats.

Apart from this regional variation, flats were not a traditional type of dwelling in England or Wales. They were found exceptionally, as in Barrow-in-Furness where blocks of flats of the Scottish type were built for shipyard workers and

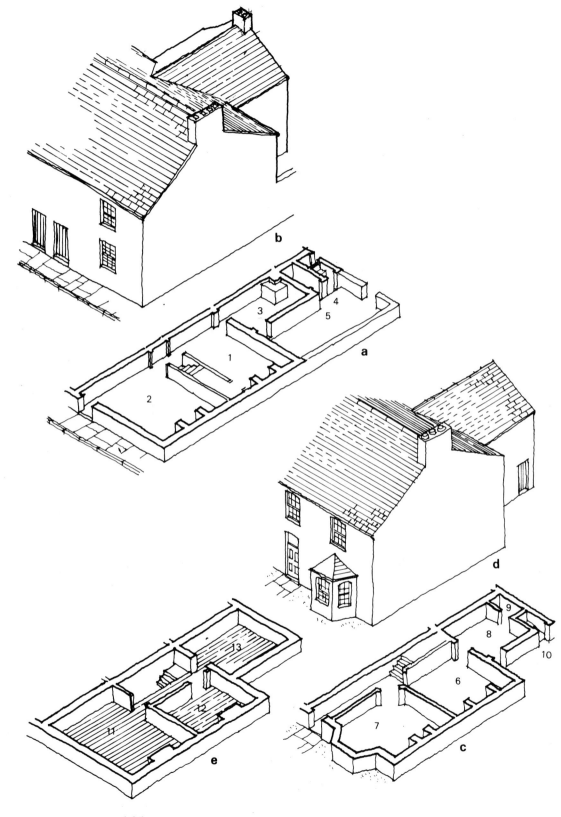

b

3
4
5
1
2
a

d

9
8
6
10
7
c

13
12
11
e

165

25 Tyneside flatted cottages

a. Ground-floor plan showing living room (1), bedroom (2), bedroom (3), kitchen (4), coal house (5), privy (6) and ash house (7). Separate front doors lead to ground-floor and first-floor flats.

b. First-floor plan showing living room (8), bedrooms (9, 10, 11) and kitchen (12) with stairs down to a separate yard.

c. Sketch to show separate doors for ground- and first-floor flats.

---

workers in the jute factories at the command of the developers of that remarkable industrial town. They were also found in London where they were built by charitable organisations to help house workers near the offices, shops, railways and workshops of the city centre. They were sometimes built experimentally in provincial cities by the municipal authorities in an attempt to combine slum clearance and social housing. The flat as a dwelling for working-class families, however, was not in the mainstream of house design in England and Wales. 18

Later developments

It has been seen that access to the rear part of the site has always been a problem in urban house design. Medieval urban house planning was affected by the need to provide access to the gardens and yards, workshops and kitchens, etc., that occupied the extensive rear areas of the narrow-fronted plots. Later and smaller houses had short plots of ground and paved yards rather than the orchards, stables, cesspits and service buildings of earlier houses; but regular and speedy removal of night-soil from the privies and ashes from the increasingly numerous coal fires became a necessity, compounding rather than diminishing problems of access. In single-cell dwellings and back-to-back cottages, ashpits and privies had been grouped; this continued for the early two-up-and-two-down cottages, but in later cottages of that type and in tunnel-back houses access to individual sanitary and refuse points was needed. It was met by provision of entries between cottages, access to communal yards, and by way of back alleys. As more and more land was transferred from farming to housing and as sanitary arrangements became more and more standardised, the back alley running between rows of dwellings facing on to parallel front streets became more and more the norm.

The gridiron pattern of front streets and back alleys, long straight rows and regular cross-streets so familiar in parts of London and in the big industrial towns and cities seemed to have been perfected by the end of the 19th century. In this perfection, however, were the seeds of the reaction of the early 20th century, not only against the monotony of the pattern but also against the cost of what was seen as extravagant street paving, against the use of narrow frontages limiting house planning, and against the high local densities that prevailed. This reaction, beginning with isolated gestures as at Bourneville and Port Sunlight, continued with several imaginative and elegant experiments in the first decades of the century, but led to the rash of suburban houses of the inter-war period. These solved some of the architectural and planning problems but created their own monotony.

Although many detached and semi-detached urban and suburban houses were

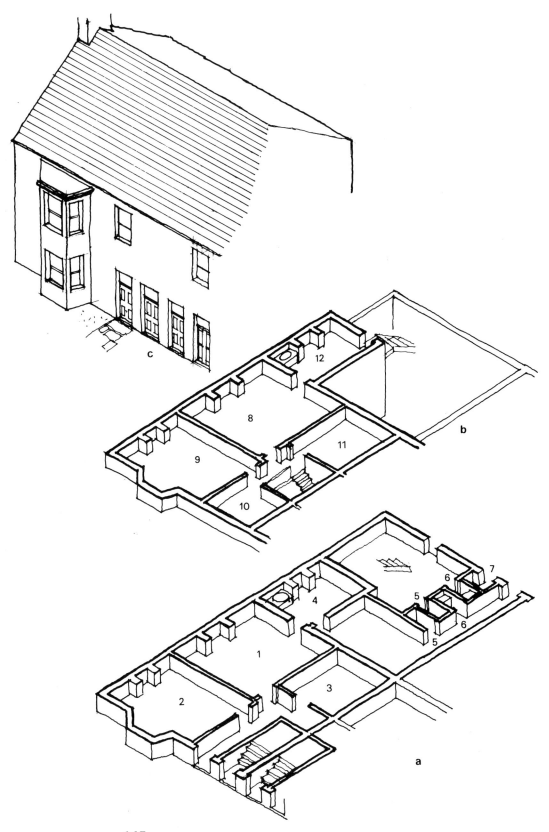

167

26 Semi-detached houses and bungalows

a. Ground-floor plan of a pair of semi-detached houses showing parlour (1), living room (2), hall and staircase (3) and kitchenette (4); this example has an attached garage (5) with a utility room behind (6).

b. Sketch to show the reflected pair of houses.

c. Ground-floor plan of one of a pair of minimal semi-detached houses of the type often known as the 'sunshine semi': living room and parlour are combined into one room (7) which runs from front to back of the house and so gains sun from two aspects. There is a very small kitchen (8) having no fireplace since cooking is by gas or electricity; hall and staircase (9) are of minimum dimensions.

d. Floor-plan of a detached bungalow of the type built in seaside towns: from the entrance hall opened parlour (10) and living kitchen (11), two bedrooms (12 and 13), bathroom (14) and WC (15).

e. Sketch showing the prominent roof covering such a deep plan.

---

built to individual designs during the 1920s and 1930s, the basic plan was standardised and repeated endlessly. Houses were built in semi-detached pairs, often included a garage, and although enjoying waterborne mains drainage were built on plots sufficiently wide to allow access to the dustbins. Recessed within a porch, the front door opened into a lobby or hall that gave access to the parlour at the front, the living room at the back and the regrettably small room that served as kitchen, scullery, breakfast room and often wash-house – containing sink, gas or electric cooker, storage units and, in the southern counties, a coal-burning stove to heat the water (in the northern counties water was heated by way of a back boiler to the living-room fireplace). From the lobby rose a staircase serving the two main bedrooms, the bathroom and WC and the small third bedroom or box-room over the lobby. Built in reflected pairs with chimney-stacks grouped in the middle, these houses were familiar, popular, cheap to build, and facilitated the layout of housing estates based on the cul-de-sac and the curving street.

At the same time there was an explosion of demand, especially among the elderly, for single-storey dwellings – bungalows as they came to be called from the Anglo-Indian term denoting, literally, 'a house in the Bengal style' – especially in seaside towns. Bungalows were built individually or in pairs, but on a wide frontage, so that the principal living room and the bedroom faced the street across the front garden while the kitchen, bathroom and WC and second bedroom faced the garden at the rear. 19

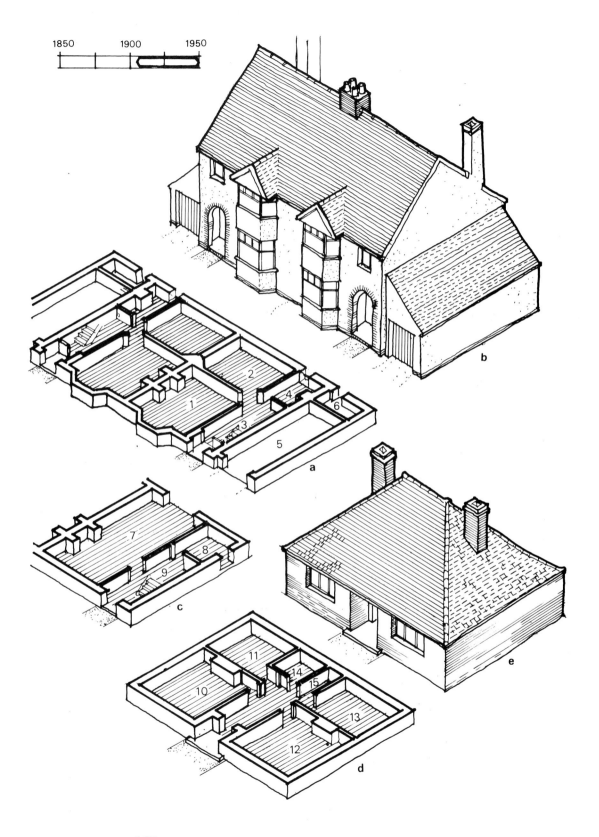

1850 1900 1950

169

Chapter 4

Materials and Construction

Introduction

In looking at a house or cottage, one tends to see the building first and think
about its plan second: the bricks or stones, tiles or thatch are observed and then
(if at all) the relative disposition of doors and windows, floor levels and chimney-
stacks. The architectural character of a village or town may appear to be determined by building materials and methods of construction rather than by house
planning: the mellow rubble walls and stone-tiled roof seem more significant than
the incidence of cross-passages and the use of dormers to light the loft. It is unlikely,
to say the least, that the designers of houses, whether magnificent or humble,
thought of it in this way. It is much more likely that they had a set of planning
requirements to meet, practical and emotional, and that they met these requirements by arranging spaces in plan and section according to tradition and fashion,
mixed as circumstances indicated. They then defined, enclosed, protected and
served those spaces with a structure and set of building materials chosen primarily
for economy, but with tradition and fashion also in mind.

Taking England and Wales as a whole, a considerable variety of building
materials has been available to house-builders. The land provided stone of all sorts,
clay and timber, and could be made to provide brick, tiles and thatch. Building
materials being expensive to move, it has until recently been customary to use
locally available materials for all except the most important buildings (usually
monumental ones such as churches and castles). But often there was more than
one material to hand – timber growing above stone, straw for thatch being reaped
from clay lands suitable for tile-making – so the choice of material was a matter
of more than mere economy. The study of houses involves the deduction of a
sequence of construction, unravelling the layers of materials used as well as discovering the plan and section and deducing the way of life that such an arrangement of forms accommodated.

The structural methods used for house construction have been, and remain,
either frame or mass. In frame construction the loads of roof and intermediate
floors are conducted through the relatively small number of vertical elements of
the frame safely to the foundations and the supporting ground. The wall serves
simply as an enclosing element, keeping out rain and cold, keeping in heat, maintaining privacy. Except in so far as members of the frame may also be elements
of the wall, the enclosing envelope could be eliminated and the frame would
subsist; indeed construction is usually a matter of frame first, walls last. In mass
construction the loads of roof and intermediate floors are conducted through the
wall to a foundation which carries both the load of the wall itself and its imposed
loads. Without the wall, roof and floors could not be carried; the wall is built first,
floor and roof construction follow. These points are obvious enough, but it is easy
to be fascinated by constructional detail and less easy to concentrate on structural
essentials.

Timber-framing

Frame construction has been almost entirely of timber. In box-frame and post-and-truss construction the structural members also formed part of the wall; in cruck construction the structural members were concealed and the wall could be of any material – wattle and daub, flint, cobble, pebbles, brick, clay or earth in its various forms. Timber-frame construction seems to have been the normal method of building over virtually the whole of England and Wales, and in some parts it has persisted right up to the present day. Stone succeeded timber-frame for quite humble buildings in certain parts of the country, remaining in use until the later 19th century. Brick, while occasionally used for medieval Large Houses, was generally introduced for complete house construction during the early to mid-17th century. Clay and earth are of ancient use, but survived in various forms until well into the 19th century.

2

61. House at Smarden, Kent
The use of tall, narrow panels in timber-framed construction is illustrated here, as is the use of a jettied upper storey.
(Peter Crawley)

Cruck construction

In cruck construction, pairs of stout inclined timber members spaced at intervals along the building collected roof-loads by means of ridge purlins, side purlins and wall-plates and transmitted them to the ground through padstones or by way of

62. Inn at Nantwich, Cheshire
By contrast, square panelling is illustrated here. Most of the panels are actually rectangular rather than square, but the shape of each panel is determined by its position in the wall. There is no structural indication in the layout of the panels of the position of the intermediate floor.
(Peter Crawley)

63. Cottages at Farm Fold, Styal, Cheshire
Though now converted into cottages, this may have been a set of single-storey farm buildings when first built, the prominent dormers probably having been added quite recently. The truncated crucks in the gable suggest that the roof was originally half-hipped.
(G. Wheeler)

a continuous sill. Each cruck truss consisted of the two inclined cruck blades together with one or more horizontal members acting as tie-beam, collar or yoke according to position between floor and ridge. The tie-beam normally projected beyond the blades in order to carry wall-plates; the collar sometimes projected to help carry the side purlins; the yoke in some cases needed to support the ridge purlins. The blades, often sawn from a single tree-trunk to make a matching pair, might be straight or distinctly elbowed, but were usually tapered and slightly curved from base to apex. Although the heavy purlins gave longitudinal restraint, straight or curved members were sometimes introduced between purlins and cruck blades as 'wind-braces' or 'sway-braces'. Cruck frames of this standard type have been used for houses and farm buildings in the countryside (and sometimes in the towns) in all of England and Wales, apart from a closely defined portion of eastern and south-eastern England, from the early medieval period until quite late in the 18th century.

One variation associated especially with late medieval Large Houses is the base cruck. This consists of stout, inclined, slightly curved timber members joined by a heavy collar above which there is a separate roof construction. Another variation associated particularly with part of west Wales and with the south-western peninsula of England, but found elsewhere in rather crude buildings, has the cruck blades in two parts either joined or scarfed together. Within a cruck-trussed structure there are variations in which the tie-beam is omitted to make an open truss where headroom would otherwise be obstructed. There is another variation in which the truss at each end of a building is truncated at collar level in order to permit a thatched roof to be swept around half-hips. Upper crucks (yet another variation) provided a sequence of development in which the blades did not run down to ground level, but terminated in a horizontal beam that was carried by some type of mass wall; the curved feet of the inclined members acknowledged the cruck tradition, but the structure was essentially that of the independent roof-truss.

The walls, which in normal cruck construction carried no loads except their own weight, could be either mass or frame. Stone and clay were the usual mass walls, but occasionally brick was used, probably as a substitute for some earlier material. In each case the walls were constructed quite conventionally and there need be no indication from outside the building that they do not carry the roof-loads. Timber-framed walls, comprised of vertical studs and horizontal rails with plastered panels between, may also conceal the cruck trusses, except on the end walls where the inclined cruck blades show themselves clearly enough. Timber-framed walls usually included posts that were joined into the cruck feet where appropriate and steadied either by the ends of the tie-beam or by spurs running out from the cruck blades. Often the timber-framed walls were rather more than one storey in height: then they carried a wall-plate and through this some of the roof-loads.

Cruck trusses were usually assembled on the site and then 'reared' vertically into position. Cruck-trussed buildings were quick and easy to erect and, although sometimes cusped and moulded, the trusses had very simple joints and made few demands on the carpenter's skill. They were inflexible, however, could not conveniently be used in multi-storey structures and were not easily extended laterally. Some trusses were of considerable span, especially in barns – Leigh Court Barn in Worcestershire spans thirty-four feet (10.36 m) – but such spans required immense trees selected or cultivated to the cruck shape.

172

173

Cruck construction

a. Diagram showing roof-loads carried through frame to ground.

b. Cruck frame concealed by mass walling.

c. Cruck frame revealed at end of timber walling.

d. Diagram showing cruck trusses reared into position.

e. Two-bay cruck frame with closed cruck trusses (1), central open truss (2), cruck blade (3), tie-beam (4), collar (5), ridge purlin (6), yoke (7), side purlin (8), wall-plate (9), wind-brace (10) and rafters (11).

f. Full cruck with tie-beam.

g. Open cruck with cruck spurs to carry wall-plate (12).

h. Truncated cruck.

i. Timber wall-post rising from cruck blade which rises from sill.

j. Base cruck with purlins resting on collar.

k. Jointed cruck.

l. Raised cruck rising from part-way up solid wall.

m. Upper cruck tenoned into a floor-beam.

n. Timber wall carrying wall-plate; side purlin on blocking piece.

o. Cruck blades halved and crossed to carry ridge purlin.

p. Blades halved or tenoned at ridge.

q. Yoke joining blades near ridge.

r. Half cruck at end to allow hipped roof.

s. Short rafters hung on pegs from ridge and purlins.

Since cruck construction was distinguished as a structural form more than three thousand examples have been recorded, covering the major part of England and Wales. The distribution shows an abrupt boundary omitting the eastern and south-eastern counties of England and a less abrupt boundary that excludes practically all of Cornwall and south-west Wales. The structures are very difficult to date: the earliest (on documentary and tree-ring dating criteria) appeared fully developed in the early 13th century and the technique remained in use at least to the 17th century and probably later. But reuse of earlier timbers and the absence of mouldings or other architectural details make the later periods especially obscure.

Few cruck-framed buildings reveal themselves as such on external inspection: most crucks are concealed by contemporary or later walling and roofing materials. Even within a building crucks may not be easy to recognise. Sometimes the foot of a cruck or the end of a tie-beam shows in a stone or clay wall; sometimes elements of a cruck truss survive in the roof space or in the upper floor of a house when the lower portions have been cut away. Often a house will have portions of a central cruck truss preserved though all the outer walls have been rebuilt in brick or stone. Parts of cruck blades were frequently reused as lintels for barn

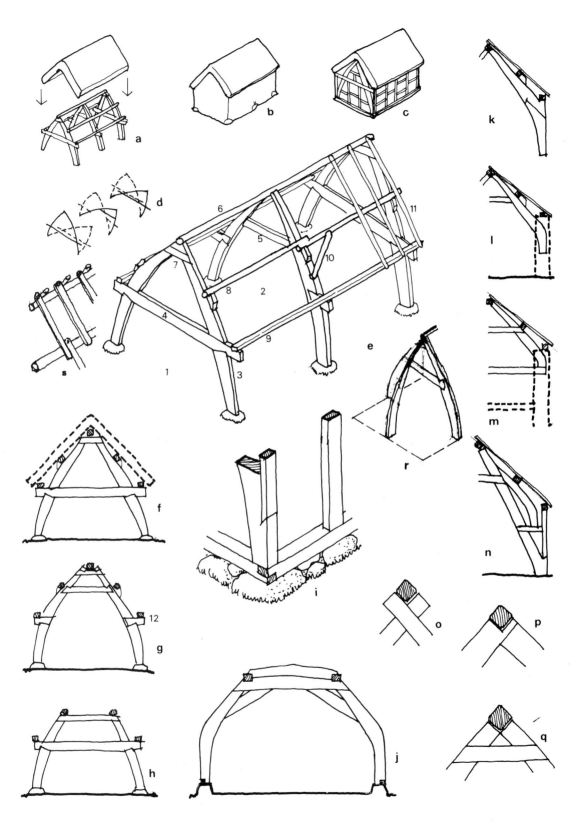

175

Box-frame construction

a. Diagram showing a two-bay box-frame consisting of posts (1) with a rising brace (2) between post and sill (3) and a knee-brace (4) between post and wall-plate (5); the posts and wall-plates are steadied by tie-beams (6); the walls, bay by bay, are divided into panels by studs (7) and rails (8).

b. Roof and walls are treated separately in this construction.

c. Roofs may be made of coupled pairs of rafters.

d. Such roofs may be steadied by a collar purlin under each collar.

e. Alternatively, at each bay a heavy principal may clasp a purlin.

f. The joint at the head of a post was carefully organised so as to keep members rigid in three directions: post thickened out in a jowl (9), wall-plate (10) jointed into a rebate in the post (11), while finally the tie-beam (12) locks both post and wall-plate.

g. Square panels in half-timbered walls consist of staves, woven wattles, and a clay or plaster daub on each side.

h. Tall panels have the same components adapted to the tall shape.

i. Timber-frame walls may be clad with plain tiles hung on laths.

j. The mathematical tile (brick tile) is a variation on the plain tile.

k. Early weather-boards were butted but most are now lapped.

l. Timber-frame walls may be entirely concealed by plaster.

m. Jettied storeys consist of stud walls rising from a sole-plate which is carried on cantilevered joists.

n. The mud-and-stud wall consists of rough posts, wall-plates and tie-beams without any of the conventional studs and rails that form panels; posts may be earth-fast rather than rising from a timber sill.

o. 'Reversed assembly' in which the wall-plate is superimposed on the tie-beam.

p. Curved brace running from post to stud.

---

doors or for cartsheds, indicating former use of the cruck system even when buildings have been renewed or replaced.

Although the general distribution of cruck construction is now well established, some pockets of apparent scarcity remain to be investigated and much work still has to be done before dating can be entirely satisfactory.

Box-frame construction

The alternative way of assembling a timber-framed building is that in which the wall is considered as an entity that also carries any roof-loads imposed on it. The method is sometimes called 'box-frame' and sometimes 'post-and-truss', though these two terms are more accurately used for particular aspects of the same timber-framing technique.

In this form of construction, studs and rails were assembled to form the frame

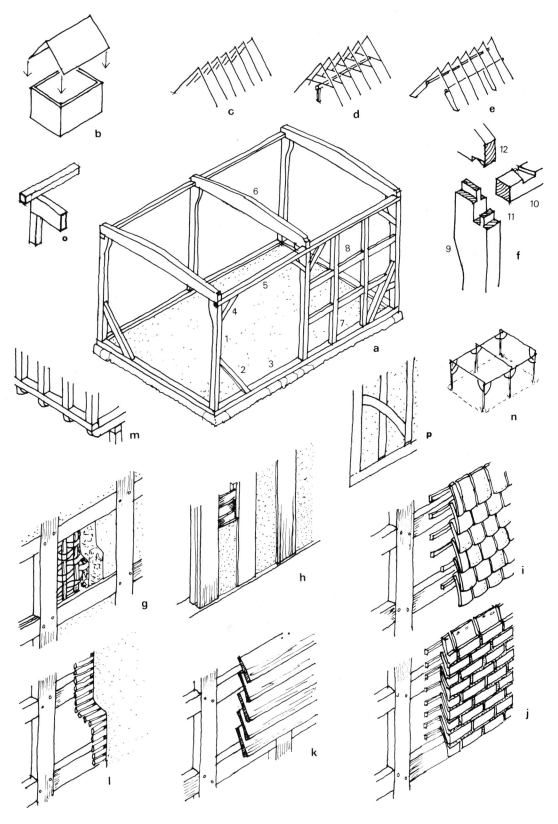

of the wall whose panels were infilled or covered with some cladding material. The studs might be of uniform cross-section, as indeed they are in modern 'balloon-framed' or 'platform-framed' timber buildings, but in the past it was more customary to divide the walled box into a series of compartments or bays marked by stouter posts and with opposite walls held together by means of heavy timber beams spanning from post to post.

The so-called 'normal method of assembly' entailed the use of a special joint at the head of the post which was widened out in order to receive first the wall-plate in one direction and then the tie-beam from the other direction. (Cruck construction, incidentally, makes use of 'reversed assembly' in which the tie-beam runs under the wall-plate.) A timber-framed structural box composed of several bays was kept rigid by having wall-plates run longitudinally at the head of each wall and tie-beams run laterally at bay intervals. There were also straight or slightly curved diagonal members that helped during the piece-by-piece erection process, bringing some of the loads back to the posts and also providing some triangulation.

Since the four walls of the building formed a rigid box, the roof was a separate item whose covering was carried on separate pairs of rafters or by a combination of rafters and roof-truss. In the 'single' or 'trussed-rafter' roof each pair of rafters was individually triangulated with the aid of a collar or by means of crossed 'scissors rafters'. This was an adequate technique in terms of carrying the roof-loads, but rather less than adequate in terms of general stability: lacking the longitudinal restraint of the purlins used in cruck construction, such a roof was liable to collapse as pairs of rafters fell apart from each other along the length of the building. Collapse could be prevented by use of the collar purlin, a heavy timber plate running horizontally underneath the line of collars and supported at each bay interval by a short crown-post rising from the tie-beam. It was customary to have pairs of inclined braces running longitudinally between crown-post and collar purlin and laterally between crown-post and collar, making a decorative growth like boughs spreading from the trunks of trees, at intervals along the roof. Sometimes the crown-post was steadied by other braces rising from the tie-beam like the swelling of roots at the foot of a tree-trunk.

In the 'double' roof, heavy pairs of principal rafters rose from each tie-beam near its junction with the wall-posts; the principal rafters and the tie-beam made a roof-truss. Between each pair of trusses, bay by bay, purlins provided longitudinal restraint and also gave intermediate support to rafters, making collars or scissors unnecessary. These purlins were usually tenoned into the principal rafter or trapped between the principal and a collar which was introduced into the truss; they were not normally trenched into the backs of principals in the way that side purlins were trenched into cruck blades.

Because the principal rafters, tie-beams and posts ran together at intervals along the timber-framed walls of a building, the structure could be regarded as an open frame of posts, trusses and wall-plates, all interlocked and with the wall spaces divided into convenient panels by means of lighter studs and rails: hence the term 'post-and-truss'.

There were many variations on the box-frame/post-and-truss technique, and elements of this form of construction were sometimes mixed with cruck construction; but generally, and especially in smaller buildings, the two main schools of carpentry are easily distinguished.

Infill and cladding

Infill is used when the timber members are exposed: so-called 'half-timber' buildings are those in which the timbering, both structural and decorative, makes a network around the light panels. There are two main varieties of half-timber work: that in which studs are placed close together to give narrow panels each rising through a full storey, and that in which a combination of studs and rails makes square or wide rectangular panels, two or three deep per storey. Tall panels predominate in the eastern half of the country and square panels in the western half; but there is considerable overlap, tall panels being used on western buildings or parts of buildings that had high status, and square panels being used in eastern buildings

where economy of timber was important or where it was intended to cover the frame with a cladding. Tall panels might be made more decorative by the introduction of horizontal or inclined rails; square panels were quite often made more ornamental through the use of extra members to give herring-bone or quatrefoil patterns. Tall panels were sometimes infilled with tiles or thin stone slabs, but were usually daubed on wattles and had a plaster finish. Square panels were sometimes filled with thin wooden boards, but usually had daub and plaster on a wattle base strengthened by staves. Nowadays, both types of panel generally display recent bricknogging as panels of brickwork replaced the wattle and daub.

Cladding occurs when the timber members are entirely concealed by a decorative or weather-protective skin. This usually consists of either plaster on laths, or plain roofing tiles, or slates or horizontal weather-boarding, though in the south of England there was also an unusual technique called mathematical tiling, or brick tiling, which used tiles especially shaped to present a brick-like appearance. Cladding materials were applied to older buildings, especially in the towns, to make them more fire-resistant, more weather-resistant or more fashionable; but many of the later timber-framed buildings in the south-eastern counties were designed to be clad, and their scrappy and inelegant timbers look particularly forlorn when

66. Detail from a house in Hertford, Hertfordshire
The plaster rendering to timber-frame construction here takes the form of pargeting, with both moulded and combed decoration.
(Peter Crawley)

the cladding is mistakenly removed in order to create an appearance which was never intended and which they never before possessed.

Jettied construction

The technique of projecting or 'jettying' successive storeys in a timber-framed building was used in both town and country from the late Middle Ages, but was probably most popular during the 16th century. Various practical advantages have been ascribed to jettying: it provided extra floor space to upper rooms, allowed short storey-height posts to be used in multi-storey buildings, simplified jointing at each floor level and made wall-loads help counterbalance floor-loads. It seems more than likely, however, that jettying, with its rich pattern of light and shade in receding surfaces, was simply a form of decoration that appealed to the late medieval mind. Certainly doubt is cast on every supposed practical advantage of jettying by the simultaneous use of conventional construction – often in the same building.

Mud and stud

The vast majority of timber-framed buildings conform to the cruck or box-framed techniques, but there is a further technique seen in some very humble buildings of late date. The mud-and-stud form of construction consists of an open framework of rough posts, either earth-fast or rising at bay intervals from padstones, connected together with equally rough wall-plates and tie-beams. Spans were short, and simple rafter roofs were adequate. The walls, being storey-height bays, were not divided into panels but consisted of clay daubing about 4 ins. (100 mm) thick and reinforced with staves.

181

Such mud-and-stud buildings are known in Lincolnshire and the coastal plain of Lancashire, and remnants may survive in other counties. They may represent the survival of a rather primitive form of construction appropriate for short-lived buildings and superseded by full timber-framing when a more substantial and durable building was required.

Solid walls

In some parts of the world and at some periods, solid timber walls have been used for house construction – the horizontal log construction of Scandinavia and the Alpine countries for instance. The remarkable survival of vertical log construction in Greensted church, Essex (incorporating logs believed to date from the 9th century), as well as more and more instances from excavated sites, shows that such walls were known in this country. No surviving domestic buildings with solid timber walls have been found here, so our study of solid walls must be confined to stone, brick and unbaked earth.

It is often assumed that timber-framing is traditional in certain heavily wooded parts of the country while stone construction is traditional to the more mountainous districts; and in a sense this is true. Where good-quality timber was cheap and plentiful one would expect it to be used since it is easily worked, readily carved for decoration and facilitates speedy erection of buildings; and where good-quality stone was abundant and cheaply quarried one would expect it to be used since it gives a substantial, rot-proof and very long-lasting wall. It is surprising then to find that, until fairly recently, solid walling was confined to buildings in which status or defensive requirements demanded its use, and that many a substantial wall in an area such as the Yorkshire Pennines, where stone is good and readily available, conceals the timber-framed construction of a previous era. Taking the long view of domestic building in this country, timber-framing is traditional and solid walling a newcomer.

Stone (including flint, cobble and pebble)

Stone has long been used for the most prestigious buildings and good-quality building stone was transported by water over some distance for that purpose. Where easily quarried, or found as outcrop, stone came into use for the construction of traditional houses and, eventually, for farm buildings. Throughout more than half of England and Wales stone is the predominant building material to be seen in houses erected before the second half of the 19th century.

The technique of masonry construction was basically the same for lesser buildings as for greater. The largest and best stones (including, where available, properly dressed stones) were placed by the mason at the corners and properly trued up. Between these alternate layers of quoins the inferior stones were laid by the wallers to show the best face outwards while tailing into the heart of the wall, interlocking where possible with the inner-facing stones. Bonding stones or 'throughs' were laid at intervals to keep inner and outer skins together and the heart of the wall

182

67. Slatestone wall, Keswick, Cumberland
This late 19th-century house has walls of the local slate-like stone. The main walling has joints so tight as to appear devoid of mortar. The quoins or cornerstones are carefully worked at the margins and laid to a uniform height.
(R. W. Brunskill)

was packed with smaller stones or chips from the larger. Stones were bedded in lime mortar where this was available or in clay where, as often, lime mortar was too expensive to be freely used. Stones laid 'dry', that is without any mortar at all, were certainly used for farm buildings in Cumbria and the most mountainous parts of Wales, but dry-wall construction was rarely used in houses or cottages. Where a stone capable of being dressed with the mason's chisel was available, it was used to form the door and window openings, but elsewhere such openings had rough stone jambs and timber lintels. Where stone was of particularly good quality and where the status of the houses would justify the expense, partially or fully dressed stone would be laid in courses, at least on the main elevation, the courses diminishing in height from base to eaves to give a subtle liveliness to the building. Where the stone was too hard to dress, or too soft to retain dressing or of poor quality in some other respect, brick was increasingly used for quoins and around openings. There are even instances of fashionable brick façades being included in buildings whose remaining walls were of stone.

At some times and in some places walls were whitewashed or rendered with plaster or roughcast. Whitewash was used with carboniferous limestone, for instance, enhancing the pale grey of the stone and helping to protect the wide joints from leaching of the bedding material. Rendering, with plaster and a painted finish, was popular in the early 19th century as an extension of the vogue for stucco in polite architecture. The application of pebbles or shell fragments to wet cement or plaster rendering as pebble-dash was a Scottish technique, apparently popularised in England during the period of the Vernacular Revival in the late 19th and early 20th centuries.

Flint is found in certain areas of the south-eastern quarter of England which lack a good building stone. It is a perfectly satisfactory material for general walling when properly bedded, but cannot be used for corners or to make satisfactory door or window openings. For the older and more pretentious flint buildings as well as those which are humble in status and fairly recent in date, brick was used for dressings. Brick lacing courses were used at intervals in the wall to tie the flint together, and it is sometimes difficult to decide whether the builder was aiming to produce a flint wall with brick reinforcement or a brick wall with flint as decoration. Irregular undressed flints were used in general walling, but split or knapped flints with the black interior facing outwards may be seen in the walls of superior houses. Flint was also used decoratively with whatever other materials might be to hand: chequer-board pattern flint and limestone panels may be seen across southern and eastern England from Norfolk to Wiltshire.

Cobble has similar virtues and defects to flint, but is found in other parts of the country. Stones rounded by ice action may be found in areas of morainic deposit, and other cobbles, rounded through the action of water, may be gathered from river beds. In the absence of any more suitable building material cobbles have been used, especially on the fringes of mountainous areas, for general walling purposes; in such cases the few available finer stones might be used sparingly for quoins, dressings and bonding stones. Cobbles may be split like flints, and a cobble wall with fieldstone admixture and bonding provided an economical wall for utilitarian buildings and quite a decorative outer surface for humbler houses.

Seashore pebbles, which are like small cobbles, have been used for the walls of cottages and farm buildings, especially on the coast of East Anglia. Pebbles are even more difficult to use as a walling material than flints, and one wonders if the neat rows of pebbles set in a network of bricks in early 19th-century cottages

Solid-wall construction

a. A stone wall of compact stones making use of quoins (1) to strengthen the corners and through-stones (2) to keep the inner and outer parts of the wall together.

b. A stone wall of thin striated stones laid without the use of quoins.

c. A cob wall showing the separate 'lifts' from each construction phase.

(and often represented in pottery models of such cottages) were selected for their constructional economy or their ornamental qualities.

England and Wales are blessed with an intricate pattern of solid geology and surface drift. Areas of some uniformity, as in parts of the Pennines, are more than balanced by other areas, as in Northamptonshire, where building stones seem to vary substantially within a few miles. Much of the attraction of domestic buildings in this country derives from the many variations of stone walling material and technique that have been composed on the limited number of themes in planning and general organisation.

Brick

While stone construction may cover the greatest area in this country, brick probably accounts for the greatest number of houses, if only because of the vast spread of this material during the late 18th and 19th centuries.

Brick construction is relatively simple, especially as brick provides the material both for general walling and for the formation of corners and openings. Much of the mason's craft consists of the accurate reduction of the rude material into the desired shape, whereas the bricklayer's craft consists of manipulating more or less standardised units. Uniformity is limited and variety ensured through bonding (i.e., the way in which bricks are put together for strength and good appearance), through care in selection of bricks for size and colour, through the nature of the joints between bricks and through the patterning which is introduced into the brick surface.

English Bond, which has alternate courses of headers and stretchers, was used comparatively little in domestic construction, though English Garden Wall Bond, with three or five, or just several stretcher courses between the header courses, was common enough. Flemish Bond, with alternate headers and stretchers in each course, was used in smaller houses quite extensively, especially on the main elevations. Flemish Stretcher Bond and Flemish Garden Wall Bond, which had extra stretchers in each course or extra courses of stretchers, were used for less important walls. Rat-Trap Bond, in which bricks were laid on edge rather than on face, producing a wall with internal vertical cavities, was economical in bricks and labour and was used, especially in the southern counties, for cottages and other humble buildings. These bonds made use of bricks which at first were somewhat irregular in size from one brickmaker to another and were irregular in shape because of poor control of the firing process.

Gradually length and width became standardised, though depth continued to

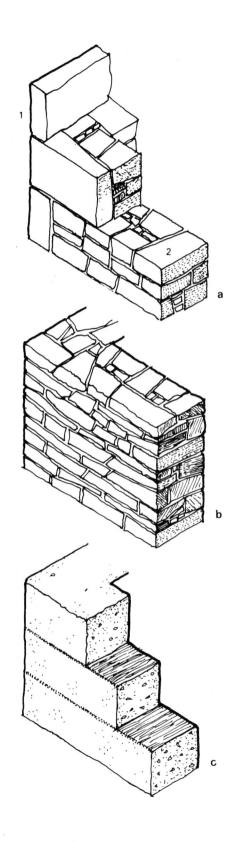

The character of Pershore derives from the brickwork of most of its buildings. This fine house has good-quality bricks in Flemish Bond to the front block-bonded to inferior bricks laid in English Garden Wall Bond to the side. The coursing of the superior bricks is not aligned with that of the inferior.
(Peter Crawley)

vary between districts and over time as outside influences, such as the Brick Tax 1784–1850, were brought to bear. Only within the last few years has the difference between deeper bricks in the north and shallower bricks in the south been completely eliminated. Colour has never been standardised. Depending on brick earth and firing methods, neither capable of being precisely determined, colour varied from site to site. This was especially so in early days, when bricks were made for each individual building and fired in clamps alongside the intended site. Even when large-scale brick-making in continuously-fired kilns became common in the second half of the 19th century, most bricks were still made and used locally. Jointing techniques were linked to the size and irregularity of bricks: irregular bricks required deep bedding and a thick joint, whereas soft bricks rubbed to precise dimensions could have almost invisible joints.

Pattern in brickwork was determined by all these elements, but there might also be deliberate selection, as in the diaper work of the 16th century, the chequer-board header pattern of the 18th century and 19th-century polychromy.

Although more and more medieval brickwork is being discovered, comparatively little is from domestic buildings and even less from small houses. Brick was generally introduced to domestic architecture through brick fireplaces and chimney-stacks in the late 16th century and throughout the 17th century, but mainly in the southern, eastern and east Midlands counties. It became even more fashionable in the mid-17th century and was used in places where perfectly adequate stone was available. By the mid-18th century it had become competitive in price, both with timber building and stone construction; brickwork made most headway, however, in those counties where structural timber was becoming scarce, but wood for firing the abundant brick earth was still available.

Earth (comprising clay, cob, mud and wychert)

The cob buildings of Devon are well enough known and form the biggest concentration of earth-walled buildings in Britain; but the technique was widespread in use, was practised until fairly recently and has been discovered to be of ancient origin.

In earth construction the usual practice was to mix clay or chalky soil, dug from the house site, with dung and chopped straw and a little water to the consistency of stiff concrete, then to raise it roughly in a wall about 3 ft (0.91 m) high, pare it down with a hay knife, allow it to set and then repeat the process until the required height was achieved. It was a slow process but, if properly conducted, produced a strong, solid wall that would last so long as a daub of plaster and a coat of whitewash kept the surface secure from attack by rain or rodents. There was an alternative quick process, used on both sides of the Solway Firth, in which 3-in. (76-mm) layers of clay alternating with thin sprinklings of straw were laid in one operation and allowed to settle under their own weight; this technique was suitable only for quite low walls. A completely different method of using earth in wall construction was to make sun-dried blocks out of the mixture and then build the wall as if with large bricks. This 'adobe' technique was used in East Anglia, though on surviving evidence it was a late 18th to mid-19th-century form of construction virtually confined to cottages and farm buildings.

Many cob houses of Devon and adjacent counties are of 16th- and 17th-century date and some are medieval, and the late 17th century is represented in clay and

187

Brick walling

a. English Bond with stretchers (1) and headers (2) in alternate courses.

b. English Garden Wall Bond with extra courses of stretchers.

c. English Cross Bond with stretcher moved half a brick.

d. Flemish Bond with alternating headers and stretchers.

e. Monk Bond with two stretchers between headers.

f. Flemish Stretcher Bond with extra courses of stretchers.

g. Rat-Trap Bond with bricks on edge rather than on flat.

h. Header Bond with all bricks laid head on.

i. Dearne's Bond with alternate courses of headers and brick on edge.

69. House at Allerford, Somerset
The lost rendering to the left of the chimney-breast reveals what is probably cob construction.
(Peter Crawley)

mud houses of Leicestershire, Northamptonshire and Cumberland. Earth construction was most extensively used, however, in the late 18th and early 19th centuries, when there was a great demand for cottages but mass production of bricks and relatively cheap transport by railway had not yet come into being.

a

2
1

b

c

d

e

f

g

h

i

189

Roof construction

Note: These forms of roof construction are shown as used on solid walls, although all could equally well be used on timber-frame walls.

a. Simple coupled-rafter roof: each pair of rafters is halved or tenoned at the apex; there is no ridge.

b. In the crown-post-and-collar-purlin roof each pair of rafters is joined by a collar (1), the collar purlin (2) runs underneath the row of collars, the crown-post (3) rises from the tie-beam to support the collar purlin, and is braced to collar and collar purlin and sometimes to tie-beam also.

c. In the kingpost roof a stout member, the kingpost (6), rises from the tie-beam to support the ridge purlin (4) which receives common rafters that are also given intermediate support by the side purlins (5); each side purlin rests on the principal rafters (7), which are themselves received by the tie-beam (8) and kingpost; sometimes there are angle struts (9).

d. In the arch-braced collar-beam truss, principal rafters (10) at bay intervals are joined by a heavy collar (11), while in between are butt purlins (12) which are joined into the principal rafters and do not rest upon them; the arch braces (13) help carry loads on to corbels down the walls (14) and also help bind all the other members of the truss into a rigid frame.

e. A simple triangular truss of two principals and a tie-beam shown with side purlins of the 'through' or 'trenched' form resting on the principals; common rafters are then carried on the side purlins.

f. Clasped purlin in which a fairly light purlin is trapped between principal rafter and collar. Here the principal rafter is 'diminished' to the dimensions of a common rafter above purlin level.

g. So-called 'Butt' purlins pass through slots in the principal rafter, whose top surface is in line with that of the common rafters.

h. 'Through' or 'trenched' purlins.

i. Crown post braced at its head to collar and collar purlin and at its foot to the tie-beam.

Roofing materials

Of all the materials that could be used to cover house roofs, thatch was at one time the most widespread. Where available, stone tiles, stone flags or slates were employed for superior houses. Then plain tiles and, later, pantiles came into common use. From the mid-18th century first Westmorland slates and then Welsh slates – waterborne by coastal ship, river flat and canal barge – became increasingly popular, especially in towns. Finally, within the past eighty years or so, tiles transported by railway or lorry have overwhelmed virtually all other materials.

Even the best roofing materials do not last more than two or three generations without needing attention, and most houses of any age have had one or two changes of roof covering. Since the roof pitch varies so much according to the roofing material, each change usually leaves some mark. Generally, the larger the unit the lower the pitch at which it can be satisfactorily used: plain tiles require a steeper pitch than pantiles, stone tiles than stone flags, and small natural slates than large mass-produced Welsh slates. Thatch sheds rain at a steep pitch, but also absorbs showers of rain to give up the moisture later.

190

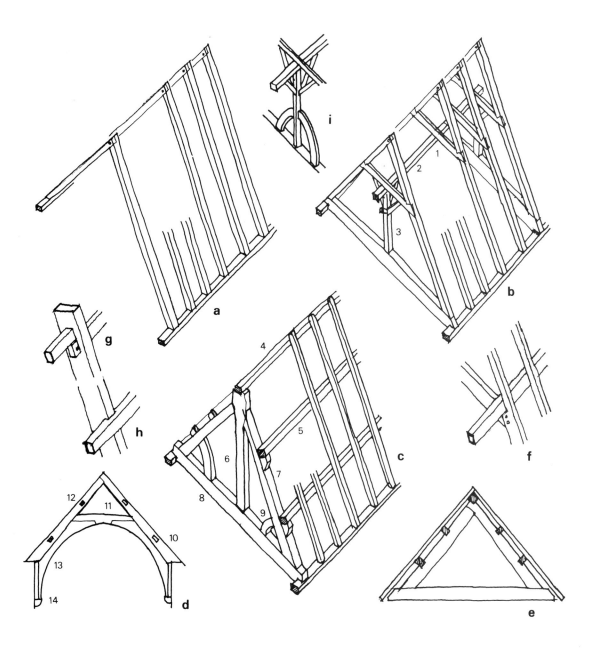

a

b

c

d

e

f

g

h

i

1
2
3
4
5
6
7
8
9
10
11
12
13
14

191

Roofing materials

a. Half-hipped thatched roof: end view.

b. Side view.

c. Gabled thatched roof.

d. Flagstones at eaves, thatch above.

e. Pantiles replacing thatch above flagstones.

f. One thatching technique represented.

g. Thick slate roof, gable of 35° pitch or more.

h. Slate with rounded head and single nail-hole.

i. Isometric sketch showing diminishing courses.

j. Thin slate, gable of $22\frac{1}{2}°$ to 35° pitch.

k. Thin slate, square head and double nail-holes.

l. Isometric sketch showing regular courses.

m. Plain tile roof, gable of 45° pitch or more.

n. Plain tile cambered in two dimensions.

o. Isometric sketch showing tiles covering joints.

p. Pantile roof showing low pitch.

q. Pantile showing subtle curvilinear section.

r. Isometric sketch showing single-lap pantiles.

s. Stone-flagged roof, gable of 30° pitch or so.

t. Stone flag with rounded head and single peg-hole.

u. Isometric sketch showing flagstones pegged over the laths.

v. Stone-tiled roof, gable of more than 45° pitch.

w. Stone tile with rounded head and single peg-hole.

x. Isometric sketch showing lighter timbering for stone tiles.

Special constructional features of urban houses

While the materials and constructional methods used for houses in the towns were generally similar to those used in the countryside, there were some differences. The most marked of these was the continued use of timber-framed construction long after it had been abandoned in the countryside, and its frequency in towns in regions where its rural use (or at least its survival) was rare. Thus towns such as Totnes and Kendal have quite a lot of timber-framing, though timber-framed construction is as scarce in the Devon countryside as it is in Westmorland. Paradoxically, the affection for timber-framing persisted even though many towns eventually had regulations controlling the use of combustible materials, while country parishes rarely made any such provision.

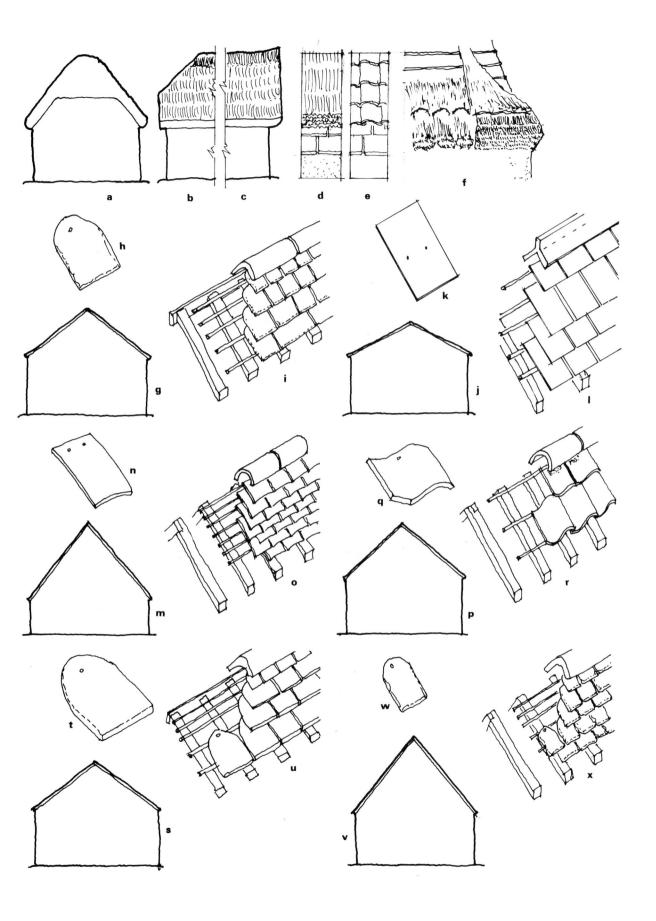

a
b
c
d
e
f
g
h
i
j
k
l
m
n
o
p
q
r
s
t
u
v
w
x

One way of resolving the conflict between the desire to use timber-framing and the need to avoid fires in towns was to use stone or brick party walls, and timber-framing for other parts of a house. Timber-framed fronts and backs were popular, such a form of construction being economical: a front could be jettied and decorated and a back could be simply framed and panelled while the stone party walls could carry floor- and roof-loads, accommodate fireplaces and flues and provide fire-stops. The 'three-quarter house' with all sides except the front built in solid walling was even more popular; here again the versatility and ease of ornament of the timber front seems to have been an important factor in its choice. Brick-fronted houses with timber party walls may also be found, however, especially where the brickwork has been applied to an earlier structure.

Stone might be used in a town of timber-framed buildings for houses of special importance or pretensions. In Salisbury, for instance, some houses had ashlar fronts and other walls of flint or stone rubble; for Exeter it has been suggested that the proportion of stone in a house indicated its importance. Partial or complete timber-framing may be found in surviving urban houses dating from the 14th to the late 17th century. In certain towns where half-timbering remained fashionable, such as Chester, the frame is exposed though usually much restored; more generally, the jettied upper storeys were underbuilt and the whole façade covered with

70. Thatched house near Beaminster, Dorset
The thatched roof to this stone-walled house is steeply pitched and set between stone gable copings.
(Peter Crawley)

71. Plain tiles at Hertingfordbury, Hertfordshire
The regular lines of the coursing are relieved by the subtle curves in length and width of the plain tiles which are laid to a pitch of more than forty-five degrees.
(Peter Crawley)

plaster, tiles or slate. Some towns, such as Lewes, built almost completely of timber-frame, have hardly a piece of structural timber in view. Like stone, brick was used for important buildings in certain towns such as Hull and King's Lynn from the medieval period, but was not generally used until the late 16th century and did not supersede timber for another hundred years. Even then, in certain towns of south-eastern England, such as Dover and Hastings, walls of timber studs were built well into the 19th century.

In roofing, the almost universal use of thatch presented a far greater fire hazard than the use of timber for structure or for decorative cornices. The enforcement of local building regulations must have been difficult, but plain tiles, pantiles, stone tiles and slate became ever more popular as roof coverings both in new construction and as replacement. The Royal Commission on Historical Monuments for England records that in Stamford stone tiles were used as early as 1389 and became common in new construction during the 18th and early 19th centuries; plain tiles and pantiles came into use during the late 17th century and slate was used after

195

1850. One further fire precaution adopted in Stamford and elsewhere was the use of a plaster floor immediately under the roof and consisting of a layer of gypsum plaster about 4 ins. (100 mm) thick, bedded on reeds and carried by laths on the floor joists. Such a floor helped protect the rest of the building from a fire in the roof, but it also warded off the draughts that blew through ill-fitting tiles and provided a flat and rot-proof floor for the storage areas in the garret space.

It is easily assumed that relatively cheap rail transport of bricks and slates from the mid-19th century onwards led to complete uniformity in materials for domestic construction. And yet a study of towns as far apart and as widely differing as Batley in Yorkshire and Bradford-on-Avon in Wiltshire confirms that other materials continued to be used in new construction long after the coming of the railways.

Roof shape, dormers, parapets and other details

As in so many other aspects of house design, roof shape seems to have been determined by the resolution of conflict between necessary function and available material, the choice being mediated by tradition and fashion. Broadly speaking, a roof may be hipped or gabled; hipped roofs are suitable for box-framed construction, in which the roof is a lid placed on the box of the building, whereas gabled roofs are appropriate to cruck construction since roof and walls are one. Many box-frame and probably most post-and-truss buildings are gabled, however, whereas some cruck-framed buildings have hipped roofs carried on half-trusses. In stone and brick-walled buildings the use of hip or gable makes no material difference to the stability of the building, but in cob or earth-walled buildings the gable triangle tends to be unstable and another material was often used here. Whatever the form of wall and roof construction, hipped roofs of low pitch were used when the aim was to conceal the roof. Thatch and plain tiles lend themselves to hipped-roof construction, whereas slate, stone flags and pantiles suggest gabled roofs. Thatch can be conveniently swept around a hip to give a complete unitary roof, and small plain tiles, easily cut and covered with half-round hip tiles (or neat bonnet tiles), also make satisfactory hips. Slate and stone flags, on the other hand, are generally too large and heavy to be cut and mitred to give a weatherproof joint at the low pitch of a hip, while pantiles are too bold in their modelling.

All materials can be used for gabled roofs, though some are more suitable than others; it was probably to help in adapting thatch to gabled-roof design that variations such as the half-hip were developed. In a half-hipped roof the end walls begin as gables, affording space for gable windows, and then continue as hips with thatch swept around; half-hipped tiled roofs often have a little extra gable termination to ease the roofing detail at the end of the ridge. Half-hipped roofs in cruck-trussed buildings are quite easily constructed using truncated trusses.

A variant of the gabled roof that is also occasionally found in hipped form is the double-pitch or gambrel roof, which is perhaps more accurately called the mansard roof in its hipped version. In such roofs a steep pitch is used at the eaves, changing to a shallow pitch to meet the ridge, thereby giving headroom where it is most needed at the perimeters of a garret or attic storey.

Apart from the flat roofs that were sometimes used to cover tower houses, house roofs were traditionally pitched, at the angle appropriate to the material, and were exposed at the point where they met the wall in what was usually quite a boldly

72. Stone flags at Hathersage, Derbyshire
Here stone flags split from local gritstone have been laid to a relatively low pitch in diminishing courses.
(Peter Crawley)

73. Stone tiles at Filkins, Oxfordshire
In contrast to the bold pattern of stone flags, the stone tiles used here make a gentler pattern of smaller units laid in diminishing courses to a steeper pitch.
(Peter Crawley)

197

projecting eaves. The flat roof of a tower house would be hidden behind a parapet which was of military appearance if not always of military value, but parapets were not generally used in house design until Renaissance precedent suggested that the roof should as far as possible be hidden and that the plain walls should run up to meet the sky at the clear, decisive line of a parapet coping. It was only with the introduction of such parapets that the collection and disposal of rainwater in houses became a building problem. Thatched roofs tended to absorb rain which was then dripped clear of the walls with the aid of a deep eaves; tiled and slated roofs threw rain straight off by means of their slope. Roofs draining to the back of a parapet, on the other hand, required gutters, rainwater heads and downpipes, all introduced as decorated features in the late 17th and early 18th centuries and then adapted to more utilitarian forms for 19th-century roofs.

Dormers are devices for adding light and increasing headroom in roof spaces. They were introduced, or at least multiplied, when floors were inserted into open halls and when such a window was the only means of lighting the upper room so created. However, they were also used in terraced cottages when any other means of lighting was impracticable, and in the garret floors of larger houses when the rooms to be lit were mainly contained within the roof space. It is a testimony to the power of tradition that so many houses were built with cramped upper floors, awkwardly lit with the aid of dormer windows, when a few more courses of brickwork or masonry would have allowed full-height rooms and conventional windows. Dormers presented all the difficulties of gabled or hipped roof construction and covering in miniature, with the additional problem that they created valleys. Until lead became freely and cheaply available, valleys could only be formed satisfactorily by sweeping thatch or lacing tiles and stone tiles; dormer roofs of pantiles had to be treated as outshuts of the main roof with no valleys at all.

Chapter 5

Rooms and Room Uses

The arrangement of the walls, floors, partitions and roof that make up a house or cottage is loud in its statement of form but largely mute in its statement of function. We are tempted to relate what is observed to what we find familiar and name rooms and assign functions according to our understanding of domestic life today and our speculations about domestic life in the past. Historical sources, on the other hand, describe activities and their related furniture and equipment but may have little to say about the placing or layout of the rooms that were the setting for those activities. For some towns and rural parishes the surviving buildings of various periods are quite numerous, but documents limited in number and scope; for others the documents abound but most of the buildings to which they refer have been altered or demolished. Occasionally an abundance of documents survives and can be related to an abundance of surviving buildings. At Stoneleigh in Warwickshire, for example, a skilled and energetic scholar has been able to build up a rare and complete picture of the relationship between the people, their life-styles and the buildings they inhabited over several centuries. [1]

The range of documents that may be available in the county record office, manorial muniment room, family archives or the Public Record Office is very great, extending from court records and other legal documents through estate records (including building accounts and contracts) to travellers' observations and family diaries. The two most useful sets of documents that are fairly generally available are the Hearth Tax returns of the parish and the wills and probate inventories for the family and its house.

The Hearth Tax returns span the period between 1662 and 1689; detailed records are available from 1662 to 1674 and the fullest return was for 1664. The tax was levied on all domestic property in town or country worth more than twenty shillings a year and was at the rate of two shillings a hearth or fireplace. Paupers were exempt. The parish constable was responsible for checking the number of hearths in a house, and this he could usually do by simply counting chimneys. The Hearth Tax returns demonstrate the disparity between castles and mansions with thirty or forty hearths and small farmhouses and cottages with only one. They also demonstrate the relative wealth of different regions and districts in the later 17th century through the proportion of dwellings with only one hearth.

In Westmorland, for example, the small county town of Appleby had one house, Appleby Castle, with forty hearths, nineteen houses with between three and six hearths, fifteen houses with two hearths and thirty-eight houses and cottages (including those exempt from the tax) with only one hearth. Excluding Appleby Castle, thirty-eight of the seventy-two dwellings (53 per cent) had only one hearth. In the nearby village of Crackenthorpe there was one house with four hearths, one with two hearths and twenty-five houses and cottages (including those exempted) with only one hearth (93 per cent). There are similar proportions throughout that part of the county. [2]

In the county of Glamorgan it has been calculated that for every 130 houses or cottages, ninety-two (71 per cent) had one hearth, twenty-three had two hearths, eight had three hearths and seven had four or more hearths. Throughout the county between 25 per cent and 40 per cent of households were classed as poor and were therefore exempt. However, there was a difference between the uplands, where (even excluding the paupers) 70 per cent of dwellings had one hearth and the lowlands where (again excluding the paupers) the proportion was 49 per cent. [3]

In East Sussex, on the other hand, only 31 per cent of dwellings had one hearth. In Warwickshire 69 per cent of dwellings (including those of paupers) had only one hearth. [4]

These examples also show the improvement in living conditions from the later 17th century, when many or most households huddled around one hearth, through the late 18th century, when most farmers would have at least two hearths or fireplaces and possibly four, to the late 19th century when any reasonably prosperous workman could expect to live in a cottage with three or four fireplaces.

Wills and probate inventories record what real estate a deceased person had to bequeath and also what chattels, in addition to money or farm produce, he possessed. Until 1858 wills, testaments and inventories were proved by church courts, though the documents are now mostly kept in county record offices. Inventories dating from the later 17th century to about 1725 tend to be the most informative in that they often list goods in the rooms in which they were kept. The evidence has to be treated with caution, however: for instance, the inventory-takers were variable in their thoroughness, and also furniture might have been assembled in certain rooms for their convenience.

Where an inventory, or better a sequence of inventories from a succession of deaths, can be related to a house that survives for study, the results can be very illuminating, as Dr Alcock and others have been able to show. [5]

The following comments on rooms and their uses are based on information collected from probate inventories. [6]

GROUND FLOOR

Living room (hall, bodystead, house, firehouse, forehouse, house-body, house-part, house-stead, living kitchen): the principal living room and the one that contained the main or only hearth or fireplace. A multi-purpose room, it was normally used at least in part for cooking and contained equipment for the fire such as fire irons, andirons, shovels, tongs, spits for roasting, a beam or bar called the 'reckan' from which pots were hung over the fire and, in the north of England, usually also a bakestone or griddle for cooking oatcakes. Furniture would include a table (such as a trestle table), forms, a chair or chairs and shelves or a dresser for crockery. It was the room in which visitors would initially be received, and as the main or only heated room was the one in which visitors and family were made comfortable.

Parlour (bower, sometimes chamber): the principal retiring room and, at first, the room that contained the principal bed including bedstead and mattress. The parlour provided privacy and usually opened off the living room. Furniture included chairs, cushions and cupboards. The parlour was also the store for valuable goods, and in small farms grain was kept here in arks and chests. At first the parlour was unheated; heat was not considered necessary in a sleeping room, but as that function moved to the great chamber the parlour acquired a fireplace and became more of a dining room with tables and chairs, though it still often contained a bed. The fireplace was not used for cooking unless the parlour was separately occupied, as by a widow or an elderly couple. Hall and parlour, public and private rooms, made up the basic house.

Pantry: a store room for dry edible goods; sometimes a space partitioned off from the parlour but with a separate entrance from the living room. In larger houses the pantry balanced the buttery, but in smaller houses the two became one. The **larder (larder house)** served a similar purpose but was originally for meat storage.

Buttery (spence, drink-house, dish-house): in the 16th and 17th centuries this was the commonest term for a cool storage place in which drink was kept, but in small houses the room might be used for a variety of storage. The term was an alternative to 'pantry' for a store room partitioned off from the parlour but separately entered. In larger farmhouses there might be more than one buttery. The room would usually contain barrels and tubs.

Kitchen: as one of several detached buildings that made up the complex of domestic structures constituting an early Large House, the kitchen – a room for cooking – was the last to be incorporated into the main house. In Large Houses of the late 17th and 18th centuries, the kitchen moved into a semi-basement. In smaller houses the kitchen was incorporated into the main block, taking cooking away from the living room. Food preparation, especially of the ruder variety, and also sometimes brewing were done in the **back kitchen** or **scullery**, which would be unheated. A kitchen would contain fire irons and cooking equipment but might also have steeping and storage vessels such as vats. In late 18th-century and 19th-century cottages, a general living and dining room where cooking was done on a cast-iron range was referred to as a kitchen.

Service room (back-house, low-house, low end, nether end): a room usually at the rear of the house for general storage of produce but also of farming equipment. There was no furniture particularly associated with such a room.

Outshot (outcast, outshut, outend) or lean-to (turf-house, toofall): a term descriptive of appearance rather than of use. The outshut was at the back of the house, covered by an extension of the main roof. Outshuts were usually unheated and were service rooms. The **turf-house** was an outshut where peat was stored.

Dairy (milk-house): a room for storage of milk and its separation into cream and conversion into butter; essentially a cool room, sometimes located over running water. The dairy contained bowls and churns. On larger farms the dairy was a separate building between the house and farm buildings; on smaller farms it was part of the house, but escaped Window Tax if the word DAIRY was displayed on the outside lintel.

Boulting house (bake-house): found attached to larger farmhouses, this room was for sieving and storing flour and preparing food such as bread for the oven.

Store room (cellar, sellar): a storage room mainly for perishables. It was usually on the ground floor, but from the late 17th century might be in a partial or complete basement.

Brew house (back-house, kiln-house, malt-house): a room in which beer was brewed. It might contain vats such as a mash vat for storing malt, querns, tubs and perhaps a copper or boiler.

FIRST FLOOR

Bedroom (chamber, bed chamber, lodging chamber): a chamber was usually a room for sleeping and was generally on the first floor. Alternatively or additionally a chamber was a store room where produce such as grain could be kept dry at first-floor level and warm above a hearth. As a sleeping room the chamber contained bed frames, beds of straw, feather or flock, bed hangings and truckle beds that slid underneath the bed. As a storage room the chamber contained chests and arks.

Loft: essentially a chamber within the roof space even though at first-floor level.

Soller: an upper floor room for retiring and storage; a term used particularly in East Anglia.

TOPMOST FLOOR

Garret (cockloft, loft, vance roof): a room within the roof space. It was mainly for storage, of apples for example, but could also provide sleeping accommodation for servants and children.

Cheese chamber (cheese room): this was sometimes in the loft space and sometimes at first-floor level, where its window was exempt from Window Tax under the same concession as for the dairy. Cheeses were stored and cured here.

Chapter 6

Examples of House Development

Introduction

For the sake of clarity the type-plans illustrated in previous chapters have been prepared on the assumption that houses were built new and survived unaltered; in only a few cases have typical modifications been shown. Many houses do in fact remain for our study and appreciation fundamentally unaltered – maintained and repaired of course, modernised to some extent perhaps, but in plan, section and elevation largely as intended by their original designers and left by their original builders. Many others, however, are up to date in outward appearance but consist of layer upon layer of alteration.

While the process of detailed improvement may have been continuous, there have intermittently been more radical changes. At one stage a plan has been transformed, at another there has been a change in section; sometimes plan and section have been changed together, sometimes the external cladding and architectural expression have been modified while plan and section remained largely unchanged. In some cases a modification has been peculiar to a particular house, but changes appear more often as waves in a great swell of improvement. Just as in recent times a fashion for central heating, for bow windows, for double glazing or for Victorian conservatories seems to sweep through the country, so in the past fashions for deep plans, tall rooms, inserted floors, multiple chimney-stacks and so on can be detected.

Alterations certainly testify to progress in housing standards – small improvements adopted slowly at first but at a more rapid rate in the late 18th and 19th centuries. But the process seems to have involved not merely raising standards, giving greater floor area or more efficient heating, etc., but also the adoption of new models. The medieval house, when modified, might conform to the new model of an almost symmetrical plan and multi-storey section. The two-unit farmhouse of one and a half storeys, when modified, might embody the double-pile plan, two storeys throughout. Very often, therefore, the idea seems to have been to change from what had been an up-to-date plan but was now old-fashioned to a new plan destined to be old-fashioned in its turn.

In some cases improved standards were achieved partly through increasing the ground area occupied by the building, i.e., by throwing out a wing or outshut, adding a couple of bays to the length and so on. In other cases, both in town and country locations, the available site area was virtually fixed and extension was confined to the vertical plane by way of additional storeys and attics.

Improvements often led to a change in use of certain of the rooms. The unheated parlour became a heated dining room at the same time as the unheated loft became the heated principal bedroom. Generally, the increasing specialisation of functions led to a multiplication of rooms. For instance, a hall in which food preparation, cooking and dining all took place became regarded as out of date; those functions were parcelled out between scullery, kitchen and dining room, leaving the hall as only a living room. Such modifications to an existing house would be following the examples set by other houses newly erected to the latest pattern.

Not all houses were improved, however, for by the process of 'filtering down', which to some extent still persists, existing houses were modified to suit a new and inferior use. Thus the manor house in the village, becoming redundant for its original purpose, might become the farmhouse of the tenant of the home farm, only to be divided later into cottages for farm labourers. Even here there was a tendency for the plan of the time to be adopted, so that the medieval manor house, perhaps already made into a multi-storey building for the tenant, would be sliced into a series of cottages one and a half rooms deep and two storeys high, according to the contemporary plans designed for cottagers. The process continues, of course, so that the set of cottages may in recent times have been converted back into a single house in which the assumed form of its medieval predecessor is combined with a plan embodying the characteristics required for illustration in the glossy magazines.

Nor may all the houses which appear to blend fashionable with archaic features actually represent modification. The distinction in status between front and back, between attic and cellar and the main part of an elevation, meant that archaic door and window styles, archaic details, and even archaic materials were used in socially inferior parts of the building. Houses of the Vernacular Revival movement must also be distinguished. While archaeological correctness was no more a hall-mark of this revival than of most other revivals, some architects and craftsmen of the late 19th and early 20th centuries did in fact rate correctness of size, proportion, detail and craftsmanship rather highly. They were also often responsible for a degree of 'built-in' history, as in their chosen mixture of materials for wall or roof or in their use of buttresses imitating those used to repair genuinely ancient structures.

Sometimes the successive modifications to a house show themselves quite clearly. This is especially true of changes in section, where gable walls reveal successive alterations in roof-pitch or front walls display changes in eaves-line or even success-ive levels of window opening. It is always advisable to walk around the whole of the exterior of a house, if at all possible, so that surface indications of radical changes may be observed. In other cases the surface changes have been so complete that the various indications can only be seen from inside. Often one needs to inspect roof timbers and assess such features as smoke blackening in order to determine the various phases of modification – remembering always that changes were very frequently from one typical plan to another. In these situations the story can only be unravelled by careful and complete archaeological examination.

A few common sets of modifications have been selected here and the various stages of development described and illustrated. Examples have been taken from the houses of people of different social levels and from urban houses as well as those of the countryside. Approximate dates have been suggested for the various major changes; in some instances a long time-span has been covered, in others a much shorter span with major changes at intervals of about fifty years. In all cases the most recent modifications have been ignored.

Development of a Large House

This sequence describes the stages whereby a medieval manor house might be transformed into a simple Georgian country gentleman's house.

Stage 1 *c*.1300   The building is of T-shaped plan and consists of an open hall with a two-storey wing placed at right angles. The hall contains an open hearth; the other rooms have no fixed means of heating. Walls may be of timber-frame, clay, stone or even brick but have been taken as stone in this example. The roof covering may be of stone, slates, tiles, shingles or thatch but has been indicated here as thatch.

Stage 2 *c*.1400   At this stage the plan is substantially of the same T-shape, but the rooms are becoming more clearly distinguishable one from another and are taking specialised functions which are recognisable. The open hall is still heated by an open hearth but is approached by a screens passage formed at the junction of hall and cross-wing. The conventional arrangement of buttery, pantry, kitchen passage and winding staircase to the solar is maintained and the hall is shown as screened with the aid of spere-truss partitions and a central free-standing screen.

Stage 3 *c*.1500   The main change at this stage is the addition of a cross-wing to transform the T-shaped plan into an H-shaped one. The two-storey additional cross-wing has private rooms on the ground floor and a great chamber above, all heated by fireplaces in the side wall of the wing. In the earlier portion of the house the only substantial change has been the replacement of the open hearth by a side-wall fireplace, improving conditions in the principal room but retaining the disadvantages as well as the fine proportions of an open hall. Externally the new wing may usually be distinguished from the earlier building by a change of masonry as well as rather more generous dimensions, but the opportunity might well be used to place a new roof covering over main block and new wing alike.

Stage 4 *c*.1600   The house has now been transformed once more from an H-shaped plan to that of a house multi-storey throughout. A floor has been inserted in the main hall, an improved staircase has been provided, all rooms have been given plaster ceilings and all main rooms are heated. The cross-passage, spere truss, etc. have gone, leaving only traces in the roof construction above the new ceilings; a new multi-storey porch and balancing bay window have been added and the eaves at the front of the open hall have been raised to accommodate a new dormer window, though the low eaves at the rear would still indicate the shape of the former open hall. There are many windows now, all fully glazed, and some with opening lights.

There is a tendency towards symmetry and a hint of the Renaissance in some of the details, both inside and out, but the feel of the building remains medieval.

Stage 5 *c*.1750   Little trace of medieval origins may be seen in the house as it appears in the second half of the 18th century. Renaissance influence predominates and neither in planning, construction nor use of materials is the earlier history of the building particularly obvious.

The house-plan has been reorganised to provide an entrance front with a main portion flanked by slightly projecting wings and a garden front with a single

Development of a Large House

a. Plan c.1300: hall open to the roof (1), open hearth (2), subsidiary rooms of indeterminate function (3 and 4) with a solar above reached by means of an outside staircase or ladder.

b. Plan c.1400: hall open to the roof (1) heated by an open hearth (2) reached by a cross-passage (3) that gives access to a buttery (4), pantry (5), kitchen passage (6) and the winding staircase to the solar above (7).

c. Isometric sketch showing the T-shaped plan as it might have been about 1400. The walls are of stone but the roof would probably be of thatch. The solar in the cross-wing has fine tall windows but the other rooms are poorly lit.

d. Plan c.1500: hall open to the roof (1) but heated by a fireplace on the rear wall (8); the cross-passage (3) still serves buttery, pantry, kitchen passage and staircase to the solar as in the T-shaped plan, but the newly added parlours (9 and 10) have transformed the house into an H-shaped plan.

e. Sketch of the house in the early 16th century showing the main hall and its two cross-wings of slightly different widths. The walls are of stone, the roofs of stone tiles and there are several mullioned and transomed windows.

f. Plan c.1600: hall now only one storey in height (1) with a side-wall fireplace (8); the cross-passage has gone and the entrance is marked by a multi-storey porch (11) balanced by a multi-storey bay window; the kitchen has come into the house (12) and has its own fireplace, but pantry (5) and kitchen passage (6) remain, as do the heated parlours (9 and 10).

g. The sketch of the house at this period shows that there is a tendency to symmetry induced by the porch and the balancing bay windows. The two principal floors are now amply lit by many mullioned or mullioned and transomed windows. There is a suggestion of Renaissance detailing about the front doorway leading into the porch.

h. Plan c.1750: the plan has been simplified as a result of modification and cladding in brick or a superior stone. The hall (1) is now a heated reception room with circulation space leading to kitchens (12 and 13), staircase (14) and reorganised dining room and drawing room (9 and 10).

i. The considerable alteration to the exterior is indicated on the sketch: a marked attempt at symmetry is foiled only by the different dimensions of the wings; similarly an attempt to give a flat-roofed appearance is successful only to the extent that the parapet walls conceal the low-pitched slated roof.

---

straight wall. The main doorway, embellished by a Renaissance surround rather than a medieval porch, leads straight into an imposing heated hall which occupies the site of the former open hall. One wing has the kitchens and the other the retiring rooms, while a wide dog-leg staircase leads to the bedroom floor above. Externally, Renaissance proportions and details have been adopted, from the tall, newly built or newly faced walls, with their cornice and string course and quoins, to the tall windows with their architraves and double-hung sashes. The bold sweep of the medieval roof has been replaced by the shallow pitch and many hips of the new roof, sinking below the parapet wall to give the building a plain silhouette and the illusion of a flat roof. Only the difference in width between the original and the later cross-wings betrays the history of the building to casual external inspection.

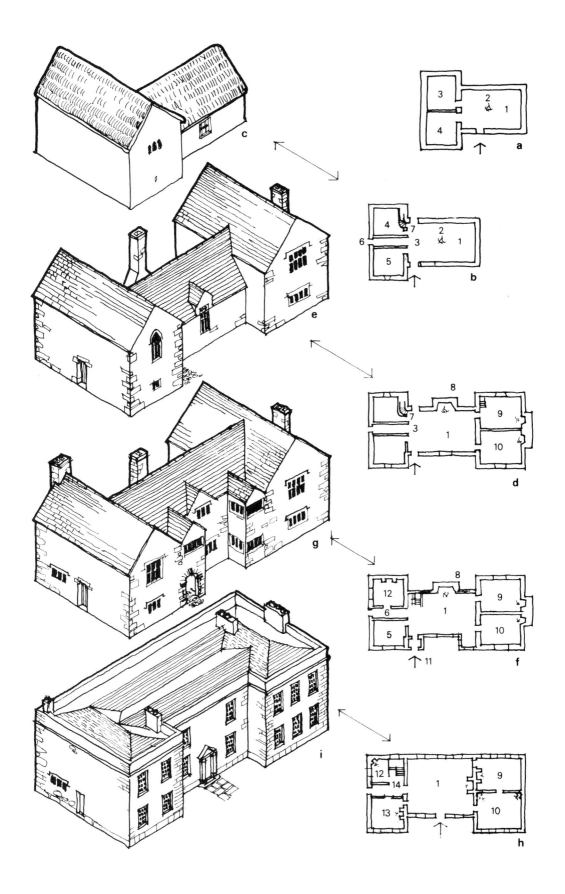

c

a
3
2 1
4

e

b
4 7 2
6 3 1
5

d
8
7
3 1 9
10

g

f
8
12 9
6 1
5 10
11

i

h
12 9
14 1
13 10

Development of a Wealden house

a. Plan c.1400: hall open to the roof (1), open hearth (2), cross-passage (3), service rooms (4 and 5) with loft over, private room or rooms (6) with loft over.

b. Isometric sketch as built c.1400 with simple rectangular ground floor and, in this example, both upper storeys jettied forward. The timber-framed walls are close-studded at the front and support a hipped roof of thatch.

c. Plan c.1500: hall still open to the roof for one bay (1), but with open hearth set against a fireback wall adjacent to the cross-passage and served by a smoke bay above (7). Service rooms (4 and 5) and retiring room or rooms (6), both sets with loft over, flank the hall.

d. Sketch as at c.1500 showing the thatch replaced by tiles in a gablet roof but otherwise with no substantial change in appearance.

e. Plan c.1600: the hall (1) is now ceiled through the insertion of an intermediate floor; a massive brick fireplace (8) blocks the cross-passage and forms a lobby entrance (9); there are service rooms (4) and parlour (6) at each end; the complete upper floor is reached by a staircase (10) rising alongside the fireplace.

f. Sketch showing the tall brick chimney rising over a retiled gablet roof which is broken by the dormer window inserted to light the newly formed chamber over the earlier hall. The timber-frame is now concealed by a lath-and-plaster cladding.

g. Plan c.1750: the hall (1) has now become purely a living room, served by a fireplace (8) and reached by the lobby entrance (9). The service room (4) has now become a kitchen with its own fireplace (11) backing on to the earlier chimney-breast. The staircase (10) has become rather more spacious and convenient for use. The parlour (6) has a brick fireplace.

h. Sketch showing the house as in c.1750 with its hipped roof of plain tiles partly hidden by the parapet of the brick wall that forms a new façade. Other walls are tile-hung. The new chimney-stacks serve many fireplaces.

i. Longitudinal section c.1500 with louvre position (12), smoke bay (7) and internal jetty of chamber into hall (13).

Development of a Wealden house

This sequence describes the transformation of a Wealden house of timber-frame and thatch into a lobby-entrance house of brick and tile.

Stage 1 c.1400   A conventional Wealden house is erected during the late 14th or early 15th century. It consists of a central hall open to the roof flanked by service rooms at one end and retiring rooms at the other end, both with lofts or chambers above. The hall is heated by an open hearth and reached by way of a cross-passage, the other rooms have no fixed heating provision. The upper rooms are reached by ladders or steep staircases from the rooms below and are not connected over the hall. In the example illustrated, the rooms are jettied to the front but in some instances the chamber over the parlour or retiring room is jettied into the hall. The building is of timber-frame construction, with a structural bay for each of the main rooms and a half-bay over the hearth and cross-passage. Between the posts of the structural bays the walls are divided by studs and rails giving a tight pattern of narrow panels on the main elevations and wider spacing

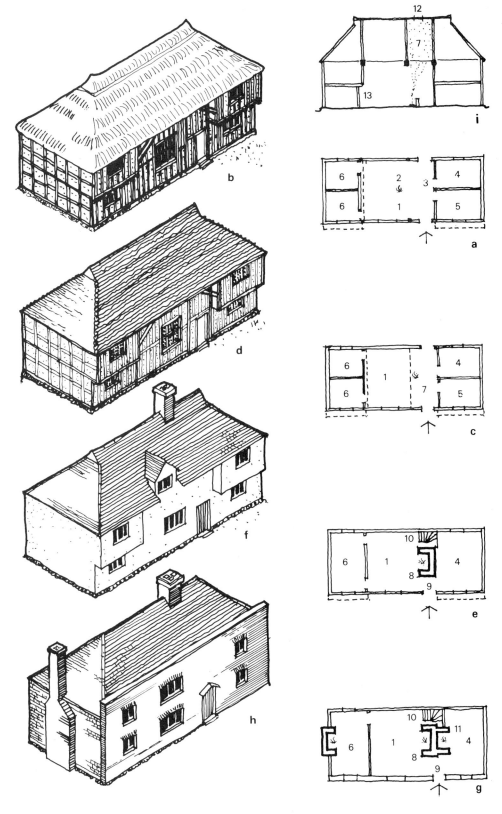

209

of panels elsewhere. Here a hipped roof of thatch is carried over hall and chambers with the aid of crown-post-and-collar-purlin trusses. As the whole roof is open and the thatch absorbs the smoke from the open fire, all the roof timbers would be blackened to some extent, though with a concentration of blackening over the hearth itself.

Stage 2 *c*.1500   The main change at this stage is the improved control of the fire on the open hearth. Its position is moved further away from the centre of the hall and towards the cross-passage, and the burning of the fire is made more effective through the use of a fireback of stone protected by a cast-iron plate. The smoke is guided upwards into a smoke bay formed by the plastered partition wall of the service rooms and chamber and a newly plastered section of the truss which was previously open and visible from the hall floor. Smoke is allowed to leave through the gaps in the tiled roof or through louvres in the gablets, or through a louvre specially formed over the smoke bay. Sometimes the smoke bay is carried downwards to enclose the hearth rather after the fashion of an inglenook. Blackening is now more heavily concentrated within the smoke bay.

Stage 3 *c*.1600   The plan is now transformed. The open hearth is replaced by a wide brick fireplace inserted into the former cross-passage, blocking the rear entrance and making the front door open into a lobby against the fireplace jamb wall. An intermediate floor is inserted, with beams and joists exposed to the room below and with a boarded floor which might be at a different level from that of the earlier floors alongside.

This new floor allows a great chamber to be formed and lit by a dormer window, proudly indicating on the front elevation what improvement had been made. The great chamber is heated by a small fireplace whose flue rises in front of the one from the ground-floor hall. The inconvenient split access formerly provided to the chambers is now replaced by a more spacious winding timber staircase. All the first-floor rooms have plaster ceilings and now suffer neither from smoke nor draughts.

At this stage improvements were often made to the timber-frame to produce both a fashionable exterior and a more comfortable interior. Sometimes the frame was clad by weather-board, more often it was covered in plain tile, but most effectively it was clad in lath and plaster which eliminated draughts and allowed both a colourful and a smart external appearance. The two flues were combined into a tall brick chimney-stack, often embellished with brick decoration or enlivened by a star shape on plan and emerging through a decorative capping to create a feature which dominated the whole house.

Stage 4 *c*.1750   There is no major change in planning at this stage. The Wealden house has already been transformed into a lobby-entrance house but the change is reinforced through the provision of a kitchen fireplace, possibly incorporating an oven, placed back to back with the earlier fireplace of the living room. The parlour no longer retains any function as a bedroom but is given a fireplace the better to establish its status and the more efficiently to encourage its new use. At the same time the chamber above the kitchen might also be given a fireplace, giving the two stacks five or six flues between them.

The most obvious changes during this period have been made to the main elevation. The characteristic Wealden house appearance with its jettied storeys and deep eaves has been transformed into a flat façade through the provision of a false elevation of brick (or sometimes timber and mathematical tiles) with completely new windows. The house is clearly recognisable as having a lobby-entrance plan, but there may be no external indication that it is of other than 18th-century date or that it originated as a Wealden house.

Development of a longhouse

This sequence describes the development of a longhouse into a farmhouse with attached farm buildings by a process of alternate rebuilding.

Stage 1 *c*.1600   It is assumed that the first rebuilding in permanent materials has occurred on a site which may long have been occupied. The outline of a previous building or several generations of buildings of the longhouse plan has been retained and one or more of the cruck trusses which formed the basic structure of earlier buildings may have been kept in place, but the walls are of stone laid as if for a permanent structure.

At this stage accommodation consists of two rooms for the farmer and his family and a cowhouse for the oxen or other valuable cattle. The domestic rooms are a hall and parlour, both open to the roof, except that the parlour may have a loft over. Only the hall is heated, and this by means of a wood or peat fire set on a hearth against a fireback wall and with smoke imperfectly gathered into a plastered hood. Both rooms are lit by unglazed mullioned windows with sliding shutters. A cross-passage gives access both to the domestic quarters and to the cowhouse; the cattle may be tethered longitudinally so that the cross-passage can act as a feeding passage also.

The whole building forms an elongated rectangle on plan. The walls are of stone and a half-hipped roof of thatch covers accommodation for humans and animals alike – in fact there is no visual distinction between the two parts of the one building.

Stage 2 *c*.1650   The process of alternate rebuilding has now begun. The cowhouse has been lengthened, allowing two rows of cattle to be tethered longitudinally so as to back on to a combined access and manure passage. Thus the cattle need no longer use the common cross-passage, though internal access between house and cowhouse is still available for the farmer. The eaves-line of this part of the building has not been changed, but the gable wall of the extended cowhouse would have a pitching hole serving a low-roofed hayloft. The domestic part remains on the earlier plan, but an intermediate floor has been inserted and a continuous loft has become available for storage or for use by children or any resident servants or farm labourers. The domestic rooms would now be much more comfortable than before: the ceiling and newly glazed windows would reduce draughts while the chimney-hood would take smoke away more efficiently from the more completely enclosed inglenook. Externally, a distinction can now be detected between parts for humans and parts for animals, though the original cross-passage located within the agricultural part still gives access to the domestic part.

Stage 3 *c.*1700   Fifty or sixty years later further changes have taken place, but in this instance the major improvement has been to the farm building. The whole of the cowhouse has been rebuilt on much the same plan as before but with better accommodation for the cattle and with a tall and capacious loft above. This would have been part of a general extension of farm buildings, for a new stable and barn would have been built early in the 18th century. Rebuilding has been done in better-quality masonry and there is an odd contrast with the earlier and less accomplished stone walling of the domestic part which still survives. As part of the rebuilding a new stone-flagged roof has replaced the former steeply pitched thatched roof.

There have been fewer changes to the domestic part. Most improvement has taken place on the first floor: a new flagged roof has been laid on the same roof-trusses as the old thatched roof so as to give raised eaves but the same ridge-line as before; this has meant that the rooms at this level are taller and suitable for use as bedrooms. They are reached by a new staircase projecting slightly from the rear of the building. On the ground floor the inner room no longer needs to double in use as the main bedroom. The principal ground-floor room continues to serve as a kitchen living room, though a new fireplace may have been inserted into the earlier inglenook now that coal is becoming available as a fuel.

At this stage the various changes in the building may be seen in the exposed masonry. The cowhouse and loft have new stone of good quality and properly laid; the domestic parts have old stone, of indifferent quality and relatively crude construction at the lower levels, but with two layers of newer and better masonry above. On the gable the various changes in eaves-line and roof-pitch may be seen.

Stage 4 *c.*1750   It is now the turn of the domestic part for considerable improvement. The whole of this part has been made taller: the ground-floor rooms (living room and parlour) are loftier and brighter as the intermediate floor has been raised and new windows of different proportions have been inserted, and the first-floor rooms are also taller and have new windows. The domestic part has been made more spacious: the main room has taken in the site of the old inglenook and the inner room has taken over space formerly used for the pantry. A lean-to roof at the rear covers a gentle staircase that rises to the first floor (and also perhaps falls to a small cellar) and has a pantry alongside. Both rooms are heated by coal-burning fireplaces. The cowhouse part remains unaltered but incorporates a cross-passage which is now redundant, for access to the domestic accommodation is now by way of a door at the front leading directly into the living room, its position emphasised by a date plaque.

Now the visual distinction between parts for humans and parts for animals is made complete. The house has a formal arrangement of doors and windows and the front wall has been rendered to conceal the various levels of masonry, yet the continuous roof recalls that of the original longhouse.

Development of a two-unit house

This sequence describes the development of a small two-unit timber-framed house into a large lobby-entrance house of brick.

Stage 1 *c*.1600   At this stage the house consists of a hall open to the roof and two smaller rooms (parlour and buttery or pantry) with a loft over. The hall is heated by a huge brick fireplace rising to a brick chimney-stack. The house is timber-framed, of box-frame construction, and is covered by a thatched roof; the front walls at least would have close studding and the roof thatch would finish at a peak on the gable wall. The arrangement is that of the two-unit plan, but the accommodation is rather mean and cramped.

Stage 2 *c*.1650   Now the house has been practically doubled in size. The original two-unit plan survives but the hall has been ceiled through the insertion of an intermediate floor and has become a kitchen living room. The balance of the plan has been completely altered through the addition of a new parlour and bedroom over; both rooms are heated and their fireplaces, set back to back with those serving the original house, make for a massive heating block which rises through the roof as a prominent chimney-stack. The upper floor of the extension has set the height for the newly raised roof over the original building, and the cramped loft has now become two quite spacious chambers.

In this case the entrance has been moved away from the fireplaces to a position near the partition wall between main room and inner rooms. The original timber-frame has been modified by the alteration to the roof as well as by the addition of the new parlour wing, and so the whole has been clad in lath and plaster – an operation that would also reduce draughts.

Stage 3 *c*.1700   The same basic outline is retained at this stage but with quite considerable alterations in room uses, construction and architectural details. The plan has become that of the conventional lobby-entrance plan. Fireplaces serving living room and kitchen and the chambers above are placed back to back and their flues combine in the one great chimney-stack. The entrance is against the jambs of the fireplaces but is protected by a porch, open at ground level and with a closet-like room above. Between entrance and fireplaces there is a framed newel staircase. The original parlour has now taken in the buttery, has gained a fireplace and now serves as a heated parlour; the parlour of Stage 2 has become quite a spacious kitchen. There are full-height heated bedrooms above and a garret storey now provides storage space. Brick and pantiles have now replaced timber and thatch, though traces of the former timber-frame may perhaps be seen internally or on the rear wall. Generally, the newly fashionable brick details and door and window forms belie the humble origins of such a house.

Development of a cross-passage house

This sequence of plans shows how an apparently homogeneous plan and section can conceal several stages of transformation.

Stage 1 *c*.1550   A mid-16th-century date has been assumed for this stage, though it could be much earlier in some parts of the country and rather later in others. At this stage the house consists of three units: living, retiring and service, in the arrangement of the conventional cross-passage plan. Heating is by means of a single open hearth. All the rooms are on the ground floor and separated by screens rather than by full-height partitions. There is a massive structural frame

Development of a longhouse

a. Plan *c.*1600: hall open to the roof (1) and heated from a hearth in an inglenook (2); the cross-passage (3) gives access both to the domestic quarters and to the cowhouse (4); the parlour (5) may be open to the roof or lofted over; a cruck truss (6) helps support the roof.

b. Isometric sketch as built *c.*1600 showing the whole accommodation contained within a rectangle of stone walls and covered by a half-hipped roof of thatch.

c. Plan *c.*1650: kitchen living room (1) now ceiled by the intermediate floor but still heated by a hearth in an inglenook and with smoke collected into a chimney-hood; the cross-passage (3) remains but there is an alternative access into the cowhouse (4); the inner room is now split into parlour (5) and a pantry or dairy (6); a ladder-like staircase (7) rises to the low loft that extends over the whole of the domestic part.

d. Sketch showing the house *c.*1650: the cowhouse part remains unaltered except for the insertion of a door for the cattle, but the domestic part has been given new windows on the ground floor and has been heightened to allow for the formation of the loft. There is a new gabled roof of thatch over the whole building, and a chimney-stack forward of the ridge serves the chimney-hood.

e. Plan *c.*1700: the kitchen living-room (1), the pantry (6) and the parlour (5) remain as before but a new staircase (7) rises to the improved first floor. The cross-passage (3) still allows internal access to the cowhouse (4) which has been heightened.

f. The sketch shows a further heightening of the roof to allow the loft over the domestic part to become a bedroom floor, but a tall storage loft has also been raised over a generally improved cowhouse. The thatch has been replaced by stone flags laid at a lower pitch.

g. Plan *c.*1750: the kitchen living room (1) now has a fireplace (2) about to be further improved through provision of a cast-iron kitchen range; the parlour (5) now has a fireplace (8); a pantry (6) extends from the rear wall alongside the staircase (7) which now rises to the further heightened first floor. The cowhouse (4) survives as does the redundant cross-passage (3).

h. As the sketch indicates, the whole building is again under one roof which has been raised so that the domestic part can have taller rooms on both ground and first floors. The new position of the front door and the formal placing of windows now distinguish domestic accommodation clearly from agricultural. The straight masonry joint, however, recalls the origins of the main elevation while the successive changes in roof-pitch are indicated on the gable wall.

---

of cruck trusses but the walling and roofing materials are relatively insubstantial: perhaps turf, clay or mud and stud for the walls and a crude sort of thatch for the roof.

Stage 2 *c.*1600   Here the main elements of the plan and structure are retained but the detailed organisation is beginning to take shape. The main room is still open to the roof and heated by an open hearth, but one whose position has been fixed by a fireback wall and which is progressing towards having a canopy and louvre to channel the smoke upwards. At one end of the main room is the cross-passage running through a structural bay which also includes the service room; at the other end is the inner room divided into parlour and pantry. The inner

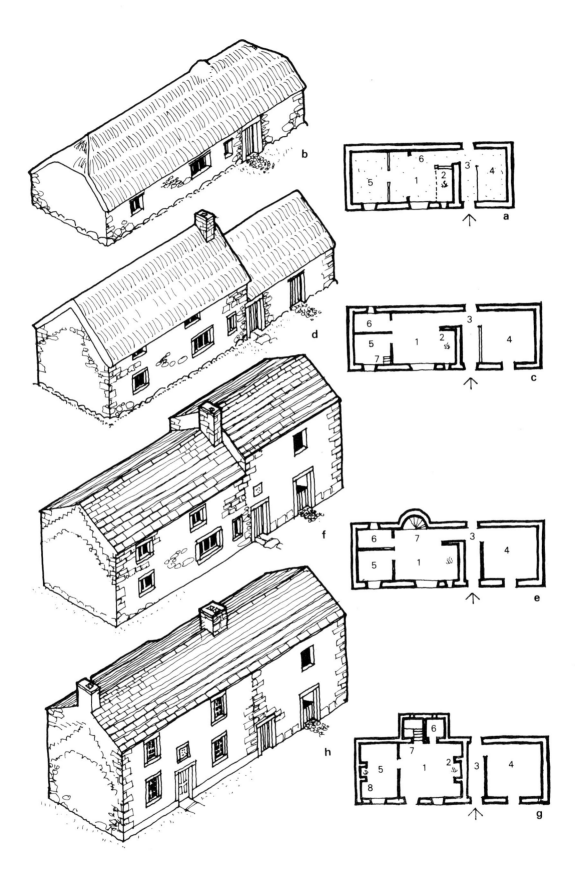

b

a

d

c

f

e

h

g

Development of a two-unit house

a. Plan c.1600: small hall open to the roof (1), heated by a massive brick or stone fireplace (2) and with a lobby entrance (3) against the jamb wall of the fireplace. The inner rooms, parlour (4) and buttery or pantry (5), have a loft above which is reached by a ladder.

b. The sketch shows the house at this stage as of half-timber construction with close studding at the front and a gabled thatched roof above.

c. Plan c.1650: the plan has now been considerably extended. The hall (1) has become a living room and kitchen combined and is served by a new fireplace (2) which incorporates an oven. There is a new entrance (6) but parlour (4) and buttery (5) remain. A new staircase (7) gives access to the upper floor which now extends over the whole of the plan. The main change is the addition of a new parlour (8) heated by a fireplace (9) and with a chamber above. The alternative position for a door at (10) would have given the conventional lobby-entrance plan.

d. The sketch shows the building extended, its timber-framed walls concealed by a plaster cladding and the massive chimney-stack rising from a newly thatched roof. The stack serves fireplaces in the hall, the new parlour and two chambers.

e. Plan c.1700: the plan has now taken lobby-entrance form. There is a living room (1) heated from a fireplace (2) and giving access to a heated parlour (4); the site of the earlier heated parlour has now become the kitchen (11). There is a range of heated bedrooms on the first floor and an unheated garret above, all reached by the framed staircase (12). The lobby entrance is both marked and protected by the porch.

f. The sketch shows how the timber-framed walls have been replaced by brick and the thatched roof by a roof of pantiles contained within Dutch gables.

---

room would normally be ceiled at tie-beam level, both to improve the comfort of the parlour and cleanliness of the pantry and to provide a loft above. At this stage the windows would be unglazed and control of draughts far from effective. Smoke blackening could occur on any of the roof timbers apart from those above the parlour and pantry. While the basic cruck trusses continue to support the roof, the walls consist of studs and rails forming wattle-and-daub panels, related to the cruck framework but not necessarily load-bearing.

Stage 3 c.1650   The main change at this stage is the insertion of an intermediate floor in the central bay of the house. This was usually done by running a beam longitudinally between the tie-beam of the truss that forms the partition to the inner room and the heavy beam or bressummer that forms part of the inglenook fireplace. The newly inserted floor was often at a rather higher level than the older floors over the inner or service rooms. At this stage the cross-passage has become a true passage, partitioned off from the service room and running behind the fireback wall of the inglenook. Externally the main change in the appearance of the building comes from the addition of the dormer window lighting the newly formed chamber; this window might often be highly decorated by means of moulded beams and plastered coves as if the householder wanted to call attention to his house improvements. A minor change may be seen in the chimney-stack rising from the top of the plastered chimney-hood and emerging forward of the ridge.

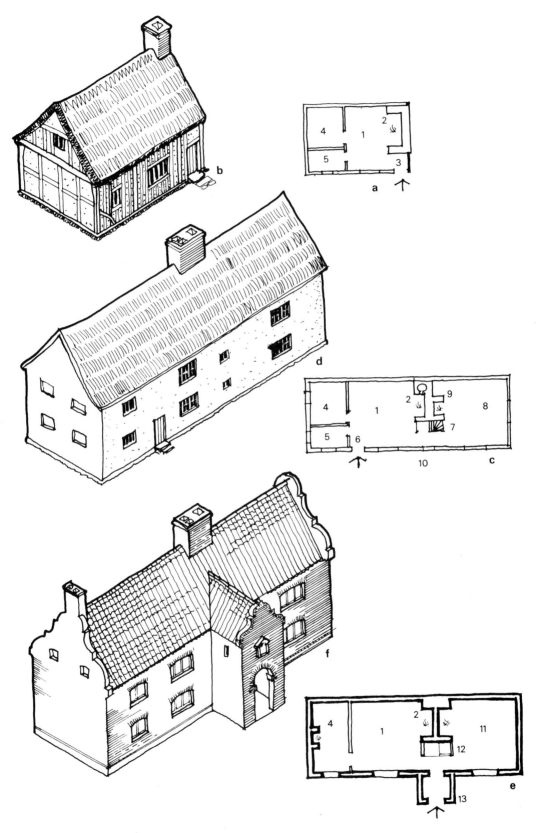

b

a

d

c

f

e

217

Development of a cross-passage house

a. Plan c.1550: a hall (1) is heated by an open hearth (2) set near a cross-passage (3) and flanked by a service room (4) and a private or retiring room (5); all are open to the roof and contained within insubstantial walls.

b. The sketch shows the cruck framework for the three-unit cross-passage house. It is assumed that there would be a half-hipped roof, but because of the lack of surviving examples of this period it is difficult to be certain of the walling material.

c. Plan c.1600: there is a hall (1) open to the roof and heated by an open hearth (2) set against a fireback wall; the cross-passage (3) leads to a service room (4) which is also open to the roof; the inner room has become a pantry or dairy (5) and a parlour (6). A ladder or very steep staircase rises to a loft over these two rooms.

d. Isometric sketch of the house as it might have been about 1600, showing the three units lit by unglazed windows. The timber-framed walls with side panels are set around the original crucks, and the half-hipped thatched roof with a saddle louvre over the hearth surmounts the walls. There is a small window in the half-hip lighting the loft.

e. Plan c.1650: the ground-floor plan remains substantially the same but an intermediate floor has been inserted in the hall to make it into a kitchen living room with chamber over. This room (1) is heated by a fire in an inglenook (2), and is still reached by a cross-passage (3) and flanked by a service room (4), pantry (5) and parlour (6) with a staircase (7) leading to the now complete upper floor.

f. The sketch shows that the only major changes have been the addition of a dormer window to light the new chamber and a brick chimney-stack serving the chimney-hood that rises from the inglenook. However, houses of this stage which survive often have brick walls to the weather sides of the building and steeply pitched slated roofs replacing the 17th-century thatch.

g. Plan c.1750: there is a living room (1) with a fireplace (2); it is entered directly from the front (8). A kitchen (4) has its own fireplace, as does the parlour (6). A new staircase (9) rises to the improved first floor.

h. The sketch shows new brick walls and a low-pitched slated roof. There is no indication on the outside of the original plan or of the cruck trusses of which elements survive within the house.

Stage 4 c.1750   The house is now substantially altered in plan and outward appearance. The three main elements of living room, parlour and service room remain, but the cross-passage has been eliminated and the entrance moved to a position between the two main rooms and into a lobby formed at the foot of a fairly convenient staircase. The service room has now become a kitchen with its own fireplace and, indeed, the former single source of heat has been multiplied into fireplaces in all the ground-floor rooms and in some of those on the first floor. Externally the main change has been the replacement of timber-frame and thatch by brick and slate. The cruck trusses survive, to a substantial extent, in the parlour partition wall and as truncated posts in the walls at each side of the fireplace. Other pieces of the former timber-frame may have been used as wall-plates or as parts of the low-pitch timber trusses that carry the roof slates. Generally the rooms have been made taller both at ground-floor and first-floor levels, and as well as being properly heated they are adequately lit and ventilated from the tall sash

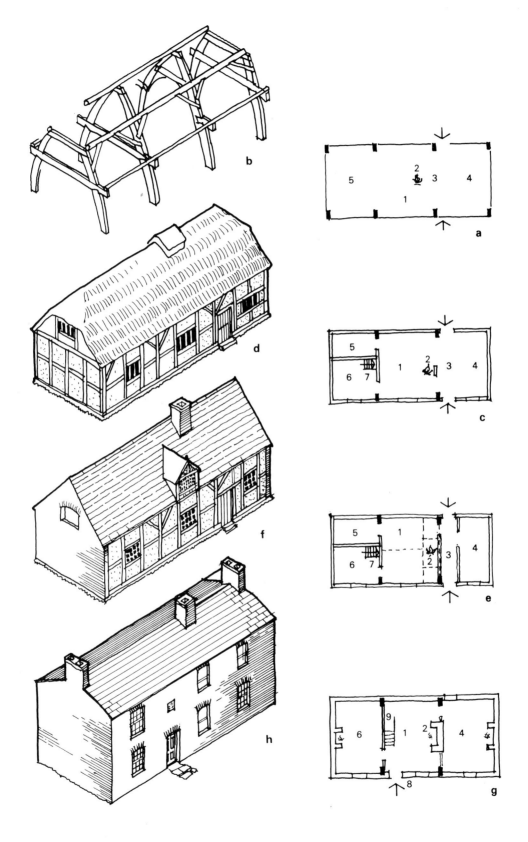

219

Development of a medieval town house

a. Plan c.1350: the building occupies a fairly wide plot facing on to a street or market place. In the front portion there are shops (1) reached from a gallery (2) approached by a flight of steps (3). As the shop level is slightly raised, a vaulted basement is sunk into the ground and approached by steps (4). The rear portion consists essentially of a T-shaped hall comprising the open hall itself (6) with its open hearth (7) and cross-passage (8), off which opens a private room (9) heated by an end-wall fireplace (10) and with a room above reached by a winding staircase (11). The passage (5) and cross-passage (8) give access from the street to the rear part of the plot (12).

b. The isometric sketch attempts to show the building complex as it might have been during the medieval period. It is assumed that the front portion was timber-framed over a stone basement, that the rear portion was stone-walled and that the whole was covered by a thatched roof.

c. Plan c.1550–1600: shops, each separately heated, are reached by steps as necessary from the new road level. A passage (5) leads to the rear portion in which the hall (6) has an inserted floor, a new fireplace (13) and a staircase (14) leading to the newly formed chamber. The passage (8), now enclosed, leads to the private room (9) as well as to the rear of the plot.

d. The sketch shows the front portion rebuilt to give two full storeys and a garret storey well lit by a line of dormer windows; access would be from the rear portion or by stairs within some of the shop units. The rear portion now has a dormer and several chimney-stacks, while the whole roof now has a covering of fire-resistant tiles.

e. Plan c.1750: the building complex has been reorganised to give two houses each two rooms deep and one room wide. A shop (1) has its own entrance (15), but another door and passage (5) lead to a rear room (6) with service rooms extending along the plot (16) and a staircase (17) leading to the upper floors. Another shop (18) is reached by way of a passage (19) which also leads to a staircase (20) and a rear room (21).

f. Just as the plan has been reorganised, the construction has been changed. Timber-frame has been replaced by brick and steeply pitched tiled roofs by low-pitched slated roofs. The exuberance of timber decoration has also been replaced by the reticence of brick.

---

windows. These changes were usually made during the second half of the 18th century, and they give no external indication whatsoever of the phases of the plan's development nor any clues to the former structure that might be concealed within.

Development of a medieval town house

Although the pressures of commerce and increased population weigh heavily against the survival of early buildings in town and city centres, some do survive, albeit heavily restored or considerably altered. Three stages in a typical progression are described here.

Stage 1 c.1350   In this instance the building complex comprises two parts on a fairly wide urban plot. Facing on to the street there is a two-storey timber-framed building raised over a stone-vaulted half-basement. The timber-framed building

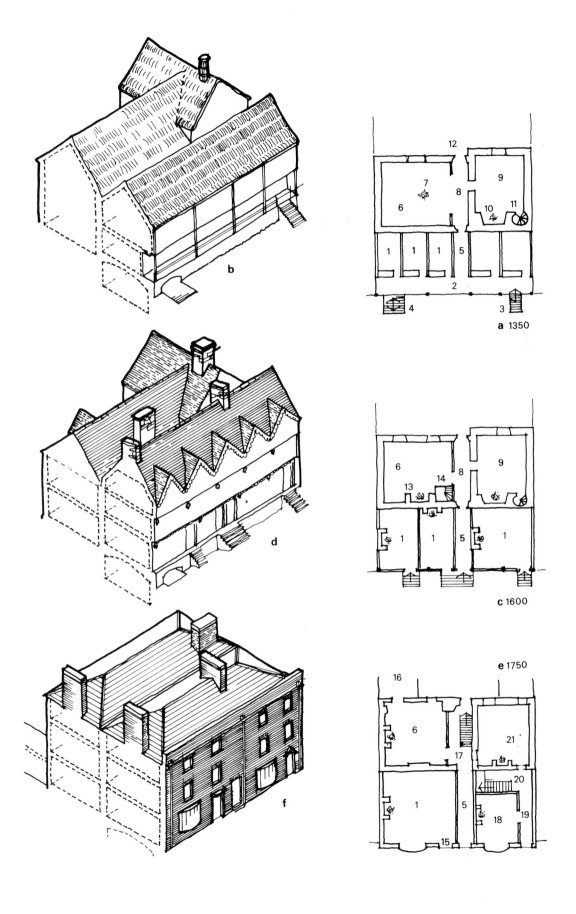

b

a 1350

12

7

6

8

9

10 11

1 1 1 5

2

4 3

d

c 1600

6 8 9

13 14

1 1 5 1

e 1750

16

6

17

21

1 5 20

18 19

15

f

consists of a series of shops with rooms over and reached by way of a gallery raised above the level of the street or market place. The stone basement is a warehouse or workshop and is reached by a set of steps dropping from street level. At this stage the demarcation of communal street and private land is still rather imprecise, and the space in front of the gallery and alongside the various steps may have been occupied by temporary booths during fairs or on market days. Facing on to the rear of the plot there is a stone-walled T-shaped hall which was probably originally occupied in connection with the cellar workshops and other shops, but may later have been in separate occupation. The T-shaped hall consists of hall and cross-wing as in rural buildings of this type, but the cross-passage at the junction of hall and cross-wing serves also to give general access from the street to the rear part of the plot.

Stage 2 *c.*1550–1600   In any successful town, commercial pressures on the best frontages increased the accommodation on the plot and led to the erection of ever taller buildings. In this instance it is assumed that the shops have been rebuilt to give three full storeys and fewer shop units of larger size. The overhanging storeys and profusion of dormer gables lend the streets of some of our older towns their familiar character. The building at the rear has also been altered. An intermediate floor in the hall and a garret floor in the cross-wing add to the available accommodation.

Stage 3 *c.*1750   By now the distinction between public street and private building plot has been established: the front portion has taken over space formerly marked by the projection of sets of steps and a new brick structure has replaced the former jettied timber-frame. At the same time the rear portion has been modified, with some original stone walls being retained and others added in brick. The two original buildings have now been reorganised to give two units at right angles to the earlier units, each being one room wide and two rooms deep and both extending along the sides of the plot in a series of service rooms. All rooms have fireplaces, so that stacks of multiple flues rise from the new low-pitched slated roofs. A parapet runs in a straight line along the street, giving a steadier and more sober impression than the gabled skyline of the previous stage.

Chapter 7

Houses and Cottages of Scotland

Introduction

Although there are sufficient similarities in the domestic architecture of England and Wales for the two to be considered as one group, the domestic buildings of Scotland are sufficiently different for them to be discussed separately. As elsewhere, the houses and cottages of Scotland are a product of geography and topography, history and economics; they reflect the culture of what was for long a separate country and one that retains its independence in important respects.

The geographical divisions of Scotland – the Southern Uplands, the Central Lowlands, the Eastern and North-eastern Coastal Plain, the Highlands and the island groups of Inner and Outer Hebrides, Orkneys and Shetlands – reflect topographical variations deriving from those solid and surface geological differences that help to determine the traditional use of building materials. Coal measures and deposits of other minerals particularly distinguished the Central Lowlands and ordained them as the site of Scotland's brief period of industrial pre-eminence.

In terms of domestic architecture, the history of Scotland extends from the medieval period when the Scottish Crown claimed, and for a time occupied, tracts of northern England, through the long series of wars between the two kingdoms when a basically weak Scotland was regularly supported by an ascendant France. The Union of the Crowns in 1603 drew the Scottish court and much Scottish talent to London while the process of assimilation of Scotland into the United Kingdom was hastened by the merging of the parliaments in 1707. Although law, education, religion and, to a large extent, language remained distinct, Scotland benefited from the Union and enjoyed a period of prosperity from the middle of the 18th century to 1914. This was reflected in domestic architecture which, while still scarcely a match in most respects for that of England, made great advances over what had been accepted before. However, the Highland/Lowland split and the isolation of the Western Highlands and the island chains from developments in the rest of Scotland meant the survival of much that was backward. Innovations tended to originate in the east and south-east, move up the east coast, then slowly move northwards and westwards. The contrast between the primitive conditions of the inhabitants of the remote islands and the relative comfort of those who lived in the Lowlands provoked comment from travellers and researchers from the early 17th century right through to the early 20th. Scottish innovators, entrepreneurs, bankers and agriculturalists left their marks on town and countryside in the late 18th and the 19th centuries, though houses generally remained smaller and less well-equipped than those of England.

Before the agricultural and industrial revolutions of the 18th century, Scotland was a land of small farms held from landowners, often through intermediaries, by peasant farmers on precarious tenure. Farming was mixed, each tenant having a few cattle and sheep to balance the cultivation of a few acres for oats or barley.

Instead of villages there were small townships of up to a dozen dwellings called 'clachans' in the Highlands and 'fermtouns' in the Lowlands. One settlement might contain the parish church but was otherwise undistinguished from the rest. Within the 'head-dyke' that separated the farmland from the waste, the 'run-rig' system of agriculture was practised. The 'infield' would be divided into strips continually cropped and fertilised; occasional crops would be taken section by section from the 'outfield', while the remainder would be used for grazing. There would also be summer grazing of the waste land high above the head-dyke. Tenancy requiring service and payment of rent in kind remained common long after it had been all but abandoned in England. The tenant was generally responsible for construction of house and buildings in spite of tenure being at will or on very short lease. With the Agricultural Revolution of the 18th century farms became fewer and larger

74. Amisfield Tower, Dumfriesshire
Built about 1600, this is a late example of a type widespread in Scotland. It has an elaborate collection of turrets at each corner and a romantic skyline of gables and chimney-stacks.
(Peter Crawley)

224

and tenancies longer. Landlords provided much improved houses and buildings in return for money rent, and about 150 new planned villages or small towns were established, mostly in the Lowlands, between 1750 and 1850. In the Highlands the revolution was marred by clearance and social unrest, and attempts to establish new balanced communities, mostly on the coast, met with very mixed success.

Until the late 18th century, Scotland apart from Edinburgh was a country of small, widely dispersed rural towns. The success of the Industrial Revolution, however, promoted Glasgow above Edinburgh in size and prosperity, making it the second city of Empire, while many other towns, especially in the Central Lowlands, became large, prosperous and well-built.

Large Houses of the countryside

As in the rest of this book, the Great Houses of royalty, the nobility and the powerful in town and countryside will not be discussed. This brief account begins with the Large Houses of the smaller landowners.

Little survives of the equivalent of the medieval manor house in England. There are a few upper-hall houses of the late 12th, 13th and early 14th centuries with a hall open to the roof and raised over an undercroft. Rait Castle, Nairnshire, is an example, with its first-floor hall formerly reached by a timber forestair with separate access to the undercroft.

The tower house is the most characteristic Large House type in Scotland. Even if it had not been the basis for the design of hundreds of fanciful 19th-century 'castles', it would still have set the character for the most dominating buildings in the Scottish countryside. Tower houses range in date from the 12th to the 17th century, and the Union of the Crowns did not in itself halt the construction of defensible dwellings. The main period was from the late 14th to the late 16th century. Examples may be seen throughout lowland Scotland, with some concentration in the counties bordering England but also in Fife and the richer counties of the Central Lowlands. Few tower houses are to be found in the Highlands and Islands. Their design always represented a balance between defence and comfort, with the former predominating earlier and the latter in more recent times. Although a tower house was self-contained in terms of its domestic accommodation, it was usually just one element in the barmkin or walled enclosure that contained other domestic and service buildings as well as farm buildings.

Early tower houses were simple rectangles three or four storeys high with a stone-vaulted basement at ground level, a hall at first-floor level and chambers at second-floor and garret levels. The various storeys were connected by staircases within the basic rectangular shape. Entrance was usually at first-floor level, though sometimes at ground level. The door was secured with a drawbar and often supplemented by an iron-barred 'yett', while the small windows of the upper storeys were barred with iron. There was a projecting parapet at the top of the wall but no provision for more active defence: the occupant relied for security on the thick stone walls and the stone-vaulted basement.

Later towers were L-shaped, the projecting wing accommodating a more generous staircase and freeing the principal rooms on each floor. More spaces were

225

taken out of the thickness of the wall. There was often a 'caphouse' or gabled attic chamber incorporating the top level of the staircase. This, together with prominent chimneys, crow-stepped gables and round turrets at each corner of the battlements, made for an eventful skyline enhanced still further in later examples by the elaborate surrounds to dormer windows. At the same time windows generally, especially in the upper storeys, were enlarged and generously decorated. Elsieshields, Dumfriesshire, mainly of the late 16th century, is a good example.

The final development, after about 1570, was the Z-plan, so called because of the projection at each corner of the basic rectangle. The best-known example is Claypotts, near Dundee, of 1569–88. Here the corner projections are almost circular but convert to square shape at the highest level. The gables of these projections, together with those of the main block, the caphouse and the pedimented dormer windows, create a lively skyline. Entrance is at ground-floor level but protected by gun loops, and the rounded turrets are pierced for handguns.

Tower houses seem to have been designed more and more for purely symbolic rather than serious defence. They came to be the fashionable outward and visible signs of wealth and status even at a local level. At all times they were distinct from the great castles; they could not provide serious protection against invasion from England, but they could provide appropriate security in a countryside subject to local unrest, especially during periods of weak government and powerless kings. [2]

At a rather lower social level, defensible farmhouses for the more prosperous farmers have recently been discovered, corresponding to the 'bastle houses' on the English side of the border. The typical Scottish bastle house (previously known only from documents), as found in the upper Clyde valley in the late 16th and early 17th centuries, was a two-storey rectangular building with walls of substantial thickness having accommodation for animals on the lower floor and the family on the upper floor. There were separate entrances at the two levels and an internal staircase to join the two, doors on both levels being protected by drawbars. The roof was quite steeply pitched, sometimes thatched though the more appropriate covering was slates or stone flags. Only a handful have been discovered as yet, but more may emerge as their design is better understood and recognised. [3]

As defensive needs diminished and the symbolism of the tower became less potent, so the lairds' houses of the 17th century developed as simple rectangular blocks, one room deep and two or three storeys high. They had unprotected doors and large partly or fully glazed windows. Often the block was extended by a staircase tower or wing giving a T- or L-shape. When the staircase tower was at the front of the building it included the front door and contained a gently winding 'turnpike' stair; sometimes the tower was in a round or polygonal form. One variation of the L-plan incorporated a staircase of flights around a newel of stone in the angle of the L. [4]

During the 18th century and early part of the 19th, the typical laird's house was rectangular with a central timber staircase behind the front door and one room (or later two) on each side. Although there were some two-storey houses of status there were usually at least two full storeys with an attic and often a semi-basement as well. Later and larger houses were of double-pile plan, but this layout never achieved the dominance that it had in England and Wales. [5]

Small Houses of the countryside

The study of Small Houses in Scotland is complicated by three main factors: the fundamental and comprehensive nature of the agricultural improvements of the 18th and 19th centuries, the small size of the average farm before improvement had taken its full course, and the considerable time lag between the adoption of new features in the more advanced parts of the country and their dissemination to more backward areas. Many of the houses that have interested travellers and scholars over the past two centuries have been typologically early but chronologically late.

Before the Improvements, the typical Scottish farmhouse was an elongated single cell open to the roof with a common entrance for humans and animals (mainly cattle) but no cross-passage. The animals were separated from the humans, if at all, by a flimsy wattle partition. In the house part, sleeping accommodation was provided by a bed recess in the wall or later by a box-bed in the room. A fire burning on a hearth in the middle of the floor provided warmth and heat for cooking; the smoke from wood or peat fuel accumulated in the roof space or drifted up to a.makeshift chimney in the roof.

The primitive nature of such a house-and-byre combination may be explained by the general poverty of small farmers on their very small, inefficiently farmed holdings, and by their insecurity of tenure – whereby at worst they were tenants-at-will and at best they had very short leases, so they might have to shift house sites from time to time. In any case, because of the long-lasting tradition of payment of rent to the landlord or his representative by service or in kind it was almost impossible to accumulate the capital to invest in building, even if insecurity of tenure had not made such an investment unwise. The farmer by custom usually retained possession of his house timbers and hearthstone whether rebuilding on the same site or moving.

From the mid-18th century onwards many tenancies were amalgamated into large farms run on economical lines and with substantial farmhouses and farm buildings provided by the landlord. For a time in the 19th century experienced Scottish farmers accustomed to running such estates were in demand in those parts of England and Wales where the Agricultural Revolution occurred rather later. But small farms did remain, more efficiently run and with improved accommodation.

The change was more in quality than in size. Small farmers continued to live in one-storey dwellings; but as the animals were moved into cowhouses and stables, space became available in the basic rectangle of the plan for a living room and a parlour/bedroom (though box-beds remained popular). The typical small farmhouse of the late 18th and early 19th centuries was thus a single rectangle on plan, with two rooms open to the roof and a single hearth set beneath a chimney canopy.

Developments in the late 18th and 19th centuries gave more and better accommodation by way of section rather than plan. First part of the house was lofted, then the entire floor area: this resulted in a one-and-a-half-storey cross-section with the extra accommodation being entirely in the roof space or, later, partly in the roof space and partly below raised eaves. The extra space was lit either by small lights in the roof slope or later by dormer windows, which might be elaborate polygonal windows above the eaves or tall dormers taking the main wall above

76. Small House at Ruthwell, Dumfriesshire
This single-storey house of only two rooms is typical of so many smaller houses and larger cottages throughout Scotland.
(Peter Crawley)

the eaves. It was uncommon to light the loft through the gables, or indeed through the back slope of the roof. Heating was at first still by a fire burning on a hearth backing on to a gable wall, but later a fireplace in the parlour/bedroom was added. All this led to a standard elevation of a gabled rectangular building with a central doorway flanked on each side by windows, perhaps with dormers above, and with one or two gable chimney-stacks.

77. Houses at Gairloch, Ross and Cromarty
The accommodation has here expanded into the roof space with bedrooms lit by dormer windows.
(Peter Crawley)

The more substantial farmhouses had two storeys and even, in the better farming areas, two and a half storeys and sometimes a cellar. They were still usually one room deep: the four-square double-pile farmhouses that spread over England and

7

Wales in the late 18th and early 19th centuries had relatively few counterparts in Scotland.

In the Highlands and Islands, where not subject to clearance, farmsteads of older type survived until very late. In one version the single-room house-and-byre combination was flanked on one side by a barn and on the other by a porch and bed outshut. In areas of severe climate such as the Orkneys, house, byre, stable and barn in one line culminated in a round, beehive-shaped corn-drying kiln. The 'black houses' of peat or mixed construction were built as late as the closing years of the 19th century and probably later. They were occupied until recently, though with a fireplace rather than a central open hearth. According to one report, houses on St Kilda had tall walls so that the winter accumulation of dung and ashes could build up before being scattered on the fields in the spring.   8

As in England and Wales, developments in heating and cooking methods affected design in plan and section. Early Small Houses and late survivals of that type in the North and West had a single open hearth near the middle of the house with a peat fire burning on a hearthstone and able to heat a cauldron for porridge or a griddle for oatcakes. Among superior houses this was superseded by a hearth in an inglenook projecting to the rear of the main living room, including a stone flue but also providing a warm 'room within a room' for the comfort of the family. Among the general run of Small Houses the workings of the hearth were improved by the provision of a chimney canopy or 'lum', sometimes suspended over the hearth but later, and much more commonly, moving with the hearth to a gable wall. This arrangement was somewhat similar to the wood-and-plaster hooded chimney and inglenook of England, but in Scotland the canopy was supported by cantilevers from the gable wall rather than carried on a heavy beam and there was no suggestion of the room within a room. The 'hanging lum' was suitable for curing meat, and Bruce Walker has found evidence of farmers and cottagers renting out their peat smoke to richer farmers whose modern coal fires were unsuitable. Eventually coal-fired ranges were more generally adopted, but the scarcity of coal beyond the Central Lowlands and the difficulty and expense of bringing coal by rail or sea, let alone by road, meant that peat remained in use very late in the more remote areas.   9

The sleeping arrangements already mentioned reflect a different attitude to privacy from that which developed in England and Wales. In Scotland it was the bed recess, the bed outshut, the 'bed neuk' and the box-bed that gave privacy. Any one of these opened off or was located in the principal living room. The private bedroom was a relatively late indulgence for the ordinary farmer. In England and Wales the four-poster bed with its curtains offered privacy equivalent to that of the box-bed, but even when in the parlour such a bed was at least located in an inner room. The idea of placing sleeping quarters upstairs came late to the Scottish farmhouse, even though it was long-established in the tower house.

Cottages of the countryside

As farms were generally small and worked by the family there was not much of a cottager class until the period of the agricultural improvements. Nevertheless there were cottagers who, like the tenant farmers, supplied labour to the land-owners as rent for their cottages. Their accommodation was minimal, consisting of one room open to the roof with no separate provision for cattle. In 1808 these were described as 'mean and wretched hovels'.

The Improvement period brought benefits to the cottager class. Some became day-labourers on the larger farms and were provided with one and a half rooms on one storey or in a lofted one-room plan. Cottages were built in pairs or in rows or with the new farmsteads. Other cottagers became textile workers, especially with the development of linen manufacture, Scotland's staple industry after 1707. The typical textile worker's cottage would have one room, perhaps lofted, for the family and another room, unheated, to the side or at the back for the loom. There was little or no development of basement or attic loomshops, so that the long ranges of 'weavers' windows' found in England are not to be seen. When the looms were removed and the loomshop taken into domestic use, there might be no sign that a cottage had once had an industrial function.

The tradition of single-storey living was strong within the larger-scale rural industrial settlements of the Central Lowlands; New Lanark, for instance, had its workers' accommodation in flats rather than houses. Many of the blocks at New Lanark were originally designed around one-room dwellings repeated to a height of several floors. This is in contrast to rural industrial communities in England, such as Styal in Cheshire, where the terraces of cottages were based on the two-up-and-two-down plan. In Scotland many seeming double-fronted houses in industrial communities actually contain one-room flats with bed closets or box-beds, the front door leading to a common staircase and so to the flats.

Houses and Cottages in the towns

As in England and Wales, so in Scotland houses in towns differed from those in the countryside. This reflected a difference of function: the dwellings were occupied by merchants and craftsmen rather than by farmers and labourers. But it also reflected the siting: narrow burgage plots rather than the more open farmstead sites. The medieval towns of Scotland, however, were even smaller than those south of the border. Even Edinburgh in the early 14th century is estimated to have had only about 2,000 inhabitants (even though its population had risen to an estimated 20,000 by the early 17th century), while Glasgow in the mid-15th century had an estimated population of 1,500 and Stirling about half that number. Although they were only the size of a present-day village, it is assumed that the towns had an urban character because plots fronting the commercial streets and market places were relatively valuable and came to be intensively developed. Few elements of the medieval dwellings survive; the older parts are of late 16th to

78. House at Biggar, Lanarkshire

Here is a two-storey house with the curious placing of a chimney-stack at the apex of the front gable which is found so often in Scottish towns. The use of Ionic scrolls to terminate the various gable copings is a delightful touch.
(Peter Crawley)

79. House at St Monance, Fife

Here the forestair is prominent. The thatch of the roof has been replaced between the crow-stepped gables by pantiles with slate at the eaves.
(Peter Crawley)

232

left **80. House at Pittenweem, Fife**
This 19th-century town house is two rooms deep, double-fronted, and has two and a half storeys and a basement. The characteristic forestair of the Scottish town house has been retained in miniature.
(Peter Crawley)

81. Houses in Pittenweem, Fife
This group of town houses has enclosed forestair blocks. The houses are several storeys high and have a broken skyline of chimney-stacks and crow-stepped gables.
(Peter Crawley)

233

early 17th-century origin, but all towns now have a 19th-century character, so radical was development and rebuilding during that period of unprecedented prosperity.

11

Urban houses

It appears that an early medieval merchant's house would consist of a booth or booths at ground level opening into the street with a loft or dwelling space above reached by an external timber staircase rising from the street. An entry alongside the booths gave access to the rear of the plot. Post-medieval development led to an increase to two or three storeys with attics; a forestair, frequently of stone, rose from the street and often emerged into a projecting timber gallery which gave access to rooms above and shelter to booths below. The entry, now called a 'close', led to a succession of courtyards with houses and other buildings called 'lands'. Some towns sooner or later acquired fortifications; but Edinburgh was the biggest and most vulnerable, and so development – especially during the late 16th century and the 18th century along the High Street – meant even taller buildings with dwellings on each floor, all reached by a winding 'turnpike' staircase rising directly from the street or at forestair level. There were, of course, many single-family dwellings large and small on the outskirts or in the commercially less attractive parts of the towns, but the convenience and prestige of central locations meant that important families as well as commercial tenants concentrated at the heart of the town.

Tenement flats

When development and redevelopment occurred on a large scale in the big towns (especially Edinburgh, Glasgow and Dundee) in the 18th and 19th centuries, it was by way of flats rather than individual houses. Notwithstanding similarities between Georgian streets in Edinburgh and London, front doors in the former city were likely to lead to communal stairs while in the latter they invariably led to private stairs used by a single family. The lavish scale of horizontal living in the north matched that of vertical living in the south. Expansion in Edinburgh began when builders leapt over the old Nor' Loch, in a first phase from 1770 and a second from 1820, and built the New Town, an event that corresponded to the development of Bloomsbury and other districts in London.

The characteristic Scottish town house is the tenement flat. The term 'tenement' has a wider meaning, but in this context a tenement is taken to be a self-contained dwelling on one floor within a larger building and reached by a common access stair; a 'flat' in English terms. In Edinburgh, blocks tended to be up to five storeys high with attic and basement, but the fall in some sites meant that they could rise to as many as fourteen storeys. In the Georgian New Town the common stair and landings were just inside the front wall; in later Edinburgh blocks the staircase was internal and top-lit. In Glasgow, tenement blocks were usually four storeys in height with an internal staircase. In Dundee the blocks were three or four storeys in height with a projecting turnpike staircase at the rear and open galleries giving access to flats at each level.

12

The smallest flats had one 'apartment' or habitable room, indeed one room only, with no kitchen or scullery let alone bathroom; others had two apartments. By 1939 nearly 60 per cent of Glasgow's dwellings were of this type. More commodious flats had three or four apartments, sometimes more, with an individual WC but neither a separate kitchen nor a scullery, the sink being in the living room.

234

The flats were either 'through', stretching from front to back of a tenement block and so capable of through ventilation, or were placed back to back without this possibility. In Edinburgh a common arrangement was to have two pairs of back-to-back two-apartment flats on each floor, all served by a central staircase. In both cities, the larger and later flats of three or four apartments had individual WCs and sculleries. In Edinburgh, Glasgow and the larger towns such as Dundee and Aberdeen substantial tenement blocks were erected with these arrangements between about 1890 and 1914, while construction of back-to-back flats was permissible until 1925.

Since 1945 wholesale clearance has reduced the number of tenement blocks and altered the character of Scottish towns accordingly, but the survivors are now increasingly cherished and are being brought up to modern standards of accommodation.

Of course all Scottish towns had numbers of conventional houses built, especially on the outskirts. One common plan was to have one room on each side of a central straight-flight staircase, as in Stirling in the early 18th century. In Edinburgh, wherever land was available, substantial double-pile houses were erected in the second half of the 18th century.

Materials and construction

The overwhelming impression of Scottish buildings, fostered by the tourist industry, is of dour gritstone or sandstone tenements in Edinburgh and Glasgow, white-rendered cottages between romantic tower houses in the countryside, and pastel-coloured houses crowding the little ports of Fife. In so far as the overwhelming majority of traditional dwellings are of stone construction, the impression is understandable; but some of the rendered walls are not quite what they seem, and the impression gained by travellers before the second half of the 19th century was rather different.

Scotland is a country of cruck construction, though in contrast to, say, Worcestershire, hardly any crucks are exposed to view. The crucks are simple, in fact crude, related to roofs of fairly low pitch and often jointed. In many cases they were no doubt the timbers that the landlord provided for the tenant and that the tenant used in his rebuildings. The use of half-crucks, as in the end wall of a building in Corrimony in Inverness-shire, showed that hipped roofs as well as gabled could be used in cruck construction. Documents refer to crucks as 'couples', while purlins were 'pans' and rafters 'cabers'. Post-and-truss and box-frame construction is rarely found in Scotland, except that many town houses of the 15th and 16th centuries – and probably earlier – were timber-framed, either completely or more commonly with just a timber-framed street front, the back and party walls being of stone. 13

In the countryside an old and persistent technique was the use of thick 'feals' of turf either around a cruck frame or to make load-bearing walls. Such turf walls continued to be built at least until the early part of the 19th century, and the technique survived into the latter half of that century in remote northern parts. The walls were raised on a stone base wherever stone was available. They were not

235

long-lasting, either because of problems with stability or because of vulnerability to the weather. The frequently reported custom of rebuilding a house every two or three years, after spreading the remains of the dismantled house on the fields, related mainly to turf construction. The replacement houses were built in two or three days.

In parts of Scotland – certainly in the South-West and around Dundee – solid clay-wall construction, comparable to the cob of Devon, was used. This involved either a slow process of raising 'lifts' of clay, letting it dry and then raising more lifts until the desired height of wall was reached, or a quicker process, described in Dumfriesshire at the end of the 19th century, whereby thin layers of clay separated by a sprinkling of straw were raised in one day to the required one-storey height. Clay walls had to be rendered with clay or lime to be made weather-resistant.

Another technique was to build in alternate layers of clay and stone or of turf and stone. Since fieldstones were used, this made for a more substantial wall without requiring a mason's skill. The 'Clay and bool' method used a composite material of stones and clay for every layer.

A quite different technique was to use clay within permanent shuttering of stone inside and outside, or with a pattern of stones on the outside embedded in clay set in shuttering. The result may not be easy to distinguish from solid stone walls mortared in clay.

Yet another method was 'stake and rice'. This involved staves of storey height, a horizontal weave of wattles, and then daub applied to both sides. This technique was certainly used for internal partitions and could have been used for the upper parts of external gable walls.

In solid-stone construction there were two quite distinct methods. In one, associ-

236

237

84. Dwellings at Ullapool, Ross and Cromarty
The house on the left has slate covering the main roof; the dormers that light the bedroom are partly in the roof space. The cottage on the right, with its roof at the same pitch, has corrugated-iron covering, presumably replacing thatch.
(Peter Crawley)

85. Cottage at Cullen, Banffshire
The eaves are so low in this dwelling that the door penetrates into the roof. The pantiles (presumably replacing thatch) are characteristic of the eastern and north-eastern coastal communities.
(Peter Crawley)

ated with the 'black houses' of the Hebrides, the wall was very thick – 5 or 6 ft (1.52 or 1.82 m) or even 8 ft (2.43 m) in thickness – and had a flat top only partly covered by the roof. Inner and outer skins were of fieldstones laid dry and the core was of earth mixed with stone, also laid dry. Such a wall was stable up to head height and well insulated. Indeed, later and structurally superior walling and roofing techniques were sometimes compared unfavourably with the older ones in the latter respect. In the other method, associated with the 'white houses' that succeeded black houses, walls of 2 ft (0.6 m) were built as conventional masonry walls either laid dry, or bedded in clay mortar or even bedded in lime mortar where it was available and could be afforded. In the 19th century any

238

86. House at Auchindrain, Argyll
The remarkable survival of this community of 18th- and 19th-century farmsteads illustrates the use of jointed cruck construction with drystone walling (here whitewashed) and simple thatching (replaced here and there by corrugated iron).
(R. W. Brunskill)

dampness or poor insulation was relieved by plastering on laths nailed to studs rather than direct on to the wall.

Except for conventional masonry walling none of the techniques described was really suitable for more than single-storey construction, but as that was what was wanted at the time this was not a serious defect.

For weatherproofing and improved appearance, these solid walls were often rendered or 'harled' and then lime-washed. Bruce Walker has shown that these renderings were traditionally drab rather than colourful. The pebble-dash finishes that disfigure so many British houses built in the first half of the 20th century may have originated with the Vernacular Revival in Scotland, but do not seem to have been traditional there.

Although brick- and tile-works were established quite widely as a result of the agricultural and industrial revolutions, brick never seems to have been a popular material in Scotland; the many brick council houses built after 1920 appear thin and insubstantial when compared to those that use more traditional materials.

Roofing shape and materials as seen at the present day are no more characteristic of the Scotland of the past than contemporary walling materials. The simple gabled roof with a chimney at each gable and a covering of slate or tile is a technique little older than the 19th century.

Except in tower houses, most roofs were of thatch of some type laid on a hipped or gabled roof with a rounded or almost flat ridge. Roofs were plain, with few valleys, but sometimes enlivened with crow-stepped gables or tall dormer windows rising from the eaves. One curious detail sometimes found is a front gable terminating in a chimney-stack – even a false one here and there.

Thatching materials included 'divots' or squares of turf used as an underthatch

Scottish houses 1

a. Map showing areas of distribution of tower houses. The densest concentration is double-hatched.

b. Plan of early tower house, lower floor.

c. Plan of early tower house, upper floor.

d. Ground-level plan of later tower house.

e. Upper-floor plan.

f. Sketch showing the L-shape with projecting stair turret.

g. and h. Plans of late tower house.

i. Plan of bastle house.

j. Sketch of bastle house.

---

or as the waterproof layer; straw laid loose and held by ropes, or later either laid in conventional thatching techniques or, in Ayrshire, finished with a mixture of lime mortar and chopped straw; rushes and reeds pulled from the fields but sometimes cultivated for the purpose; and finally broom and heather. In the North and West thatching materials were laid on the roof without any great skill and secured by ropes weighted with stones suspended over the eaves or, in the black houses,

87. Detail of wall at Auchindrain, Argyll
The use of fieldstones without mortar is illustrated here.
(R. W. Brunskill)

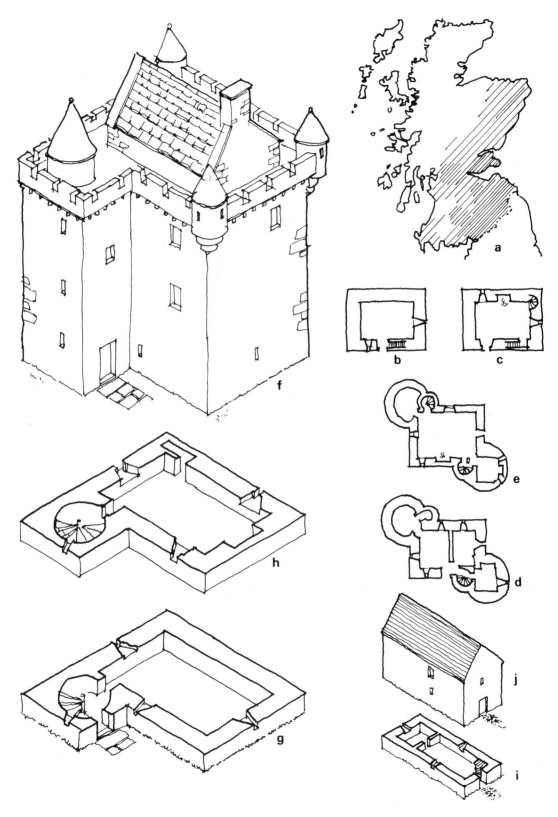

241

Scottish houses 2

a. Plan of typical black house showing main house with living kitchen (1), bedroom (2), cow-byre (3) and outshut or barn (4).

b. Elevation of black house.

c. Cross-section showing thick double walls.

d. Plan of house with living room (5) and a bedroom (6) loosely partitioned off, and 'hanging lum' fireplace (7).

e. Sketch of black house.

f. Plan of house of the improvement period with living room (8) and parlour (9) and with a press (cupboard) (10) and a staircase leading to bedrooms in the roof space.

g. Elevation of (f).

h. Upper-floor plan of Edinburgh-type tenement showing box-beds (11) opening off living kitchen (12) and bedroom (13).

i. Elevation of such a tenement block.

---

with stones laid on the exposed top of the thick wall. Alternatively, roofs were stob-thatched into turf. The life of such thatched roofs varied from a year to several decades. Contemporary accounts often describe how every year, or every two or three years, the whole roof was stripped and consigned to the midden while new thatching was laid in the space of a day or two. No elaborate thatching technique would result in such a short life or allow such quick and easy replacement. At the opposite extreme, reed was regarded as a superior thatching material lasting twenty or thirty years, while a roof thatched in heather was reputed to last forty or fifty years – even though in England heather was regarded as inferior to straw, just as oat straw was regarded as much inferior to wheat straw for thatching.

14

An alternative material, superseding thatch in the East and South-East, was slate: local slate as from Ballachulish, Cumbrian slate in the South-West, Welsh slate in the South, near the border. All were introduced in the late 18th century and used increasingly in the 19th. Stone flags were introduced at the same time, but were only used in small areas such as parts of Caithness and Sutherland where this heavy material was quarried. English travellers noted that slate (and perhaps stone flags) were laid on a close-boarded roof rather than on slating battens. One interesting material observed as early as the end of the 18th century was tarred felt or paper, but its use on houses was not common.

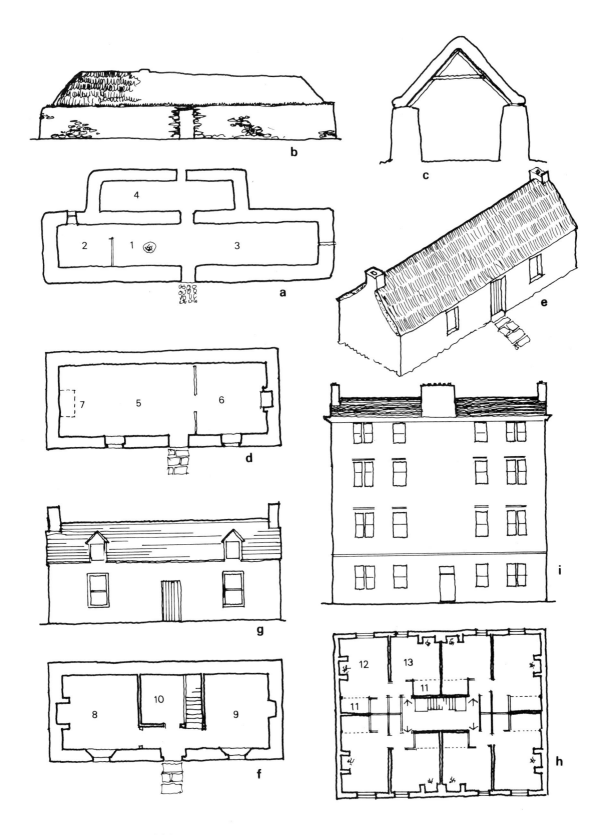

243

Scottish houses 3

a. Cross-section showing walls of double thickness stone and infill and with net (1) over thatch (2) over turf (3).

b. Cross-section showing crude cruck construction and conventional thatch.

c. Cross-section of wall with alternate layers of stone and turf.

d. Cross-section of wall with stone and clay.

e. Elevation of wall in Aberdeen bond.

Postscript

Investigation of the domestic vernacular architecture of Scotland has proceeded apace during the last twenty years or so. As in England and Wales, historians, archaeologists, geographers and folk-life students have all made contributions. The balance between the study of the fascinating and picturesque black houses of the Highlands and Islands and the far more numerous white houses of the greater part of the country is being restored, and year by year more research is exploring and explaining the basis for the distinctiveness of Scottish domestic architecture.

This distinctiveness lies initially in the different house-plans. In the countryside it is clear that the tower houses of Scotland differ more than superficially from their English counterparts while the long, low single-storey houses and cottages lend their signature to many parts of the country, having comparatively few contemporary counterparts in England and Wales. In the towns the urban character of quite small communities is given distinctiveness by designs based on the projecting forestair and upper-level entrance, while the tenement flats and the spacious sets of apartments of the middle classes distinguish the large cities of Scotland from all their English counterparts except, perhaps, for London.

These are just a few of the Scottish house-plans but the same distinctiveness can be seen in their construction and in the use of materials. It is not that the materials available in Scotland are fundamentally different from those in England and Wales, rather that those available for use varied so much. Structural timber became scarcer at an earlier date; brick became fashionable at a later date; turf, clay, heather and peat remained in wider and longer use in Scotland than in the rest of Britain. Many other aspects of construction and use of materials are characteristically Scottish.

As studies progress that special character which comes from choices in siting, planning and building the vernacular architecture of Scotland will be made ever clearer both for the country as a whole and for its several regions.

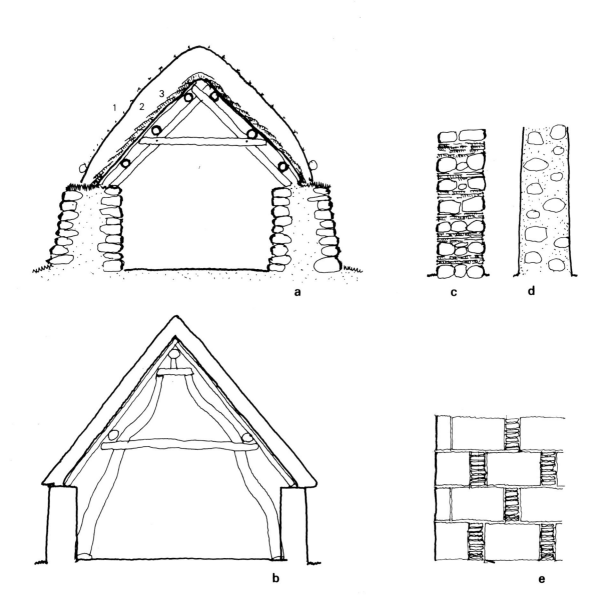

a

c   d

b   e

245

Conclusion

The archaeological and documentary study of existing houses proceeds with ever-increasing momentum. It pushes back the limits of our knowledge of the oldest houses; but it also adds to our knowledge of comparatively recent and humble cottages such as are liable to be demolished so much more completely by the 20th-century bulldozer than any villa or hut destroyed by Saxon or Scot. At the national level the Royal Commissions on Historic Monuments, allied with English Heritage, Cadw and Historic Scotland, continue to set high standards for the study of an ever-broadening range of house-types, particularly through the lists of buildings of special architectural or historic importance.

At the regional level the county archaeology units supported by local and national government spread professional expertise and supplement the more intermittent work of some university departments. Amateurs, on whom so much archaeological and documentary work has depended, add to the records of existing buildings while working through the county and local archaeological and historical societies. More recently they have banded together to promote the study of smaller houses and farm buildings through the work of recording groups such as the Domestic Buildings Research Group (Surrey), affiliated to the national Vernacular Architecture Group.

Not only does the study quicken its rate and extend its limits, it continues to deepen. When houses are, sadly, demolished it is possible to make a record not only of the structure above ground but also of the layers of debris and foundations below ground through excavation. Thus at a few sites we are already able to see something of the precursors of our standard house-plans, and to distinguish the various stages of modification or the sudden acts of innovation that produced the plans we recognise. Admittedly few such total studies have yet been made, but more are to be expected.

Through the expansion of the work of the National Monuments Records we now have an archive wherein all the material may be deposited. This archive is essential, since very little of the rapidly increasing amount of recorded information is ever likely to be published in the conventional way. But with the aid of this archive, study can move forward from the stage of collecting data and writing commentaries on individual houses.

Since recording and analysis are alternating processes (one needs to record in order to analyse, but one also records on the basis of previous analysis), the swiftly expanding collection of records will enable more analysis to be undertaken and make it better founded. One result will be new and more comprehensive classifications; there will also be a better appreciation of the links between plan-types, of the process by which one type succeeds another, and of the diffusion of plan-types from one region to another. Eventually, we shall also have a better grasp of the rules for proportioning of plan and section that were used by the designers.

An improved understanding of houses as archaeological specimens and historical entities ought to enhance our appreciation of the effects of social, economic, historical and cultural factors on domestic planning. The widening and deepening horizons of the archaeologist have matched similar extensions of prospect for those working in other disciplines. Broad classifications of house-plans will, one hopes, be matched by even broader explanations of the interaction between domestic design and the many facets of domestic life in both the distant past and more recent years.

Finally it is worth mention that, for an architect, the archaeological study of houses may be much more than an end in itself. The better we understand the characteristics of the houses of past centuries, the better we can establish criteria for their preservation, develop administrative and technical processes for their conservation, and learn how to design new houses that match the houses of the past in quality and bear a seemly relationship to them.

Notes and References

Chapter 1

1. Fox and Raglan, 1951–4.
2. Barley, 1961.
3. Brunskill, 1987, Council for British Archaeology, 1980, L. Smith, 1985, Swallow et al., 1993, all give advice on measuring of buildings and recording generally.
4. But see E. Wiliam, 1988 and Aldsworth and Harris, 1982.
5. Among published typologies intended for general use as well as for regional or local use are those in Eden, 1969, Machin, 1978, RCAHMW, *Glamorgan*, Vol. IV (ii), 1988, RCHME, *West Cambridgeshire*, 1968, and *Stamford*, 1977, and P. Smith, 1988.
6. For houses occupied by the professional classes see RCHME, *North York Moors*, 1986, Ch. 3.
7. For amplification of this point see P. Smith, 1980.
8. Hoskins, 1953 and 1965, and Machin, 1977. Hoskins suggested that there was a housing revolution that took place in the English countryside generally between about 1570 and 1640 (but a century later in the four northern counties) involving the complete rebuilding or substantial modernisation of the fabric of houses and an increase and improvement of their furnishings and equipment. This has come to be called the Great Rebuilding. Machin looked at the concept again in the light of more recent research and suggested that an 18th-century rather than a 17th-century rebuilding was quite widespread. However, he questioned the whole idea of a single Great Rebuilding and suggested that we should look at successive waves of rebuilding at different times and in different regions. More recent writers such as Harrison and Hutton, 1984, and Wrathmell, 1984 and 1989, share doubts about the idea of a Great Rebuilding. Argument has continued in volumes of *Vernacular Architecture* but has been somewhat confused by the relationship between 'impermanent' and 'flimsy' construction. Interesting comment appears in Johnson, 1993, pp. 7–14. Johnson and others have been concerned about the extent to which surviving houses represent those that formerly existed.
9. For aspects of planning theory see P. Dickens in D. L. Clarke (ed), *Spatial Archaeology*, 1977, pp. 33–45, W. Hillier and J. Hanson, *The Social Logic of Space*, 1984, and F. E. Brown, 1990, for example. Johnson, 1993, comments in his Ch. 3, especially pp. 33–8.

Chapter 2

1. Further discussion on siting appears in Roberts, 1974 and 1978, and M. W. Beresford, 1979.
2. For recent discussion of ground-floor halls, including aisled halls, see J. T. Smith, 1992, pp. 12–29 and Pearson, 1994, pp. 24–30, also RCAHMW, *Glamorgan*, Vol. III (ii), 1982, pp. 121–58; for their use in Yorkshire see Harrison and Hutton, 1984.
3. For recent discussion of first-floor halls see RCAHMW, *Glamorgan*, Vol. III (ii), 1982, pp. 158–78.
4. Discussion of bastle houses has been complicated by disagreement about the suitability of this term. However, it has come into general use since publication of Ramm and others, 1970, to describe this version of the first-floor hall. The type seems more common than was at first thought. For recent accounts see Dixon, 1979 and 1993, and Ryder, 1990 and 1992. For Scottish examples see Ch. 7. Wales seems to be without bastle houses.
5. It is often difficult to distinguish a formerly free-standing tower to which other buildings have later been attached from the solar wing of a single-ended hall that has lost its hall range. For discussion see Blair, 1993. There is an interesting distribution map of tower houses in the British Isles in P. Smith, 1988, p. 338, and the matter was developed in P. Smith, 1980.
6. See P. Smith, 1988, p. 232.
7. P. Smith, 1994, p. 291, recalls a Small House in the Conwy Valley uplands with a hall still open to the roof and an inscription recording its erection as late as 1854.
8. See J. T. Smith, 1992, pp. 32–3, Pearson, 1994, especially pp. 9, 80–1 and 121–3, also Harding, 1976.
9. G. Beresford, 1979, pp. 98–158, including turf walling.
10. Mercer, 1975, p. 42.
11. 'Lobby entry' and 'baffle entry' are terms coined by students of vernacular architecture and are often used interchangeably. Mercer, 1975, and P. Smith, 1975, prefer 'lobby entry' and Mercer reserved the term 'baffle entry' for an entrance at the front corner of a house against the jamb of a gable fireplace.
12. Examples appear in Machin, 1978, pp. 68–91, P. Smith, 1988, p. 252, and RCAHMW, *Glamorgan*, Vol. IV (ii), 1988, p. 251.
13. See P. Smith, 1975, p. 158.
14. See Neave, 1971, pp. 18–19, and Harrison and Hutton, 1984, pp. 63, 80–1 and 116.
15. See R. W. Brunskill, 'Lowther Village and Robert Adam', *Transactions of the Ancient Monuments Society*, Vol. 14, 1966–7. For the *ty-unnos* cottage built overnight and as found in Wales see E. Wiliam, 1988, p. 13.
16. I am indebted to R. Harris for discussion of this plan.
17. For example see Lowe, 1985, pp. 6–7, and P. Smith, 1988, p. 326. This is preceded by observations on the late emergence of cottages in Wales generally.
18. For discussion of use of single-storey cottages in Yorkshire see C. D. Newton, 'Single-storey Cottages in West Yorkshire', *Folk Life*, Vol. 14, 1976, pp. 65–74.
19. Stell, 1965, p. 20 and Addy, 1975, Ch. 4.

20. P. Smith, 1963, p. 432, also Stell, 1965, Mercer, 1975, pp. 32–3 and 45–6, expanded in RCHME, *Rural Houses in West Yorkshire*, 1986, pp. 178–83.
21. In Daniel Defoe, *A Tour through the Whole Island of Great Britain*, 1724–6, Penguin edition, 1971, pp. 491–3.
22. RCAHMW, *Glamorgan*, Vol. IV (ii), 1988, p. 33, 'The "squarson" is a feature of 18th-century rather than 17th-century building.'
23. Pantin, 1957, and RCAHMW, *Glamorgan*, Vol. III (ii), 1982.
24. Barley, 1961, pp. 90–5.
25. Barley, 1961, p. 29.
26. For inns and public houses locally see RCHME, *Houses of the North York Moors*, pp. 126–37.

Chapter 3

1. For the contrast between pre- and post-17th-century site development, compare Taylor, 1974, and Summerson, 1945.
2. The great fires that ravaged many provincial towns as well as London inevitably took their toll of early houses, especially those of timber construction, and hastened their replacement by more up-to-date houses. An example is Blandford Forum, Dorset, whose appearance stems from rebuilding after fires of 1713 and 1731. The relationship between survival and attrition by fire was examined by C. R. J. Currie in *Vernacular Architecture*, Vol. 19, 1988, pp. 1–9.
3. Faulkner, 1966.
4. For the special case of the Rows of Chester see R. H. Lawson and J. T. Smith, 'The Rows of Chester: a problem and two solutions', *Journal of the Chester Archaeological Society*, Vol. 67, 1958, pp. 1–42. The subject was developed at length in that same journal, Vols. 67, 1984–5, and 69, 1988. Further comment is in R. C. Turner, 'Early carpentry in the Rows of Chester', *Vernacular Architecture*, Vol. 19, 1988, pp. 31–41.
5. The Lincoln houses are remarkable in being double-pile.
6. Pantin, 1962–3; S. R. Jones, notes distributed to Vernacular Architecture Group members; Faulkner, 1960.
7. Pantin, 1962–3.

8. 38 King Street, Sandwich, described by E. W. Parkin to Vernacular Architecture Group members.
9. Pantin, 1962–3; RCHME, *Stamford*, 1977, Type 8a and p. 152.
10. Summerson, 1945, p. 34. See also Kelsall, 1974, p. 88; RCHME, *Stamford*, Class 14, and RCHME, *York*, Vol. III, 1972, Nos. 57–9 Micklegate of 1783, and RCHME, *York*, Vol. IV, 1975, No. 38 Monkgate, pp. 89–90.
11. See RCHME, *York*, Vol. IV, 1975, p. 90, and Vol. V, 1981, p. 109.
12. However, the situation in London is illuminated by survey plans made by Treswell in 1612; examples are illustrated in Schofield, 1984, pp. 144 and 159.
13. See Portman, 1966, p. 3. Single-storey, though not single-*cell* cottages continued to be built in north-eastern England quite late: see Muthesius, 1982, pp. 102–6.
14. Pioneering work by M. W. Beresford, for Leeds, in Chapman, 1971, developed by Chapman himself for Nottingham; by Lowe, 1977, pp. 13–15, 38 and 39 for Wales; by Caffyn, 1986, pp. 16–17 and 41–5 for the West Riding of Yorkshire (introducing the term 'through-by-lights'); and generally by Muthesius, 1982, pp. 106–23.
15. See e.g., W. J. Smith in Chapman, 1971, Ch. 7, expanded in W. J. Smith, 1987; D. Smith, 1965 for Leicester; Barke, 1979, and Caffyn, 1986, pp. 9–15 and 55–7 for the West Riding of Yorkshire; Timmins, 1979, for Lancashire; Chapman, 1991, pp. 146–51 for Nottingham; and Lowe, 1977, pp. 35, 40–2, 44 and 54 for Wales. A recent study of handloom weaving in Lancashire (G. Timmins, *The Last Shift: The Decline in Hand-loom Weaving in 19th-century Lancashire*, 1993) has shown that the advance of power-loom weaving in factories was not as swift and complete as might be thought, and that hand-loom weaving survived in many areas long after 1850. Hence the late construction of many cottages for domestic industry.
16. For this type generally see Muthesius, 1982, pp. 123–30, and Lowe, 1972, for Wales. Morgan, 1990–3 gives a detailed account of Preston,

a typical industrial town. For dwellings over dwellings see Caffyn, 1986 and especially pp. 15 and 73, and Lowe, 1977, pp. 17–20.
17. Illustrated in Rasmussen, 1960; Hall, 1973; Muthesius, 1982, pp. 90–7.
18. Muthesius, 1982, pp. 130–8; for Barrow-in-Furness examples see J. D. Marshall, *Furness and the Industrial Revolution*, 1958, pp. 348 and 413.
19. Inter-war developments reviewed in Edwards, 1989, Ch. 3; for the special case of the bungalow, see King, 1984.

Chapter 4

1. For building materials and construction generally see Clifton-Taylor, 1972, and Brunskill, 1987.
2. For timber-frame construction generally see Brunskill, 1994, and the works listed in its bibliography. An excellent outline of the subject is Harris, 1978.
3. For a detailed account of cruck construction see Charles, 1967; for distribution of crucks see Alcock, 1981, with amplification of Welsh examples in P. Smith, 1988, pp. 394–403. An early study of the dating of crucks was E. A. Gee, 'The chronology of crucks', *Transactions of the Ancient Monuments Society*, Vol. 22, pp. 9–27, but the use of dendrochronology has transformed dating. Reports on dates for timber members, including crucks, appear regularly in *Vernacular Architecture*.
4. The distinction is examined in R. Harris, 'The grammar of carpentry', *Vernacular Architecture*, Vol. 20, 1989, pp. 1–8.
5. See Roberts, 1974, and Watson and McLintock, 1979.
6. See Brunskill, 1990, and the works listed in its bibliography.
7. For clay and cob construction see J. McCann, *Clay and Cob Building*, 1995, and J. R. Harrison, 'The mud wall in England at the close of the vernacular era', *Transactions of the Ancient Monuments Society*, Vol. 28, 1984, pp. 154–74.
8. For construction of houses in towns generally see RCHME, *Stamford*, 1977, pp. lxviii–xix, etc., and *York*, Vols. III, IV and V, 1972, 1975 and 1981.

Chapter 5

1. Alcock, 1993.
2. J. C. Curwen, *The Later Records of North Westmorland*, 1932, p. 62.
3. RCAHMW, *Glamorgan*, Vol. IV (ii), 1988, pp. 23–9.
4. Alcock, 1993, p. 20.
5. Alcock, 1993; Barley, 1961 was pioneering on a national scale.
6. Based originally on Barley, 1963, with additional material.

Chapter 7

1. Dunbar, 1966, p. 34.
2. Dunbar, 1966, Cruden, 1960, Fawcett, 1994, RCAHMS, *Argyll*. Elsieshields is illustrated in the handbook to the Scottish Vernacular Working Group Dumfries Conference, 1983.
3. T. Ward, 'The elusive Scottish Bastle House', *Vernacular Building*, Vol. 17, 1988, p. 50 ff.
4. Dunbar, 1966, pp. 81–4.
5. Dunbar, 1966, p. 84, and RCAHMS, *Argyll*, Vol. I, 1971, p. 185.
6. For short life and frequent rebuilding before the Improvement, with tenants reusing main components, see Dunbar, 1966, p. 223, also for late construction of archaic house-forms. For house-and-byre dwellings, see *Vernacular Building*, Vol. 13, 1989, pp. 23–33. For travellers' descriptions see, e.g., C. Lowther et al., *Our Journey into Scotland in 1629*, ed. of 1894, p. 11 (at Langholm 'we lodged at Jon o'Foord's . . . where the fire is in the middle of the house'), or later, Robert Forsyth, *The Beauties of Scotland*, Vols. I–V, 1805–8 (e.g., Vol. V, Cromartyshire, 'The greater number, by far, of the farmhouses and offices of the tenants and cottagers are near wretched hovels . . .').
7. Naismith, 1985, illustrates many examples and comments on planned villages. Forsyth, 1805–8, contrasts houses and cottages of the Improvement with those surviving or recently superseded (e.g., Vol. I, Berwickshire, p. 533, Midlothian, p. 273, Vol. II, Tweed-dale, p. 177; cf. Vol. V, Argyllshire, p. 419, 'The houses of the little farmers are still here very miserable parcels of stones, huddled up to the height of five or six feet, without mortar, or with only mud instead of it').
8. For St Kilda see Forsyth, Vol. V, 1808, p. 337.
9. For one sort of inglenook see R. Marshall, *Vernacular Building*, Vol. 8, 1983–4, pp. 29–48.
10. Forsyth, Vol. 11, p. 177, Tweed-dale, 'deserve no better appellation than miserable huts'.
11. Dunbar, 1966, p. 170 ff.
12. J. Butt, 'Working-class Housing in Glasgow, 1851–1914', Ch. 2 in Chapman, 1971; P. Robinson, 'Tenements: a pre-Industrial Urban Tradition', in A. Fenton (ed.), *Review of Scottish Culture*, Vol. I, 1984, pp. 52–63; Scottish Housing Advisory Committee, *Modernising Our Homes*, 1947, pp. 36–9.
13. For material and construction generally see Scottish Vernacular Buildings Working Group, *Materials and Construction in Scottish Building*, 1991, and B. Walker, 'The vernacular buildings of NE Scotland: an exploration', in *The Scottish Geographical Magazine*, Vol. 95, 1979, pp. 45–60. For one traveller's description see Lowther, op. cit., p. 11, Langholm: 'We laid in a poor thatch'd house, the walls of it being one course of stones, another of earth.'
14. Forsyth, Vol. II, 1805, Ayrshire, pp. 461–2, describes a local technique of mortared thatch.

Bibliography

S. O. Addy, *Evolution of the English House*, 1975 (facsimile of ed. of 1933)

N. W. Alcock, *Cruck Construction: An Introduction and Catalogue*, 1981

N. W. Alcock, *People at Home: Living in a Warwickshire Village 1500–1800*, 1993

N. W. Alcock and M. Laithewaite, 'Medieval houses in Devon and their modernization', *Medieval Archaeology*, Vol. 17, 1973

N. W. Alcock and others, 'Devonshire farmhouses', *Transactions of the Devonshire Association*, various issues from 1962 onwards

F. G. Aldsworth & R. Harris, 'A medieval and 17th-century house at Walderton . . .', *Sussex Archaeological Collections*, Vol. 20, 1982

J. Ayres, *The Shell Book of the Home in Britain*, 1981

M. Barke, 'Weavers' cottages in the Huddersfield area', *Folk Life*, Vol. 17, 1979

M. W. Barley, *The English Farmhouse and Cottage*, 1961

M. W. Barley, 'A Glossary of Names for Rooms in Houses of the Sixteenth and Seventeenth Centuries', in L. I. Forster and Alcock, *Culture and Environment*, 1963

M. W. Barley, 'Rural housing in England', contributions to J. Thirsk (ed.), *The Agrarian History of England and Wales*, Vol. IV, 1500–1640, 1967, and Vol. V (ii), 1640–1750, 1985

M. W. Barley, *Houses and History*, 1986

P. S. Barnwell for RCHME, *The House Within: Interpreting Medieval Houses in Kent*, 1994

P. Beecham (ed.), *Devon Building*, 1990

G. Beresford, 'Excavation of a moated site at Wintringham', *Archaeological Journal*, Vol. 134, 1978

G. Beresford, 'Three deserted settlements on Dartmoor', *Medieval Archaeology*, Vol. 23, 1979

G. Beresford, *Goltho, the Development of an Early Medieval Manor*, 1987

M. W. Beresford and J. K. St Joseph, *Medieval England, an Aerial Survey*, 2nd ed., 1979

J. Blair, 'Hall and chamber: English domestic planning 1000–1250', in G. Meirion-Jones and M. Jones (eds.), *Manorial Domestic Buildings in England and Northern France*, 1993

F. E. Brown, 'Analysing small building plans', in R. Samson (ed.), *The Social Archaeology of Houses*, 1990

E. Brunskill, *Some York Almshouses*, 1960

R. W. Brunskill, *Illustrated Handbook of Vernacular Architecture*, 3rd ed., 1987

R. W. Brunskill, *Vernacular Architecture of the Lake Counties*, 1974

R. W. Brunskill, 'Traditional domestic architecture of South-west Lancashire', *Folk Life*, Vol. 15, 1977

R. W. Brunskill, *Traditional Farm Buildings of Britain*, 2nd ed., 1987

R. W. Brunskill, *Brick Building in Britain*, 1990

R. W. Brunskill, *Timber Building in Britain*, 2nd ed., 1994

L. Caffyn for RCHME, *Workers' Housing in West Yorkshire*, 1986

C. Carson, 'Segregation in vernacular buildings', *Vernacular Architecture*, Vol. 7, 1976

S. D. Chapman (ed.), *The History of Working-class Housing*, 1971

F. W. B. Charles, *Medieval Cruck-Buildings*, 1967

V. M. and F. J. Chesher, *The Cornishman's House*, 1968

A. Clifton-Taylor, *The Pattern of English Building*, ed. of 1972.

S. Collier with S. Pearson for RCHME, *Whitehaven 1660–1800*, 1991

R. A. Cordingley and R. B. Wood-Jones, 'Chorley Hall', *Transactions of the Ancient Monuments Society*, new series, Vol. 7, 1959

Council for British Archaeology, *Recording Old Houses*, 1980

H. Coutie, 'How they lived on Hillgate', *Transactions of the Lancashire and Cheshire Antiquarian Society*, Vol. 88, 1994

S. Cruden, *The Scottish Castle*, 1960

A. L. Cummings, *The Framed Houses of Massachusetts Bay, 1625–1725*, 1979

S. Denyer, *Traditional Buildings and Life in the Lake District*, 1991

P. Dixon, 'Tower houses, pelehouses and Border society', *Archaeological Journal*, Vol. 136, 1979

P. Dixon, 'Mota, aula et turris: the manor houses of the Anglo-Scottish border', in G. Meirion-Jones and M. Jones (eds.), *Manorial Domestic Buildings in England and Northern France*, 1993

J. Dunbar, *The Historic Architecture of Scotland*, 1966

C. Dyer, 'English peasant buildings in the later Middle Ages (1200–1500)', *Medieval Archaeology*, Vol. 30, 1986

P. Eden, 'Smaller Post-Medieval Houses in Eastern England', *East Anglian Studies*, 1968

P. Eden, *Small Houses in England, 1520–1820*, 1969

A. M. Edwards, *The Design of Suburbia*, 1981

G. Fairclough, 'Meaningful constructions: spatial and functional analysis of medieval buildings', *Antiquity*, Vol. 66, 1992

P. A. Faulkner, 'Medieval undercrofts and town houses', *Archaeological Journal*, Vol. 123, 1966

P. A. Faulkner, 'Domestic planning from the twelfth to the fourteenth centuries', *Archaeological Journal*, Vol. 95, 1960

R. Fawcett, *The Architectural History of Scotland, 1371–1560*, 1994.

A. Fenton, *The Shape of the Past*, 1985

R. Forsyth, *The Beauties of Scotland*, Vols. I–V, 1805–8

Sir Cyril Fox and Lord Raglan, *Monmouthshire Houses*, Vols. I–III, 1951–4

E. Gauldie, *Cruel Habitations: a History of Working-Class Housing, 1780–1918*, 1974

C. Giles for RCHME, *Rural Houses of West Yorkshire*, 1986

W. H. Godfrey, *The English Almshouse*, 1955

P. Gray, *Charlwood Houses*, 1978

J. Grey, 'On the building of cottages for farm labourers', *Journal of the Royal Agricultural Society for England*, Vol. V, 1845

I. and E. Hall, *Historic Beverley*, 1973

L. J. Hall, *The Rural Houses of North Avon and South Gloucestershire, 1400–1720*, 1983

J. M. Harding, *Four Centuries of Charlwood Housing*, 1976

R. Harris, *Discovering Timber-framed Buildings*, 1978

B. Harrison, 'Longhouses in the Vale of York, 1570–1669', *Vernacular Architecture*, Vol. 22, 1991

B. Harrison and B. Hutton, *Vernacular Houses in North Yorkshire and Cleveland*, 1984

M. Hartley and J. Ingilby, *Life and Traditions in the Yorkshire Dales*, 1968

C. A. Hewett, 'The development of the post-medieval house', *Post-medieval Archaeology*, Vol. 7, 1973

W. G. Hoskins, 'The Rebuilding of Rural England, 1570–1640', *Past and Present*, Nov. 1953; also in *Provincial England*, 1965, by the same author

C. F. Innocent, *The Development of English Building Construction*, 1916 (and 1971)

M. Johnson, 'The Englishman's House and its study' in R. Samson (ed.), *The Social Archaeology of Houses*, 1990

M. Johnson, *Housing Culture: Traditional Architecture in an English Landscape*, 1993

S. R. Jones and J. T. Smith, 'The houses of Breconshire', Parts I–V, *Brycheiniog*, 1963–9

A. F. Kelsall, 'The London house-plan in the later 17th century', *Post-medieval Archaeology*, Vol. 8, 1974

A. D. King, *The Bungalow*, 1984

P. Lawson and J. T. Smith, 'The Rows of Chester: two interpretations', *Journal of the North Wales Architectural, Archaeological and Historic Society*, Vol. 45, 1958

D. Lloyd and others, *Historic Ludlow*, research papers, 1978–

J. B. Lowe, *Welsh Industrial Workers' Housing*, 1977

R. Machin, 'The Great Rebuilding: a reassessment', *Past and Present*, No. 77, 1977

R. Machin, *The Houses of Yetminster*, 1978

C. McWilliam, *Scottish Townscape*, 1975

D. and B. Martin, *Historic Buildings in Eastern Sussex*, Vols. I–VI, 1977–91

R. T. Mason, *Framed Buildings of the Weald*, 1964

E. Mercer, *English Vernacular Houses*, 1975

K. Miller and others, for RCHME. *Beverley: an Archaeological and Architectural Study*, 1982

R. N. Millman, *The Making of the Scottish Landscape*, 1975

N. Morgan, *Vanished Dwellings: Early Industrial Housing in a Lancashire Cotton Town*, 1990

N. Morgan, *Deadly Dwellings (Preston, 1840–1919)*, 1993

S. Muthesius, *The English Terraced House*, 1982

R. Naismith, *Buildings of the Scottish Countryside*, 1985

V. Neave, 'Living-in in the East Riding', *Vernacular Architecture*, No. 2, 1971

W. A. Pantin, 'The development of domestic architecture in Oxford', *The Antiquaries' Journal*, 1947

W. A. Pantin, 'Medieval priests' houses in south-west England', *Medieval Archaeology*, Vol. 1, 1957

W. A. Pantin, 'The merchants' houses and warehouses of King's Lynn', *Medieval Archaeology*, Vols. 6–7, 1962–3

W. A. Pantin, 'Medieval English townhouse plans', *Medieval Archaeology*, Vols. 6–7, 1962-3

V. Parker, *The Making of King's Lynn*, 1971

S. Pearson for RCHME, *Rural Houses of the Lancashire Pennines, 1560–1760*, 1985

S. Pearson for RCHME, *The Medieval Houses of Kent: an Historical Analysis*, 1994

D. Portman, *Exeter Houses, 1400–1700*, 1966

A. Quiney, 'The lobby-entrance house: its origins and distribution', in J. Newman (ed.), *Design and Practice in British Architecture*, 1984

A. Quiney, *The Traditional Buildings of England*, 1990

A. Quiney, *Kentish Houses*, 1993

Lord Raglan, *The Temple and the House*, 1964

H. G. Ramm and others, *Shielings and Bastles*, 1970

S. E. Rasmussen, *London, the Unique City*, 1960 ed.

B. K. Roberts, *Rural Settlement in Britain*, 1978

B. K. Roberts, *The Making of the English Village*, 1974

D. L. Roberts, 'The vernacular buildings of Lincolnshire', *Archaeological Journal*, Vol. 131, 1974

J. Roberts, 'The provision of housing for the working classes in Manchester 1780–1914', *Journal of the Manchester Literary and Philosophical Society*, Vol. 124, 1986

Royal Commission on the Ancient and Historical Monuments of Scotland (RCAHMS), *Inventories* especially *Argyll*, 1971 on.

Royal Commission on the Ancient and Historical Monuments of Wales (RCAHMW), *Inventories*, especially *Glamorgan*, Vol. IV, Pt ii, 1988

Royal Commission on Historic Monuments of England (RCHME), *Inventories*, especially *City of Cambridge*, 1959; *West Cambridgeshire*, 1968; *Dorset*, Vols. I–IV, 1970–5; *City of York*, Vols. III, 1972, and IV, 1975; *The Town of Stamford*, 1977; and *Northamptonshire*, Vol. VI, 1984

Royal Commission on Historic Monuments of England, *Houses of the North York Moors*, 1986

P. Ryder, 'Vernacular building in South Yorkshire', *Archaeological Journal*, Vol. 137, 1980

P. Ryder, 'Fortified medieval and sub-medieval buildings in the north-east of England' in B. E. Vyner (ed.), *Medieval Rural Settlement in North-east England*, 1990

P. Ryder, 'Bastles and bastle-like buildings in Allendale, Northumberland', *Archaeological Journal*, Vol. 149, 1992

D. Rubenstein, *Victorian Homes*, 1974

J. Schofield, *The Building of London from the Conquest to the Great Fire*, 1984

D. Smith, *Industrial Archaeology of the East Midlands*, 1965

J. T. Smith, 'Medieval aisled halls', *Archaeological Journal*, Vol. 112, 1956

J. T. Smith, 'The evolution of the English peasant house to the late 17th century', *Journal of the British Archaeological Association*, Vol. 33, 1970

J. T. Smith, 'Lancashire and Cheshire houses: some problems of architectural and social history', *Archaeological Journal*, Vol. 127, 1971

J. T. Smith for RCHME, *English Houses 1200–1800: the Hertfordshire Evidence*, 1992

L. Smith, *Investigating Old Buildings*, 1985

P. Smith, 'The longhouse and the laithe house', in Foster and Alcock (eds.), *Culture and Environment*, 1963

P. Smith, 'Rural Building in Wales', contributions to J. Thirsk (ed.), *The*

Agrarian History of England and Wales, Vol. IV, 1500–1640, 1967, and Vol. V (ii), 1640–1750, 1985

P. Smith, 'The architectural personality of the British Isles', *Archaeologia Cambrensis*, Vol. CXXIX, 1980

P. Smith, *Houses of the Welsh Countryside*, 2nd ed., 1988

P. Smith, 'British vernacular architecture in a continental context', *Archaeologia Cambrensis*, Vol. CXLII, 1994

W. J. Smith, *Saddleworth Buildings*, 1987

F. W. Steer, 'Smaller houses and their furnishings in the 17th and 18th centuries', *Journal of the British Archaeological Association*, Vols. 20–1, 1957–8

C. F. Stell, 'Pennine houses', *Folk Life*, Vol. 3, 1965

J. Summerson, *Georgian London*, 1945

P. Swallow, D. Watt, R. Ashton, *Measurement and Recording of Historic Buildings*, 1993

C. Taylor, *Village and Farmstead*, 1983

R. F. Taylor, 'Town houses in Taunton, 1500–1700', *Post-medieval Archaeology*, Vol. 8, 1974

J. G. Timmins, 'Handloom weavers' cottages', *Post-medieval Archaeology*, Vol. 13, 1979

J. Warren (ed.), *Wealden Buildings*, 1990

R. C. Watson and M. McLintock, *Traditional Houses of the Fylde*, 1979

E. Wiliam, 'A Welsh cruck barn . . .', *Transactions of the Ancient Monuments Society*, Vol. 32, 1988

E. Wiliam, 'Yr Aelwyd: the architectural development of the hearth in Wales', *Folk Life*, Vol. 16, 1978

E. Wiliam, *Home Made Homes*, 1988

M. Wood, *The English Medieval House*, 1965

R. B. Wood-Jones, *Traditional Domestic Architecture in the Banbury Region*, 1963 (reissued 1986)

J. Woodforde, *The Truth about Cottages*, 1969

S. Wrathmell, 'Peasant houses, farmsteads and villages in north-east England' in M. Austen, D. Austin and C. Dyer (eds.), *The Rural Settlement of Medieval England*, 1989

Bibliographies

All published by the Vernacular Architecture Group.
Sir Robert de Z. Hall (ed.), *A Bibliography on Vernacular Architecture*, 1972
D. J. H. Michelmore (ed.), *A Current Bibliography of Vernacular Architecture 1970–76*, 1979
I. R. Pattinson, D. S. Pattinson and N. W. Alcock (eds.), *A Bibliography of Vernacular Architecture*, Vol. III, *1977–89*, 1992

Note

This bibliography is limited to those works that have been especially useful in the preparation of this book. Among other books and articles occasionally consulted, mention must be made of the many descriptions of individual houses that appear in the pages of national and local archaeological journals. The bibliographies by Hall, Michelmore and the Pattinsons and Alcock are arranged regionally and references to most of the available descriptions may be found therein.

The principal national journals that publish such descriptions are:

The Antiquaries' Journal (Society of Antiquaries of London)
The Archaeological Journal (Royal Archaeological Institute)
Folk Life (Society for Folk Life Studies)
Journal of the British Archaeological Association
Medieval Archaeology (Society for Medieval Archaeology)
Post-medieval Archaeology (Society for Post-medieval Archaeology)
Transactions of the Ancient Monuments Society
Vernacular Architecture (Vernacular Architecture Group)
Vernacular Building (Scottish Vernacular Buildings Working Group)

However, most such articles appear in the transactions of regional or local archaeological societies ranging from *Archaeologia Aeliana* (Society of Antiquaries of Newcastle upon Tyne) to *Transactions of the Woolhope Club* (Woolhope Naturalists' Field Club).

Index

Holmfirth (Yorkshire) 162
hooded chimney 51
H-shaped hall, *see* double-ended hall
Hull (Yorkshire) 195

infill panels in timber framing 176–7, 180
inglenook 51, 72, 90, 210, 214–15
inns 106
internal cross-passage houses 71–2, 74–5
Inverness-shire 235

jettied timber-frame construction 52, 176–7, 181
Jones, S.R. 118

Kendal (Westmorland) 192
Kent 24, 53
King John's Houses 28
king post roof truss 190–91
King's Lynn (Norfolk) 100, 122, 195
Kirkleatham (Yorkshire) 102
kitchen 201

laithe houses 92, 98–101
Lancashire 62, 152, 182
Lancaster 102
larder 201
Leeds (Yorkshire) 150
Leek (Staffordshire) 152
Leicester 152
Leicestershire 104, 157, 188
Leigh Court (Worcestershire) 173
Lewes (Sussex) 195
Lincoln 117
Lincolnshire 66, 70, 106, 182
living room 200
lobby-entrance houses 62–9
loft 202
log construction 182
London 102, 110, 112, 113, 138, 142, 144, 166, 234
    Bloomsbury 112, 234
    Chelsea 102
    Gt Queen St 110
    Greenwich 102
    Grosvenor Square 112
    Lincoln's Inn Fields 110
London terrace houses, central stairs 144, 146–7
London terrace houses, rear stairs 142, 144–5
longhouses 58–61, 198, 211–12, 214–15
loomshop 152–7
louvre 37, 50, 53, 218–19
Luddendon (Yorkshire) 98

Macclesfield (Cheshire) 152, 157

Manchester 99, 150, 152
mansard roof 196
mass wall construction 170
mathematical tile cladding 176–7, 180, 211
men's end 80
Midlands 78, 82, 152
Monmouthshire 56, 71
mud-and-stud construction 176–7, 181–2
mud walling, *see* earth walling
multi-storey cottages 94–5, 98
multi-storey large houses 40–43, 205
Muthesius, S. 164

Nairnshire 225
narrow-frontage urban houses
    with back-to-back fireplaces 133–7
    with cross-passage 122, 124–5
    with end-wall fireplaces 135, 140–41
    with internal hall and undercroft 117–19
    with longitudinal passage 124, 126–7
    with stairs between fireplaces 146–7
New England 66
Norfolk 70, 188
normal method of timber-frame assembly 179
Northamptonshire 184, 188
Northumberland 149
Norwich (Norfolk) 122
Nottingham 152

one-and-a-half unit rural cottages 88, 90–91
one-room rural cottages 88, 90–91
one-room urban cottages 148–51
open hearth 23–5, 30, 34–5, 37–9, 50, 51–5, 205, 211
Orkneys 230
outshut 80–83, 201
Oxford 108, 118, 122, 124, 128, 135

Palladian window 99
pantile roofing 192–3, 196
Pantin, W.A. 104, 118, 122
pantry 201
Parbold (Lancashire) 99
parlour 200
pebble walling 182–4
Pembrokeshire 56
Pennines 24, 40, 92, 99, 156, 182, 184
plain tile cladding 176–7
plain tile roofing 192–3, 196
plaster cladding 176–7, 180
plaster flooring 196
Port Sunlight (Cheshire) 166

post-and-truss construction, *see* box-frame construction
priest's houses 104, 106
principal rafter 178, 190–91
purlins 178, 190–91

Raglan, Lord 13
reversed timber-frame assembly 178
roof construction 190–91
roofing materials 190, 192–3
roof shapes 196, 198
Rossendale, Forest of 99
rural houses generally 18–21

saddle louvre 218–19
St Albans (Hertfordshire) 102
Salisbury (Wiltshire) 194
Sandwich (Kent) 126
Semi-detached houses 166, 168–9
service room 201
Sheffield (Yorkshire) 99
Shoreditch (London) 102
single-ended hall 30–35, 205–7
single-storey cottages 89, 92–3
siting of houses: rural 18–20, 213–15
    urban 112–13, 166, 168, 234
Skipton (Yorkshire) 99
slate roofing 190, 192–3, 196
small house with lateral chimney 56–8
small houses generally 50–51
smoke bay 51
smoke hood 51
Snowdonia 72
solar (soller) 202
Somerset 56
Southampton (Hampshire) 117
stake and rice walling 236
Stamford (Lincolnshire) 117, 122, 128, 135, 159, 195–6
Stell, C.F. 98
Stirling 231, 235
Stockport (Cheshire) 152
stone flag and stone tile roofing 190, 192–3, 196
Stoneleigh (Warwickshire) 199
stone walling 182–5
Styal (Cheshire) 231
Suffolk 24
Surrey 53
Sussex 24, 53
Sutherland 242

Taunton (Somerset) 108, 126, 135
tenement flats 234
Tewkesbury (Gloucestershire) 109, 126
thatch roofing 190, 192–3, 196–8, 239–42, 244–5
three-quarter urban houses 194
through by lights plan 150